D1452530

A Short Thousand Years

A Short
Thousand
Years

A CHILDHOOD IN THE THIRD REICH

ROBERT HALLMANN

FONTHILL

In memory of my beautiful wife, Maureen, and my daughter, Renate, and with grateful thanks to my daughter, Tessa, and her family, Steve, Minna, and Theo, for their constancy and support.

Fonthill Media Language Policy

Fonthill Media publishes in the international English language market. One language edition is published worldwide. As there are minor differences in spelling and presentation, especially with regard to American English and British English, a policy is necessary to define which form of English to use. The Fonthill Policy is to use the form of English native to the author. Robert Hallmann was born and educated in Germany; therefore British English has been adopted in this publication.

Fonthill Media Limited
Fonthill Media LLC
www.fonthillmedia.com
office@fonthillmedia.com

First published in the United Kingdom and the United States of America 2019

British Library Cataloguing in Publication Data:
A catalogue record for this book is available from the British Library

Copyright © Robert Hallmann 2019

ISBN 978-1-78155-735-8

Typeset in 10pt on 13pt Sabon
Printed and bound in England

Foreword:
Start of a Journey

There was ample seating and there were few passengers, but I was far too excited to sit down. The whole journey through, I stood by a window, letting the experience wash over me. My destination was 'abroad'.

I had left my home and the town of my former employment in the 'land of a thousand hills', the Sauerland in southern Westphalia, and watched the landscape rolling by, flat and uneventful now, sometimes beautiful countryside, sometimes forests, sometimes bland and damaged urban towns and villages. There were still the traditional homes and hamlets dotted about the countryside, though there was much rebuilding, stark and functional. Some were still ruined. It did not matter. When you are twenty and the future lies ahead of you, every new scene is a new adventure.

That is the beauty of trains travelling through Europe, but it might have been anywhere in the world and that feeling would most likely have been the same. Views change constantly. No sooner do you encounter a blot on the landscape and it has passed. It was all new to me, and it was the first time I had made so long a journey, though it was little in the larger way of things. Some of my schoolmates had never even left the village. From the green woods, meadows, little fields, and the traditional black-and-white timbered homes and farmsteads of my home through the banality of commercial and stark housing of post-war cities that want to make you egg on the rattling caterpillar of the train to greater speed. Except that would shorten the pure pleasure of the journey.

We crossed the mud-brown waters of the Rhine I knew from earlier trips by bicycle, but that had been to the Rhine of grape-stock-covered banks, with inns and wine cellars, lofty high castles, and romantic castle ruins on picturesque crags. Then the water might well have been wine. I got a glimpse of the majestic medieval towers of Cologne Cathedral that still rose from its bomb-ravaged surroundings in spite of its many hits, as it must once have done from the mud-plastered thatched dwellings of the populations that built it. I had been there with school friends—an age-old reminder that man can aspire to better and loftier things if the will is there, but also that mankind has learnt little since.

Bombing—i.e. punishing the civilian population—had continued long after Germany's aggressive forces of a totalitarian regime were beaten and Allied victory was assured. Cologne had been visited by 262 separate air raids by the Allies during the war. Burnt-out houses, factories, offices, and hollow-eyed ruins hugged the ground, but there were also many signs of rebuilding—of a new beginning. In the middle of that sea of ruins, the twin spires of the cathedral rose dark and accusing to the sky, a dinosaur from another age. Christianity is supposed to be all about love, especially love for your neighbour. Cologne Cathedral was made a World Heritage site in 1996. With its twin spires at 157 metres, it is the largest Gothic church in Northern Europe.

Looking back, the whole journey was a leap of faith. It was just ten years from the end of a war that had seen my country invading and running roughshod over its

Cologne on the River Rhine had been a repeated target for the Allies during the Second World War. There were numerous raids, but on the night of 30–31 May 1942, some 1,096 Allied bombers dropped about 1,500 tons of bombs on the city, obliterating or damaging 30,000 houses. Worse was to come. An assault on 29 June 1943 ignited a devastating firestorm to rival those at Hamburg and Dresden. In all, 1.5 million bombs flattened Cologne. Many people had moved out. Before the war, Cologne was home to 770,000 people; at the end, 40,000 remained. Only the cathedral stood proud.

neighbours with military might. I had lost two uncles in that war, one on the way into France and one on the Eastern Front. My own father had returned from being a prisoner of war in Russia's Ural Mountains only in 1948.

My blind faith can only be explained by my youth and belief in my own innocence, mixed with a prowess inspired by my training in what we called '*die schwarze Kunst*'—'the Black Art'—owing to the traditional reliance on black ink in printing. I was a compositor and a proud one. My hero was Gutenberg—the inventor of individually movable letters. Now I was on my way to take up a job in one of the invaded countries, in Haarlem in Holland.

I did not feel responsible for what a previous generation had done, though I was anxious how I would be received by the formerly invaded.

Outside the train, the scenery rolling by like a film was back to banality and flatness, a green, man-manipulated flatness, where most of the waterways do not flow in undulating curves, but stand in straight linear monotony from horizon to horizon. Yet from ground level, Dutch canals can be handsome, even pretty in a comely sort of way. Maybe our sensibilities have been influenced by painters in past times that recorded those landscapes and its people with such deft assurance.

Standing in the corridor of the train to Amsterdam, I was bombarded with impressions. The nostalgia for that which was left behind diminished with distance and was replaced by the excitement of the new: the challenge—an adventure, mixed with trepidation. Yet this was not a trip into the unknown, nor a holiday sojourn. I was expected.

It was a Saturday. My previous employ—indeed, the place where I had learnt my craft, had worked my apprenticeship, and spent two years as journeyman—had terminated the day before. On the Monday ahead, I would start my new job in a large printing house, also as a typesetter, but working in another language. I spoke some Low German as my parents did among themselves and the villagers, and that was akin to Dutch, but only slightly. Apart from that, I would have to learn fast. It was all part of the adventure.

Acknowledgements

Thanks to Karen Bowman, Tessa Church, James Fanthorpe, Antje Fuchte, Johannes Geck, Josef Gierse, Gisela and Heinz Hennecke, Ursula Jung (Stadtarchiv Meschede), Gottfried Kortenkamp, Ludwig Kortenkamp, Gary L. Moncur, Craig Moore, Vladimir Okhotin (RussiaTrek.org), Marianne Rettler, Bernd Schulte, Peter Smith, Michael Stratmann, Ute Tolksdorf (Westfalenpost), and Rodney Young.

Efforts have been made to gather permission for the use of photographs from a variety of sources. Should any comments need to be incorporated, this will be adhered to in future printings.

CONTENTS

Introduction

Perhaps it is because of the traumatic times into which I was born that the past is like a locked image. As I was not there later to watch the village evolve in an ever-changing present and without actually witnessing that change except for short visits, it stayed in my subconscious perhaps more than it might have had I stayed.

Germany had been punished at the end of the First World War to the point that there was great hardship. It was almost inevitable that people welcomed the rhetoric and promise of better things to come by a murderously charismatic leader. Austrian Adolf Hitler even managed to be accepted as sole ruler. It was a good start, and at first, it actually worked. Hitler cut down on unemployment with schemes like building the first motorways in the world. Then he resumed conscription and rearmament and led the nation into all-out war, defiled its name with hatred, murder, and genocide, and caused the deaths of tens of millions. Germany today is much smaller than it was in his time.

His boasted promise was a German Empire that would last a thousand years. It ended in 1945—when I was ten years old.

The Nazis had come to power on 30 January 1933 when Adolf Hitler became Chancellor. The Reichstag building, home of the German parliament, had been burnt down, possibly by the Nazis themselves as an excuse to clamp down on any opposition. New early elections were called. Meanwhile, the Nazis (*Nationalsozialistische Deutsche Arbeiterpartei*) had unleashed a campaign of violent terror against all opposition, parties, trade unions, communists, and, very soon, Jews.

On 5 March 1933—two years to the day before my birthday on 5 March 1935—federal elections were held in Germany following the Nazi seizure of power.

By the time I arrived, it was too late—the die had been cast—not that I particularly tried to change anything, as, being a sickly child, I would not be much use to such a go-ahead future. Just like Trump in America and the protagonists of Brexit—the break with the European Union by Britain—Adolf Hitler promised the people to make the country 'great' again, a promise heartily embraced by many in Germany following the humiliations and deprivation in the wake of the First World War.

'*Ein Volk, ein Reich, ein Führer!*' ('One People, One Nation, One Leader') was the new slogan. Hitler became omnipotent.

War is usually encouraged by older men who then send younger men to fight and die for them. Luckily, I was then far too young.

My parents, Maria and Robert, in later life, looking from a window in the house they built in 1949, surrounded by my father's work in slate as a *Schieferdecker*—a master roofer.

1
Remblinghausen: A Village in Wartime

Now I am past eighty years old, I look back on the events of my early years and realise how much they affected the rest of my life. It was a rough awakening from the first moments I remember, asthmatic and usually found warmly dressed with shawl and long stockings. In-between all the ugliness of the times, there was a childhood not quite in sylvan glades—well, such moments were there, of course, between times of sadness and terror, but as a child, all of that is beyond your capability to bring about change. Events simply steamrolled over us, largely self-inflicted by the grown-ups who ran the country.

Winters I remember most, and sloshy, muddy days. And death, or the possibility of it. Death was a constant companion: never far away, clinging like a shadow, permeating every aspect of life. A sister had died just over a year old and my grandfather also, though he was 'old'. My father was away 'in the War', in Belgium and France at first and then in Russia from 1944. Three uncles were also 'in the War', like most of the men in the village.

People both dreaded and waited for the post lady to deliver, or they might call at the Post Office if they were desperate for news. A call from the post lady, who herself hobbled along with a stiff knee, might mean a letter from a loved one or it might mean an official notification of a death or a 'missing, believed dead'. In one instance, I found out only later, the message had been: 'Your son was no German'. He had been shot at dawn for not wanting to kill people.

Death was in the news, in conversations, and it sometimes came from the air indiscriminately, children not excepted.

In the previous war, it had been up to the village priest to deliver official war news, and women might begin to scream just when they saw him approaching the house.

Left: The official blazon of the village of Remblinghausen features St James the Elder (*Jakobus der Ältere*), the local patron saint, and the lower half contains wheat ears, a reference to agriculture. The arms were granted on 28 February 1936.

Below: View north into the village in 1928. The house on the left is still standing today, not the shed. To the right, the old house was about to be torn down while a new one is rising on extreme right. That is where we lived when my father returned from the war. That house, too, has long since been replaced by a newer one.

Two images of the centre of the village, the oldest found from early last century. Timber buildings with straw roofs.

2

Tales from the Tailors' Parlour

Maybe it is because I have recalled them so many times—the voices, the sounds, the three languages—but I remember some of those early days as if they were yesterday. To us children and to visitors, adults spoke in High German, but among each other, they spoke in the old local vernacular—Plattduitsk—that was almost another language and changed a little from village to village. In catechism classes and in church services, we were exposed to Latin, though we did not always know exactly what we were chanting. Much of that has been forgotten today, the old words and the old songs. So much has changed, so many new influences, radio, television, the digital media, and travel, and much of that influence is a result of the war.

Yet when I am alone and listen, I can still hear and feel and smell those times, those early, almost forgotten days, when the old house was full of life and activity, when my grandfather and my uncles sat on large tables, legs crossed and sewing, though I only barely remember my grandfather. My memory of him is as an ailing old man, sitting close by the tall warming range in the tailors' parlour draped in a greatcoat against the cold.

The old house was not my home. Our home was in the middle of the village, a rented house between the churchyard and the main street, where my father kept most of the paraphernalia of his trade as a master roofer. There were two rooms upstairs and two downstairs. The one at ground level at the churchyard side had been the sleeping quarters of an apprentice until my father was called up. It was unheated, I believe.

The old house was my grandparents' house where we spent much time while my father was absent.

Sometimes, my uncles would come down from those tables—or was it just one table? Everything seems larger to a child. With giant scissors, they would cut the cloth around paper patterns that were fastened to the cloth with pins. Or they marked on to the cloth with white tablets of chalk. They had made coats and waistcoats and best suits for the villagers. Brown paper patterns of all kinds of shapes hung on the walls.

Above and right: Grandfather Adam as a young man with friends on the plot that had been in the family since 1640 and his pocket watch with his engraved name. Grandfather Adam sits second from right.

Grandfather and grandmother's wedding, Adam and Maria Schütteler, 16 July 1896. On *Opa*'s arm, his mother had vowed not to let him go.

Relatives and neighbours at another wedding. We find grandfather third below the highest man in the background straight down past another man with hat and moustache. He is partly covered by the head of my grandmother, who stands between two darkly head-wrapped elderly ladies behind what might be the bride's seated father.

Right: Grandmother and grandfather, Maria and Adam Schütteler.

Family portrait. *From left to right, back row*: Uncle Josef (Jupp), Wilhelmina (Minna), and Theresa. *From left to right, middle row*: my mother Maria, grandfather Adam, grandmother Maria (the baby on her lap might be Johannes or Willibald, who died young), August, and Robert (who died in France). Seated in front is Aunt Anna. My mother recalled the reason for her pout was that her borrowed shoes did not fit.

Above: In almost the same place as my grandfather and friends, Uncle Josef (Jupp), standing second from left, and Uncle August, seated, first left.

Below: Grandparents' house: Copy of a document of 12 January 1640 when Hans Schomacher received a plot of land '*auff der Knippen*' from Wilhelm Ditherich Kloidt at the big house near the village.

When the church was painted in 1926. The old school to the right and in the distance the big house of Cloidts outside the village.

The Singer sewing machines, black and decorated with letters and scrolls of gold on their ornamental cast iron stands, were buzzing with activity when keen feet worked the treadles and busy hands fed material and lining under the zigzagging needles.

In those earlier, happier days, people would just drop in, men particularly, from near and far, to try on their orders or just for a chat. Sometimes, especially on Saturdays and before holy days, they would call in for their haircuts.

There was usually much conversation in the parlour in those days. So many stories were told and retold and made up. Everybody knew each other and everybody had time for a few tales. Everything that happened in the village and in the rest of the parish would be discussed sooner or later in the tailors' parlour, particularly on long winter evenings. Often I used to sit there, open-mouthed and quiet in a corner. I was a good listener and there were so many stories, like that stormy evening when Uncle August recollected the experience of a creepy Alpine night. He may have embroidered some of the event, but the core of the story was true. As a young man in those bad and hungry days following the First World War, he had been sent, like so many others from 'the land of a thousand hills', the Sauerland, to travel south to the Alpine regions to sell iron wares that had been forged in local foundries from locally mined iron. There was iron in those mountains of the Sauerland.

A rare visitor rapped on the door that evening and entered the tailors' parlour.

'Good evening, everyone.'

'Oh, good evening, Dr Padberg. What brings you into the neighbourhood? And on a night like this, when one wouldn't let a cat out of the house. It's beginning to feel like winter. We have to switch on the light much earlier and black out the windows. Come in and take a seat. I trust you could not see any light outside?' *Verdunkelung* meant light-tight covers that blacked out the windows.

'No, you are fully blacked out. The house looked deserted.'

'Oh, good, then the bombers won't find us.'

Uncle August, the younger of the two brothers, climbed down from the table, took the visitor's hat and coat, and placed them on a rack of hooks near the door that led from the stone cobbled hallway into the parlour. Uncle Jupp nodded and smiled his welcome, but stayed conscientiously with his task.

'Well, you know,' Dr Padberg said as he sat down on one of the chairs that lined the walls, 'whenever I know there is going to be an opportunity to visit Remblinghausen, I let my hair grow, just to have an excuse to come and visit here.'

'You don't need an excuse to come and see us,' Uncle August joked, 'you know you're always welcome. Did you have a pleasant journey? Is your family with you?' Uncle Jupp just smiled. His name was Josef, but everyone called him Jupp.

The visitor answered pleasantly and Uncle August said he hoped they might all meet up again sometime soon, not forgetting the good doctor's beautiful wife and sisters.

Aunt Anna (second from left), on an outing with friends, must have tried to join in the latest fashion here in November 1938. On returning home, she had been admonished for being so extravagant with her money.

Right: Uncle Robert, who died in Northern France.

Below: Family and friends in the tailors' parlour under a lamp that could be lowered for precise needlework, *Verdunkelung* (blackout curtains) on windows, a fresh air vent on the wall, and a map of the Middle East and the Holy Land. Uncle August (second from left), then *Oma*, Aunt Anna, her beau Franz, neighbour Josef Nelle, Aunt Minna, and my mother. On the left is Mrs Muteng (or Moutain), whose husband most likely took the flash picture.

Uncle August seemed to have a soft spot for the doctor's 'beautiful wife and sisters', though there were children as well. While talking, he had placed a chair in the centre of the room. Dr Padberg sat down on it the wrong way around, his legs either side of the backrest, which then became an armrest for the doctor's crossed arms. A large white sheet enveloped the sitter like a Bedouin tent, the top tucked into the gentleman's collar, so that only the head rose from the white pyramid. From an unrolled linen cloth cover appeared scissors, combs, and hand cutters with two rows of teeth that clicked when pressed by the barber's hand.

'The usual?' Uncle August said, rather than asked.

'Yes, please, the usual. You know me well enough,' said the visitor. There were only two choices, short and shorter.

It occurred to me then that the doctor lacked the horizontal dividing line most usual visitors carried along the forehead. I had often wondered at the white line farmers and farmhands bared when the inevitable felt hats had to be removed at hair cutting time. Above the hat-line the skin just never saw the sun and remained pale pink in contrast to the rough, weatherworn, leathery faces and occasional necks of rolled fat that glowed almost red in summer. Dr Padberg had no such line.

Someone kicked his boots clear of soil before stumbling into the room with a tearful red-rimmed eye, and grandmother was called urgently into the parlour: 'Mother, can you come here for a moment? Fritz has caught something again that's a little too small for me.' Grandmother had a reputation for her gift to locate and remove foreign objects that might settle under eyelids, especially frequent at harvest time in those days before protective goggles.

Uncle August remained serious, though he could barely suppress his mirth. Something like that is not laughable. Gran greeted Dr Padberg with amiable friendliness as one greets some exalted personage and old friend, and turning to the latest visitor, she tried to look him in the eye on tiptoe. The ceiling was high enough, just; even so, Fritz had to bend low to avoid the beams. Uncle August pushed a chair towards him and he sat down and then gran had to bend down a little.

'How did you manage it? So deep under the lid?' she said, as if she did not already know the answer.

'We were threshing.' Tears ran down freely from the affected eye, 'and then.'

'Oh,' *Oma* said. It happened every autumn, like clockwork. 'Hand me a clean hanky.' Fritz had no clean hanky. Not even a dirty one. Uncle Jupp found a scrap of clean soft linen and the operation began with much rolling of eyes and several failed attempts close to an illuminating light bulb, when *Oma* lifted the affected lid and turned it over inside-up until the offending speck of rye husk was found and safely removed.

'That's it,' she said with a gesture of triumph, as she offered the scrap of linen to the tearful visitor. 'A souvenir. But don't rub the eye anymore, that'll only make it worse.'

'Easier said than done,' sighed Fritz, trying to stay his hand from his grime-streaked face. Gran had already vanished back to the kitchen. He breathed deeply, like someone who has lost a heavy weight from his heart, or in this case, from under his eyelid.

'Thank you, I owe you,' he said at last, a little clumsily. 'Only I haven't got any money on me … in my working clothes.'

'Pre-sales service,' laughed Uncle August, 'you'll need a new suit sometime soon, won't you? Don't forget the big purse then, the one with the lock on it.' Fritz was not listening. He had a better idea.

'You know you're mentioned in the Bible?' he said, knowing the Good Book practically by heart, only his understanding might not always tally with the real meaning. 'Why beholdest thou the mote that is in thy brother's eye, but considerest not the beam that is in thine own eye?' Only now did he recognise the other visitor: 'Ah, Doctor, don't you believe anything you hear here.'

The good doctor sighed: 'But that's why I like to come.'

Uncle August had cut and combed and cut along a comb to ensure straight and even lines. Brown locks had fallen to the floorboards like leaves in autumn.

'If my mother had a beam in her eye, she might not have been able to see yours.' Uncle Jupp, who was the elder and perhaps also the more sensible, now added to the conversation. Fritz laughed a shy laugh, a laugh that was well known in the neighbourhood.

'The story with the beam reminds me,' Uncle August said, 'of an evening in the lower Alps—the Voralpen—when I was still down there trying to sell scythes and sickles and grindstones.' Uncle Jupp sighed deeply. He would have heard it all before many a time.

'Doctor, Sir, I warned you,' said Fritz. Even so, he himself tarried by the door instead of taking his leave.

'Is that correct, so, *Herr* Doctor? Will your ladies be happy with the result?' Uncle August held a mirror in position behind the freshly shorn head, so that the client could appreciate the result in the wall mirror opposite.

'That's fine,' said the client.

Uncle August found a few more hairs to trim, hairs that seemingly had escaped him earlier, just to drag out the moment. 'We'd done good business, my partner and I,' he continued eventually, 'climbing up to the high farms with their Alpine meadows and persuading the farmers they'd need new scythes at last. It was hard work and sometimes it was impossible to part those stingy farmers from their money. Or they might perhaps just take a grindstone after one had sharpened their old scythes in order to explain how easy it was with our wares.'

Fritz chuckled almost silently. This was a course of action he could appreciate.

Uncle August continued undaunted: 'But every now and then one found a young farmer who appreciated that the old scythes his ancestors had used, had to be replaced someday.'

Fritz bit his lip.

'That's how it was that evening, when I came to a lonely tavern and knocked, in the hope of finding a cot for the night. Nights up there were black as a cat's stomach without a moon and my colleague had wandered down into another valley, because up there were too few farms for two salesmen. I have to say, it was a creepy area, high, dark fir trees and amongst them this lonely inn. I can still see it in my mind's eye, it made such an impression on me. First there was no answer, but I could hear voices inside. Shave, Dr Padberg? Or is that good, so?'

'Yes, please. Carry on, August.'

Fritz had quietly sat himself down in a corner. Now he cleared his throat with a short cough, but he said nothing.

'Yes, good,' said Uncle August, 'can't leave you half finished. Now, where was I?'

'At the door. At the front door,' coughed Fritz who had never left the village.

The doctor grinned as he watched him in the wall mirror without noticeably turning his head.

'Oh, yes, it was getting late, but eventually there was an answer. Several locks clicked and bolts jammed as they were pushed until the door opened just a sliver and a rough voice asked: "It's late. Who are you?" In the local dialect of course.'

'Of course,' smiled Dr Padberg.

'But he let me in. It was then I saw him for the first time. A heavily set character, with beard and muscles and a torn shirt that had seen better days, stood there in the light of the lamp. Gaslight and storm lanterns were still in use there. He only had one free bed, he mumbled, and that was a simple cot high up in the attic. Would that suit me?

'I was far too tired to be choosy and anyway, I intended to hit the featherbed as soon as possible. The rest of the company in his establishment looked at me with partly closed eyes as if they were gaging my worth. They all looked like refugees from justice, gallow birds to the last, and appeared even more unsavoury than mine host. I was well aware of the persistent rumours of wanderers that had vanished without trace, never to be seen again. It occurred to me I might have fallen into such a trap.'

'Hmmm!' mumbled Fritz and shifted on his chair.

While he talked, Uncle August reached for a leather strap, and fastening one end to the wall, he pulled the other end towards himself until it was taut, and with fast, well-trained movements, he sent the cut-throat razor back and forth along its length until it was sharp enough to sever a free-hanging hair, a feat which he immediately demonstrated.

With a boar-bristle shaving brush in an old cup, he produced small clouds of foam, which soon covered the lower face and throat of the customer to resemble a St Nicholas beard.

'"Did I want to order breakfast?" asked the landlord. I thought, "they only want to know if I have money about me," but I said "Yes" all the same. And I would very much appreciate a bite to eat before I excused myself. The man growled something about the lateness of the hour, but he thumped a mug of beer, a lump of bread and some cheese in front of me.

'Later the landlord lit part of the way, for only a ladder reached up to that top room. I did not fully undress and stuck the front supports of the cot in my boots, as was the way to ensure they would still be there in the morning. My money belt

I kept close in my bed. It was a simple mattress on wooden planks, but I would have slept anywhere, I was that tired—walking all day in that thin air. The noise downstairs lasted into the small hours. In spite of my tiredness I couldn't sleep, even though I had put out the lamp immediately. When it finally got quiet downstairs, I was still awake.

'The first thing I heard was a door squeak. It's weird the way even the slightest sound gets amplified when you're listening at the still of night. A finger of light passed through the flap in the floor that led to my attic room. I hardly dared to breathe when the ladder creaked under a weight. Then, through barely open eyes, I saw a storm lantern and a hairy arm. That was followed by a shiny head, then another arm with a long knife that glistened in the beam of the lantern.'

The extra sharp curved cutthroat razor gliding over the visitor's skin left wide tracks like furrows across the white face. Uncle August pressed the doctor's head back so that the pale throat was exposed. There followed another foamy covering to scrape possibly forgotten stubble.

'At that moment I really thought I had sold my last scythe,' sighed Uncle August. 'I froze, especially when the figure's shadow loomed twice as large with the closeness of the light. He bent down to stand the lantern on the floor and reappeared in my view with a small bench or footstool that he placed across and straddled my chest. My arms were pinned tight by my side then and I couldn't have moved, even if I had not been rigid with fear. I silently said a couple of "Our Fathers" without daring to open my eyes more than the slightest glimpse. There was nothing I could do. Nothing at all. Screaming would have been useless even if I had found the air to shout. In a cold sweat I watched the landlord—for that's who it was—climb on to and kneel on that footstool and … right, *Herr* Doctor, that's it. Smooth as a baby's bottom.'

With that, Uncle August removed the last vestiges of foam from chin and throat with a hand towel.

'N-not finished!' grumbled Fritz in his corner, as outside the harvest wind could be heard whipping the branches of the old lime tree.

'I do believe you forgot a small patch right here under my chin.' Dr Padberg grinned and pointed to a bare patch on his throat and Uncle August laughed, perhaps a little pleased with his prowess as a storyteller.

'Ah, yes,' he said, 'mine host. He seemed out of breath, then very slowly he balanced on the stool and stood up, somewhat shakily, quite a feat for such a large man. The long butcher's knife glistened in his hand. The old bedstead creaked under the weight. I couldn't scream. There was simply no air in my lungs.'

'Can imagine,' coughed Fritz with a constricted throat. 'Yes.'

'My eyes were open wide then as they were used to the light and …'

'No, not that,' gasped Fritz.

'… and I saw above me, below the roof, hanging from hooks on long stakes, there were sausages and cured hams and sides of bacon fat. The landlord cut down a nice red sausage and climbed back down. All without saying a word. I saw that sausage again the next morning at breakfast, nicely sliced and spread on a platter, with brown bread and Alpine butter.'

'Excellent. The shave, too,' the doctor said by way of appreciation, sliding a hand over his chin, before he paid and waited as Uncle August brushed his shoulders and collar down with a handled clothes brush. 'Perhaps we can meet on Sunday, if you have time? My wife and sisters would be delighted. Perhaps a wander over the mountains with a few chances for yodelling? And perhaps refreshments at one of your excellent Remblinghauser inns?'

'They're too expensive,' interrupted Fritz. 'Now I really have to go. You have kept me late again. Knew it wasn't true right away, otherwise you wouldn't be here today, would you? *Wiederseh'n*!' He thanked once more for the service, or rather, he hoped they would pass on his thanks to grandmother.

With that, he left the room and the house hastily. The two men looked at each other and smiled. Uncle August grinned: 'It'll be a rare day when he has money in his pocket and even rarer still, when he takes it upon himself to spend any of it.'

The next day, I asked Uncle Jupp just why that evening's visitor was called *Klumpenfritz* (Clod-boot Fritz).

'That's because of the clods of earth that always stick to his boots and sometimes other places, too.' Uncle Jupp pulled a face and I understood what he meant when his tailor's hand raised a trouser leg on which he happened to be working and shook it. We laughed then, both of us, like conspirators.

If I got under anyone's feet, I might be threatened with a shaving brush and a shave myself, but such threats would always end in laughter.

There were other conundrums for a child. Old Hännes with the lumps on his bald head like corks sticking up, a problem that would only ever be revealed when the hat had to be removed for haircutting and of course in church, when he could not hide his growths from his creator. I used to try and figure out if they ever got larger. Uncle August had said they would one day reveal the onset of horns as happened every year to the stags of the forest. Alas, Old Hännes's bumps always remained just bumps.

One day, I was taken to one of the bedrooms upstairs, where my grandfather lay still in a coffin, old and leathery and unmoving, a crestfallen face with a paper roll beneath the chin. On my enquiry, I was told it was to prevent the chin from sagging. Bony fingers were folded on his chest as in prayer. I later learnt he had been 'quite a lad' in his time. During the previous war, he had been a night watchman in the nearby town of Meschede, it was said, but he had served in the First World War and I have found a reference to Tempelhof and that was an up-and-coming military base in Berlin that later became an airport.

To a child, death is unfathomable—I knew from my mother's reaction just how sad the loss of my sister had made her. Maybe I was too young and I had not been close to my ailing grandfather, but his death was quite a natural event.

As for Uncle August's story, there was more than a grain of truth in it—at least the core of the story was based on fact. Like many of the menfolk from the region, in the

A new flag to get used to. A meeting of neighbours with grandmother (left) and Aunt Anna (third from left).

badly deprived years following the First World War, the time that led to the rise of Nazi ideology, Uncle August had travelled south to the Alpine region, carrying and selling Sauerland-made ironware (like scythes and sickles) that would be useful to hill farmers on small fields and sloping meadows. It is a long way to travel to hawk such heavy merchandise from the southern tip of Westphalia to the Alps.

The inflation of the years 1922–23 saw the value of the Mark fall catastrophically. One dollar, which had been worth 4.20 Mark in July 1914, by November 1923 reached the astronomical sum of 4,200,000,000 Mark. My mother recalled the time my grandfather, Adam, had been paid in cash for a gent's tailored three-piece suit. He went into the village soon after with the money in a wheelbarrow. Inflation seems to have overtaken the transaction, for he returned, having spent the money, with the grand trophy of a loaf of bread.

Besides the tailoring, gardening, and a little agriculture, the keeping of cows, pigs, chickens, and geese at one time, my industrious grandparents were beekeepers. Such must have been the proliferation of honey as part of the family diet, my mother in later life would not eat honey. Maybe it triggered too many memories?

Above: In nearby Winterberg, a statue has been erected to those peripatetic travellers like Uncle August who made long journeys between the wars to sell local iron wares.

Below: A note of inflation: 500 million Marks, issued in Berlin in September 1923.

Above: *Oma* and *Opa* with their beehives at the rear of the house, *c*. 1919. Grandmother's crisp apron had been borrowed for the picture.

Righjt: Mother and father and I proving my mother's later assertion wrong that I was so weak I could barely hold my head up, 1935.

3

Even Angels Make Mistakes

It was the depth of winter, with Christmas only days away. The cry of the fox haunted the land—the eerie cry that stifles all other sound and makes smaller creatures huddle up and quake in their respective hiding places, as if nature acquiesced and accepted that some living creature had to die that night, so that another could thrive.

A dog barked somewhere across the bare white moonlit fields. Another answered from a lonely farm as if to emphasise their vigilance. But those farm dogs had never yet intimidated the wily Raynard. Usually tethered, they were no match for a devious mind born to survive.

Farms were spread across the plateau and radiated out into the valleys beyond, nestling among their fields and meadows, among trees and brooks and hills and forests in a wide arc around the village, which in turn gathered about the steeply spired building of the church like chicks about a mother hen. No lights were showing from the small-paned, curtained, and blacked-out village windows.

In the snug two-storey wattle-and-daub cottage at the higher part of the village under a roof of slate and snow, the family of five gathered for the evening meal, though the table was laid for eight. There were only women present, and children. The men had been drafted to the war front or sent to work in war-related factories.

The youngest, we already knew, would not return. At only nineteen, Uncle Robert, my namesake, had been sent first to Poland and then into France 'for the glory of the Reich' to 'defend the Fatherland'. Or so they were told. He had been one of a small band of men in a convoy of tanks and trucks moving west. When boys are old enough to be called men, they are old enough to die. On 16 May 1940, *Panzer-Oberschütze* Robert Schütteler had been the last to leave his post and jumped down directly into an exploding bomb dropped by enemy aircraft. He had died 'a hero's death'.

His place was not laid out anymore.

To the family gathered around that joyless table, Uncle Robert was just a loss. A sacrifice, for what? One could not ask such questions openly. Only a small black-and-white photo with serrated edges, sent by a comrade, remained on the large cupboard. It showed a simple wooden handmade-in-a-hurry cross under a tree in a French meadow. That was all. The sum total of a promising young life.

I was about six or seven years old and I did not understand much of this. I had hardly known Uncle Robert. But I did know that since that message and that picture arrived, there was much sadness in the cottage and in my world.

My mother, my little sister, and I actually lived in a small rented house lower down in the middle of the village, but with my father and uncles away, my grandmother's house had become a second home to us. My father was in France, too, wherever that was, and my favourite uncle, who sent me drawings on rough paper postcards from 'the front', was even further away—somewhere called Russia. When would he return and play with me again? Another uncle, August, the one who invented funny names for everyone and made up stories that made you laugh, he was away, too, working in a factory somewhere. He was not so funny anymore, the few times he had visited. They said he had a shadow on his lung.

Now it was just my mother, my grandmother, Aunt Anna, and my little sister. Her name is Marianne, we called her Nanny for short. Aunt Minna was my favourite aunt, but on this night, she had returned early to her own apartment in the vicarage. Her husband, Uncle Emil, was also away in the war, and being childless, she would spend much time with us children. By comparison with our fairly ordinary abode and grandmother's old-fashioned one, Aunt Minna's flat, with her stylish furniture untroubled and undamaged by children, seemed to be somehow special.

My hands rested on the clean-scrubbed table. There were marks on that grained wooden surface—stab marks. They radiated out in a pattern shape of an opened hand and I had overheard my aunts talking about Uncle Robert, the one who died in France, who had sat on that very spot on his leave, idling, the fingers of one hand splayed out on the wood. With a stiletto-like knife in the other, he had stabbed at the spaces between his fingers and thumb, one after another, developing a rhythm. Faster and faster he had stabbed. A personal dare, but without ever drawing blood. It seemed a silly game. The pattern did not match. My hand was too small.

Idling, I stabbed at the space between my fingers with a blunt table knife to try it out and promptly felt a stab of pain on my hand. I had been slapped by my mother: 'Don't do that. Do you want to cut yourself?'

'Why not?' I thought stubbornly, not really meaning it.

Dinner was served, the simple meal steaming in a bowl within reach of everyone.

'Say the blessing, Robert.' Mother sat waiting, folding her hands. They all followed suit and bowed their heads. She tried to hurry me on: 'Come on, we're waiting.' Tempers were short with all the worry.

But I, though the only 'man' there, did not feel like praying. What did God ever do for anybody? God sent my father away and my uncles and made my mother cross. So often had I seen her crying quietly to herself, however much she had tried to hide her tears. God had taken my grandfather, my uncle, and my other sister. I would not talk to God. My mind was made up.

Above left: My father (on right) in Paris, 6 November 1941.

Above right: My father in March 1943, no longer the smiling young man.

'Come on, we are waiting,' repeated my mother. 'You know the words.' I shook my head and stayed silent. Mother insisted. Even her threat of taking me 'outside' made no impression. 'Outside' meant a spanking in the kitchen. I knew that. It made no difference and I remained obstinate. It became a battle of wills.

My grandmother interceded: 'I'll say it …'

My mother stopped her short: 'No, please, let him. He's got to listen.' My little sister sat demurely, hands folded. She would have said a prayer, had she been old enough to remember one. Even in the absence of a father, the boy had to be made to listen, had to be brought up, war or no war.

She reached for the hazel cane from the top of the cupboard and took me by the hand into the kitchen to save embarrassment all round. I bent over her knee in resignation. As the hazel swished down, I am sure it hurt her more than me, but it had to be done.

Returning to the dining room, I sat down quietly on my chair, my seat burning. Would I now say a prayer?

I kept my silence.

I would go without my supper!

I did not mind.

So my mother took me out of the room again and repeated the chastisement. Would I now pray? I would not. Mother was furious. What was she to do with me? She began to lose her temper.

I bit my lip, but it made no difference: 'Robert shan't pray.'

Robert would not eat.

Nor did I cry.

In desperation, my mother began to take my hand again, but before we could leave the room, her mother—herself close to tears—took her hand: 'That's enough. You're confusing the boy. Leave him alone. Can't you see he's not going to do it now? For pity's sake.'

My mother tried to calm down, her tears flowing freely. She was obviously glad for the interference, though she could not understand my persistence. What else could she do? Without a man in the house.

My little sister had tears in her eyes, too. I am certain she had felt every swish of the rod as if it had been administered to her.

I went to bed hungry and hurting. I knew my mother had to chastise me. I deserved it. I even felt sorry for her lack of success. But if you had asked me why I did not simply give in and say the prayer, I would not have been able to give you an answer. Not even to myself.

In the morning, I was still at my grandmother's house. Mother and sister had gone out, down the road to our own home by the churchyard. After the previous evening's events, I was understandably not in her favour, and I was left to my own devices. My sister is four years younger than I and was too small to be a useful playmate, though I would have looked after her and defended her had the need risen. At least in my mind, I would have.

I could hear grandmother busy in the kitchen. Then Aunt Anna bounced into the room with a basket of logs, which she proceeded to stack on top of the large, black cast-iron range that fitted into a gap in the wall dividing the narrow dining room from the larger parlour beyond—the tailors' parlour.

The tall, rectangular range fitted into its cutaway space with room above it and between its cast-iron legs. It amicably fulfilled its function of heating both rooms at once. In the space above it, logs were drying in the winter, filling both rooms with a pleasant aroma of woodland and the outdoors.

A box-shaped bucket on casters underneath held some briquettes of compressed coal dust. When placed in the range, covered with hot ashes and the air-flow device shut down, they would burn slowly and stay aglow, hopefully, right through the night.

Aunt Minna (seated front, third from right) on holiday care of the state. As a veteran soldier, Uncle Emil was sent on holidays in the Alps.

That fiery part of the range, with its door usually slightly ajar, was paired with another small door underneath, which contained the ashtray. A large square door covered the baking oven part beside them. The upper section of the range could be opened like a cupboard with more large, upright cast-iron doors, also decorated with picture images in relief. Inside, the hot range table was divided into two sets of concentric rings that could be lifted individually from the centre outward to allow varying amounts of direct access of the fire to pots and pans. Near the flue, a sunken, box-like copper container with a raised lid held a constant supply of hot water. I could hear Aunt Anna fussing with the various openings and encouraging the fire with the poker kept under the range.

At my end of the dividing wall, near the outer wall, a doorway opening without a door connected the two rooms.

I happened to be kneeling with my back to Aunt Anna on the wooden bench beside the table, fascinated by the frost flowers that covered the small glass panes, making the windows opaque in those days before double-glazing. The night's frost had formed the most wondrous shapes of ice patterns on the surface. I imagined I could see pictures in them, images of leaves and flowers and strange abstract landscapes—crystalline designs by a master artist.

Labouring with asthma, I breathed on one of the panes until the frost flowers melted and allowed for a small circular cameo view of the outside world, to the nearest of the tall oak trees that lined the gully at the side of the cottage, along the border between gran's meadow and the farm opposite.

Slowly, the first farm outbuildings came into view as I breathed and strained my lungs, my breath short, as usual. Playing outside was rarely allowed when it was damp or cold.

A few days earlier, I had watched two sons of one of the village's teacher's sneaking past, playing at soldiers. They were several years older than I, but even so, my mother would never allow that. The wet and clammy snow would soak through my shoes, I would catch cold, and my asthma would be agitated again. That is why, when I went out, I would always be warmly dressed in a long-sleeved vest and long johns and suspenders holding up thick black stockings under jumper and trousers, and I would wear a long overcoat and a scarf about my face. Luckily I liked to read and draw, and dream.

Over my shoulder, I could just look into the '*Schneiderstube*', the tailors' parlour, through the open door space without a door. Deep in thoughts, I tried to rub some warmth back into the tip of my nose. Aunt Anna had left the room again quietly. She was the youngest of my mother's sisters and still unmarried.

Kneeling by the window, I shifted a little for comfort, lest my legs would go to sleep. As the room warmed up, the windowpanes thawed, losing some of their magic.

The ice flowers melted. A bird had found something to get excited about outside in the snow and I could see the fox's tracks about the house from the night before. They were not very deep. Raynard must have been hungry still.

There would be dead birds around who had not made it through the cold. I was not sure if I ought to be sorry for the creatures that did not make it through the winter, or glad for those that did, because they were lucky.

As I stared, something moved into the corner of my vision outside the window. It could not be. I called out to gran, '*Oma*, look,' but nobody came. I rubbed my eyes. It was still there.

There, outside the window, just a few feet away, dangling on a very long string in the still air was a paint box. A large, colourful paint box. There, out there on a string.

'Oh yes, please,' I must have shouted the words. It would soon be Christmas, and the Christkind was showing me a present in advance. The Holy Child. Or maybe an angel? One of the helpers?

I jumped off the bench in my excitement. I nearly fell over, my knees were that stiff. I thought of running out, grabbing it, but first I looked again to reassure myself. It had gone. Disappeared out of sight. It had to be magic.

What a long string that must have been, reaching all the way down from heaven. I called out to gran again, and to Aunt Anna. No one else had seen the miracle. No one would believe me, but I could not tear myself away from the window now.

I pressed my nose against the cold glass. Could there be more? Everyone had said there would be no presents this year. Not with the war and all. There was nothing in the shops either. I was sorry now that I had refused to say prayers last night. Maybe this was my punishment?

I was so excited, I nearly missed it. Something else was slowly lowered down on that long, long string. A colouring book. Yes, it was a colouring book, hanging there outside the window in full view—and all the way from heaven. To a more casual observer, the flaxen string might have looked somewhat familiar, being widely used on farms on the new-fangled machinery to wind bales, tie sacks, etc.

In my bewilderment, I could barely contain my excitement. Standing on the bench, I could read words on the colourful book. Then an almost imperceptible jolt on the string and the book began to move upwards again.

Oh no, do not let it go yet. Then another jolt. My eyes must have been bulging as the book slowly slid out of the loop of the string and before it could disappear from view, it slipped the loop completely and tumbled into the snow.

There was no holding me now. Snow or no snow. Shoes or no shoes. I was outside and around to the side of the house as fast as my legs would carry me. There it was still, stuck in the snow.

I had rescued it. Now they would believe me, they would have to. I raced, short of breath, to find someone, to let them know. Gran was coming to meet me, to find out what all the excitement was about. She scolded me for running outside without shoes. Then Aunt Anna came in from the other end of the cottage, where the animals were kept under the same roof—the cows, the pigs, and the chickens.

Gran was surprised and gave me a hug, changed my stockings, and dried my feet and rubbed them warm. I was glowing with excitement anyway. Only my aunt, peculiarly, seemed almost disappointed. I put it down to the fact that she had missed it all.

The 'Christkind' had shown me some gifts in advance, but the angels had not secured the knot too well. I had rescued it from the snow: a brand-new colouring book. I hoped none of the angels would get into trouble over this.

Gran said it probably meant I was not such a bad boy after all. Aunt Anna was still covered in bits of straw from 'tending the animals', but that was not surprising. At the far end of the cottage, past the animals in their pens and sties and coops, a wooden staircase went up from the large space between the huge barn doors, which at harvest time allowed hay and straw wagons to be pulled in and out again by teams of horses. They would be unloaded through a trapdoor in the ceiling. A pulley system would even allow sacks of grain to be lowered or raised. The whole triangular roof-space could be filled from end to end with straw and hay and grain for the long winters.

In the gable end, way up above the window where the boy had knelt, there was a low, cobweb-covered window—small, but large enough for a box of paints or a colouring book to be passed through via a broom handle, on a long flaxen string.

Christmas came almost as an anti-climax that year. Among all the joyless worries of the war, nothing could ever match the joy of a present, lost by an angel and rescued by a little boy from the winter snows.

Above: An old gamekeeper's cottage on the edge of the village.

Below: Children sliding on ice on a sloping meadow below the big house.

Fastnacht (Shrove Tuesday) was a traditional evening when children dressed up and walked from house to house, singing and carrying wooden spits like pretend swords for the collection of mainly Pretzel, crisp biscuits baked in the form of a knot, but at family relations or good friends who kept their own pigs, they might receive a much appreciated small sausage to take home (*c.* 1960).

Clearing the midden on to sleds and spreading the contents on fields to enhance the next year's growth was all part of winter fun for village children.

4

A Tea-Cosy Saint Nicholas

Even without most of the trimmings in wartime Christmas was such a potentially magical time that some of my earliest memories hark back to it. We children had not been out of our own home by the churchyard for some days during the wet, cold weather, not even to gran's house, keeping ourselves amused as best we could. I had to be protected from catching cold, lest my asthma would start up again and my sister was yet too small. We sat anxiously awaiting our fate. It was the evening of St Nicholas, just a fortnight before Christmas.

There had been another sister between us in age, but I could not really remember the baby. The picture on the wall in our living room of a pale little face with large sad eyes, propped up by cushions and with small hands laying quietly on the feather bed was the only picture we had of our sister. She had lived for only a little over a year, having died in hospital at fourteen months, meningitis troubling and finally taking her short life. If God took back children at such an early age, would the war be the end of everything?

My mother still wore the dark clothes of mourning. It made her look old before her time. But with brothers, father, and a child already dead, and a husband and brother away and in danger, there did not seem to be much chance for the gay, fresh clothing of a young woman. Older women traditionally wore dark, sometimes with tiny flowers or patterns for relief, like grandmother's aprons.

Sitting on the hard settee (we called it a *chaise longue*) side by side, my sister round-eyed with anticipation, I racked my brain trying to think what wrongs I might be accused of? What misdemeanour of mine had St Nicholas or the angels noted down against me? That was the trouble with angels—and everyone had at least one guardian angel—however much you thought something had gone unnoticed and you had not been found out, the angels would know. Even your thoughts.

St Nicholas always carried a large tome about with him, a list of all our failings throughout the year, as well as the good and right things we had done. For those, his assistant carried a sack of presents, though grown-ups insisted that it was to carry naughty children away in. In those years, that sack usually had far more potential capacity than its meagre contents would require.

The assistant was Knecht Ruprecht, the servant who carried that sack of presents, but also a rod or switch, sometimes made from hazel twigs and most effective as a deterrent in the chastisement of naughty children.

Oh, and Knecht Ruprecht was usually black, an echo of the real St Nicholas, the bishop who had taken to the sea at a time of famine and returned with shiploads of provisions. Knecht Ruprecht was one of his native helpers. His position had degenerated into that of a figure of dread, with a black face and a hazel switch, usually younger and smaller than the stately bishop Nicholas with his superior air, his staff and book, and his intimate relationship with God and the angels.

Aunt Minna was there with us, our mother's older sister. She lived not far away across the churchyard, in her own flat at the vicarage. With no children of her own and with Uncle Emil away in the war, she would spend much time with us. Her soft and ample figure was always a reassuring presence.

This night they took it in turn, mother and Aunt Minna, to go outside and await the arrival of St Nicholas, whispering among themselves or just passing glances and acting mysteriously. Wondrous things, I suspected, were carried in large apron pockets. A drink was ready and some glasses. St Nicholas would need warming 'Schnapps' on a cold night like this.

The house was small and simple: two up, two down, on a basement and cellar, built on to the side of a larger, more substantial house of brick. It faced the main village street, though the long, roofed-over wooden stairs led from the higher churchyard at the back directly to the upper two rooms, which were separated by a narrow hallway.

There was a commotion on the wooden stairs outside. The clanking of chains, stamping of feet to remove snow from heavy shoes? Whispers. To us children, waiting with trepidation, it seemed an eternity. Then, heavy footsteps thumped along the corridor and there into the light from the single bulb dangling under its simple, conical shade in the centre of the room, stepped St Nicholas.

Disappointment mixed with a generous amount of awe may be the right description on my part. If I had expected a bishop, with all the gold-embroidered glamour that promised, I had forgotten to allow for the war. Instead, there was a man in a curious collection of clothes, in a long dark overcoat with the collar turned up under a covering blanket. For a stole, he wore something remarkably resembling a tablecloth wound about his shoulders. In place of a lofty mitre, his head was covered by what looked remarkably like an old knitted tea cosy, pulled about the ears. A sheep wool beard covered much of his face. There was something familiar about that face. But no, it could not be. The booming voice was at the same time familiar and frightening in its disguise.

My little sister sat open-mouthed at the edge of the settee, her big dark eyes almost popping out at the manifestations in front of us, for just as strange as St Nicholas was his helper, who strutted in, clanking chains that dangled from his midriff and brandishing a hazel switch, pleated and menacing.

'He' was dressed from head to toe in black and with a black face that glistened whenever it caught the light. Large white eyeballs rolled and stared and seeped water. This Knecht Ruprecht never spoke. The sack over his shoulder did not seem to be all that heavy, yet it had a pair of small stocking-clad legs dangling through its base. I was ashamed to admit to myself that I was glad the sack was already occupied and it made me feel safer.

When St Nicholas opened his big book, the writing troubled him. There seemed to be a separate notelet among the pages, especially about the children. Our mother had to help with the reading. Some angels obviously had pretty poor handwriting. What would their excuse be, I wondered.

St Nicholas rumbled more than spoke in his oddly guttural voice: 'This seems to be a particularly bad little boy,' and he listed some small failings and omissions, the sum of which hardly seemed to warrant such menace. Ruprecht rolled his eyes and rattled the chains. The black-stockinged, knobbly legs protruding from the sack moved as he moved, but there surprisingly was never a whimper from the child inside. 'Maybe it's tired and asleep,' I thought, and wondered which one of the village children had been so bad as to deserve being taken away. I would try and find out who was missing.

The little girl got more praise, but to her, praise and scolding meant much the same thing. When St Nicholas closed his book, she immediately slipped off the settee, away from the security of Aunt Minna, turned and offered her little bottom without being asked to. She did this again when St Nicholas came near, until Aunt Minna reassuringly placed her on her lap and held her close. I held her hand, too, but more to reassure myself. St Nicholas did not use the switch. He did not have to. We children would be good, we promised. Until Christmas at least.

St Nicholas still had trouble speaking with his unusual voice. A tongue tangling with pieces of potato pressed into cheeks, as I was to find out later, was bound to sound odd. At one time, he had to turn around out of sight to replace a dislodged piece. Even St Nicholas felt the deprivations of wartime. We children did receive some presents after all, some sweets and hazelnuts and 'Spekulatius', the home-baked thin biscuits in the shape of children and angels and animals and sheaves of wheat and Christmas trees, that tasted of cinnamon and cloves. Spekulatius were synonymous with Christmas.

When the visitors left, they refused the drink, but mother took the bottle and glasses with her outside the room, just in case. I did not realise it then, but that evening, I experienced some of my earliest doubts about St Nicholas and the massive task of his yearly journey to visit all the children on the same night. Would he be visiting those other places too, where my father was and my uncles? Could he not bring messages? Why, with his connections, could he not stop the war and let them come home and let everybody be happy again?

Unbeknown to us children, Uncle August was home on sick leave from his factory over Christmas. He happened to be back the very next day.

It was not until many years later that I learnt the story of how a teenage girl, a distant relative in the village, had spent painful hours that night, trying to remove shoe polish from her face, which had made her eyes run with water and almost peeled her delicate young skin in the effort.

Above: A snow-bound mill in a secluded valley below Sägemühle.

Left: Christmas at Aunt Minna's.

5

The Magic of Christmas

Christmas always was the most special time of the year—so private, one would not even intrude on one's nearest relatives on Christmas Day. We were luckier than most, having several homes to visit and presents to collect. On the second Christmas day, we would dress warmly and walk up the road to gran's and we would visit Aunt Minna.

A fir tree, 4 or 5 feet tall and cut from the surrounding woods, was the visual representation of Christmas in every home.

Among gran's lands were a field and a meadow and even a small piece of woodland on the larger of the range of hills that almost encircled the village plateau.

It might be Uncle August who brought our tree, but someone would always remember. On the days before the festival, men would pass from the woods with an axe in a greatcoat and a tree or two tucked under an arm—furtively and embarrassed at times in the darkness of the early evenings, if they did not own woods themselves. But usually, it was with the owner's understanding in reciprocal arrangements.

Advent built up the excitement and expectation, when for three Sundays beforehand, an extra candle would be lit each week on a small wreath of fir twigs and red ribbons on the sideboard until, on Christmas Day, all four candles together announced the arrival of the Lord.

On Christmas Eve from their year-long hiding place in or on top of the wardrobe came the baubles, the bells, the stars, and candle-holders, the glitter star for the top, and the narrow strips of silver foil called Lametta, which draped over the needle-branches like glistening tresses and would be collected again after the festivities, strand for strand, for reuse the following year. It would turn even a misshapen tree into a shining conical pleasure. Alas, there would be less and less of it as the years went by.

But first, the silvered cast-iron tree-stand had to be found and the tree secured, bolted in its tubular base, and then safely brought in to a prominent corner of the living room. A job for Christmas Eve—never earlier.

We children would help as much as we could. I found much pleasure in the even distribution of the shiny, delicate and brittle baubles and the Lametta as I got older.

The silvery metal candle holders, which gripped the green branches spring-tensed with their lower jaws and held small white tallow candles, had to be carefully placed so that higher branches could not catch fire. Those candles came shorter and shorter as the years went by, even if they were lit only on the rarest occasions, being almost impossible to replace. They were also the cause of many an accidental fire, though we were always careful (even the massed trees about and above the crib group at a baroque side altar of the village church caught fire one Christmas, causing considerable damage).

Christmas Eve was simple magic. Anticipation, rather than fulfilment, seems to carry the greatest joys in most of life's events. Simple things become rituals of quiet importance. The decorating of the tree, the hay that was laid out on the doorstep for the Christ child's donkey, and the pudding left on the table as libation for the much-travelled angels. The pudding had usually disappeared by morning, not always the hay.

For children, the night of mysteries knew little rest—at least not until late—listening for sounds, for creaks on outside steps or on the roof, until sleep spread its inevitable wing and not even the most determined of little eyes could stay open. It was not until many years later—when I myself was away from home—that I realised that there were people lonely enough to spend even Christmas Eve in public houses, away from loved ones or anybody close.

Mother would light the candles just before we got up on Christmas morning, and by their magic illumination, we would find under the tree whatever presents the 'Christkind' had been able to organise for us and our mother and gran and the aunties. Useful things. Useful clothing was a favourite, though such extravagances were becoming rarer, too.

A wooden pencil box, dolls carved of wood or made of cloth; toy wagons roughly cut from wood; small animals of wood or *papier-mâché* with houses, hedges, gates, and trees to plan imaginary villages, peopled with painted wooden postmen and farmers were favourite gifts; story and fairy-tale books on poor paper; books for colouring or printed sheets for cutting out would fire young imaginations; ducks on egg-shaped wheels—or round wheels with the axels set off-centre—that wobbled when pulled along, or sausage dogs that were jointed into snake-like movements for the little girl—most toys were handmade and most were of wood. Tin soldiers, tin cars, or wind-up toys might be well-used heirlooms. A '*Buselkatte*', or spinning top. I remember a large colourful one, made probably from thin sheet tin that made a humming sound when the plunger was depressed and it kept turning for ages.

Our mother would tell of the few such presents she received in her younger days as one of a family of nine that survived childhood in gran's cottage under the large linden tree. She would tell of the neighbourhood boy who, at a time when such presents were still possible—mechanical toys, cars, or tanks—disappeared with his presents to the barn beside his house. There he would take them to bits in a fit of discovery, hammer them into submission if necessary, then, unable to rebuild and assimilate them, he would walk about sulking and crying that he had been forgotten.

Such tales seemed hilarious, knowing the family that initiated them.

There might even be a field-post letter from our father at the 'front' or a postcard from Uncle Jupp addressed to me personally, with a Christmas fir-twig and a bauble and candle drawn on it. While our mother might be sad, our father had been away for so much of our young lives, he featured less in our consciousness as I remember.

News was getting rarer, too—especially good news. The monthly magazine that had been a favourite source of outside interests and information with photographs, stories, poems, cartoons, and puzzles thinned down year by year. Pages were getting fewer and fewer, until it became no more than a broadsheet, showing the glorious soldiers, airmen, and sailors smiling for the camera or looking grim in their gruesome war machines that became increasingly larger and more desperate.

A Christmas tradition that had survived from times past was one I rather enjoyed, even when I was older. When Christmas was past, at Epiphany, the feast of Three Kings, local lads dressed up as the intrepid followers of the star on their way to the Holy Land. The ingenuity employed when little was available in the way of kingly attire was remarkable, with paper crowns and tablecloths and such, they resembled a collection of hobos with attitude. Wise men of the east delivering gifts? Our version followed a wooden star cut out by fretsaw and via an empty wooden cotton reel and a long nail held in place on a suitably long staff. With string fastened on and wound about the reel, the attached star could then be turned first in one direction, then the other, as the string rewound itself with the momentum of the pull.

The song they delivered as they knocked on people's doors was traditional and in Low German, deft and folksy. I still remember the refrain in the vernacular: '*Het Geld, dät kamme van 'n Tuinen nit breaken/Do mut me chure Luie aanspreaken*'. An interesting sentiment, quite at odds with the scriptures. These wise men were on a pilgrimage and had to beg to survive: 'The money one can't just break off fences/Good folk are asked to help with expenses'. This of course was followed or accompanied by another homemade device, a rattling collection box.

Children still sing the old song nowadays, though it is sanitised in High German and there are not just three wise men, all the children, even the girls, dress up.

To a child, it is simple: religion and God are a certainty and being bad has consequences and brings retribution, if not now, then in the next life—and existing on the wrong side of the artist Breughel's manifestations for eternity was not a prospect to contemplate. Walking down the wooden flight of steps from our first floor home, we were on the churchyard, looking directly at the high, beautiful church, where everybody went on Sundays and holy days.

There was a chink of controversy. The owners of the large brick-built house to which our rooms were a wooden annexe were Protestants. When their daughter married in a protestant church in the nearby town, my little sister and I were invited as pageboy and girl. I did wonder if it would be OK with God for us to attend such a function, but I remember little of the actual event, except perhaps that my little sister was especially pleased as there were lots of sweet things on offer.

In these egalitarian times, it is perhaps not surprising that everyone is a king and that they follow more than just one star. A recent celebration of Epiphany in Remblinghausen.

Grocery store Soddemann and to the right the annexe in which I was born. Behind it is the church tower.

Above and below: The church had been badly neglected, but in 1926, a war memorial was erected on the west side of the tower.

Catch them early. A political rally down the main street with donkey and paper helmets.

With donkey and swastikas into the new age...

At the big house of Cloidts, they were threshing mechanically in 1938.

'Germans buy German wool!'

How farmers in outlying hamlets got about.

The end of an era. Last journey of the post coach, 28 February 1931. On the right in the right-hand window is Anna, the post lady.

6

Survival Lessons

The German concept of '*Haus und Hof*' is difficult to translate as description of my grandparents' home. Perhaps house and farm come close, because the home was only partly a farm, although they kept cows, pigs, and chickens, and the house had a large space at one end where huge barn doors allowed hay or straw wains to enter and pass through when harvest time required the bringing in of animal feed for the winter months. Animals took up the centre of the house and the people lived at the far end in the style of a Saxon longhouse. That is where the tailors' parlour was situated, divided from the dining space only by a wall without a door. The artisan's equivalent of a living room.

Like most of the houses, farms, stables, and barns in the village it was built of timber, filled in with wattle and daub, though on newer buildings the spaces would be filled with bricks. The roof, like most roofs in the village, was covered in blue slate that was readily available in open mines further out in the mountains. On the roadside, close by the animals and the barn doors lay the usual midden, its unavoidable contents to be ploughed into fields after harvest time. Behind the house lay a large meadow with two gardens where fruit trees and vegetables provided the main crops. Apart from that '*Hof*', which today has been divided into some eight plots with houses, they owned fields and another large meadow outside the village, plus a piece of woodland on the mountains that partly encircle the village.

For a child, the old house and surrounds were full of hiding places that excited the imagination, a playground inviting adventures, of little spaces and wide-open vistas. Nature and the seasons dominated the cycle of activities, church and religion were important and everybody knew everybody.

It could have been a paradise, had it not been for wars and their consequences.

Aunt Minna owned an exotic seashell about the size of a small fist. If you held it to your ear she would say: 'Can you hear the ocean?' It's probably the echo of one's own heart one hears roaring and whooshing in the hollow chamber, not an ocean, but to a child the illusion was real enough.

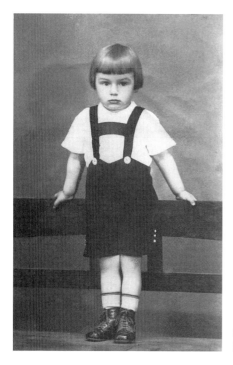

Childhood should be fun and games, not illness and war. The author in younger years.

One spring, I was allowed my own personal allotment in a corner of gran's kitchen garden. Aunt Minna encouraged me as usual with her impish sense of humour.

'Why grow something ordinary, something the grown-ups grow aplenty already?' conspired Aunt Minna confidently. 'Why not grow something much more useful? Like chickens for instance.' It was only a small plot, less than a metre square, but you do not need vast spaces to plant chicken and cockerel feathers. I conscientiously collected only the finest and stuck them into the brown earth, watered them and eagerly awaited progress. When my crop failed, I began to question adult wisdom.

Spring through autumn traditionally were the times of planning for leaner times. Food was a little more plentiful then, as much could be grown in gran's garden and some came free in woods and along hedgerows. Young nettles made a spinach-like vegetable when cooked—green and plentiful. They were not among my favourite fare, though they were particularly recommended for their content of 'iron'.

'You want to be big and strong, don't you?' Gran would say as she dished out the veg.

Chickens were scratching a living and supplied eggs if one could find them. It was always worth keeping an eye open for the free-ranging hens' hiding places, for quite likely a broody hen would find her own secret roost, shunning the predetermined and accessible sites decreed for such purposes by humans. Except, of course, that a fox might find her.

When somebody in the village declared a surfeit of young rabbits for sale, my mother bought two of the cuddly little long-eared creatures in a practical anticipation of rabbit stew. Uncle August found and cobbled together some wooden boxes with mesh-covered lattice frames instead of lids. Turned on their side, the mesh doors formed the front. Leather patches provided pliable hinges. I then raided my savings from visitors' parting gifts and secured access to the fluffy things with real locks from an ironmongers, quite ignoring the fact that a determined thief only needed to sever the leather hinges or lift up the boxes themselves. It was a part of my chores to feed the leverets with lettuce leftovers, grass, and dandelion leaves.

On good days, the rabbits could roam and feed with some freedom under a mesh frame of a square meter or two, which would be moved along the uncut lawn to fresh pastures. The frame had to be lifted on one end when the rabbits were to be returned to their hutches, worrying moments, especially on the many occasions when they took it upon themselves to escape and it needed several hands and adult connivance to return them to captivity.

Inevitably, the fast-growing creatures took on the role of pets, too close an association was not encouraged, but unavoidable. When the time came for the plump bunnies to fulfil the destiny for which they had been fattened, no one had the heart to kill them, let alone eat them, but there were families with fewer qualms and greater need and my mother finally gave them away.

Grandmother had to be of sterner stuff where animal husbandry was concerned. Almost everybody at least kept chickens and they did not arrive oven-ready as today. It was up to Gran to catch, render unconscious, and behead the chosen one on the wooden executioner's block that held the firewood axe.

Around the village on occasion, the first part of the ritual—that of catching the cockerel or chicken—could be an entertaining, if uninvited spectator sport, when old rheumatic hands and aged legs failed to be equal to the task, causing ribald comment or secret giggles when entertaining neighbours with their attempts at catching flighty fowl or even wayward piglets.

It was a sudden, painless death, a matter of necessity, probably preferable to the slow suffocation of today's upside-down hanging production lines. There was one drawback, especially in winter, when the headless chicken had to be brought indoors for plucking.

How it happened was difficult to say afterwards, but gran had come in to the house to complete her task and momentarily put down the lifeless bird in order to attend to something urgent. Perhaps it was the indoor warmth or the wearing-off of the stunned effect that produced the resulting phenomenon, but all of a sudden the headless body took to the air and entered the dining room voiceless but on noisy wings.

Soon, several people were chasing the feathered ball on legs and wings that bounced on past the large cast-iron heating and cooking range into the tailors' parlour, dripping blood and feathers. The saying, 'running around like a headless chicken' was proven that day to indeed have its foundations in real life.

Equally exciting days came at pig slaughter time. That was something requiring specialist equipment and male muscle, and either the poor pig was taken to the local butcher's abattoir and returned in manageable chunks or in the majority of cases a part-time slaughterer would come to the house.

The remarkably fast-moving victims, which had been fattened over the preceding months in daytime outdoors in an enclosure behind the old house, came to the end of their life of privilege usually before winter would draw in with its white encumbrance and before feed became too scarce.

A bolt shot into the poor creature's brain was the preferred and most humane method. There was little time and space for small people at such times when water was boiled and kettles poured steaming liquid over the tough surface as a funnel-like metal scraper depilated the large beast in sturdy fists.

While the main dissection and dismembering would be taken care of by the visiting slaughterer, all the preparations, the salting and curing, etc. would be handled by the women of the house. The sausage mincer, firmly secured to a table top, would receive the raw meat at the top and via a handle, the internal screw mechanism would cut and push the contents forward and into a spout over which well washed and scrubbed intestines were pushed, inside-out, only to be released slowly as they were filled. Sausage length was determined by the type of filling, when a sudden twist allowed for a break in the supply of the minced meat. Even a pig's bladder would be reused, split in half and sewn together and filled via a spout—if it was not blown up and dried to serve as a kind of football.

On freezing mornings, huge pale carcasses, opened like books and attached by their hind legs to the side beams of ladders, would steam, exposed to the cooling elements in yards and farmyards about the village and on the outlying farms.

Most houses and certainly all farms would have air and vermin tight room spaces where haunches of ham, sides of bacon, and a variety of sausages could hang to be cured by the smoke rising from buckets of beech sawdust, which had red hot glowing iron ingots deposited in them. As a legacy of tailoring, at gran's house old smoothing irons would serve amicably. There would be no fire, just dense smoke in the tightly shut room without an air supply, preserving and adding a special taste to the products. Westphalian ham deserves its culinary reputation.

The collecting of acorns was a welcome addition to the staple diet of pigs as they roamed in their outdoor enclosure in late summers and autumns.

On occasion at early spring times, I accompanied my mother to a gardener at a lonely house with stables and greenhouses along a single rough country track outside the village. I liked such outings. We would buy young plants, mostly vegetables, for gran's garden, and as the gardeners were also a friendly family and visitors were rare, we were invited in for the inevitable refreshment of a cup of '*Ersatzkaffee*' (substitute coffee, i.e. of roasted rye grain).

That is when the teasing started. What did I want to be when I grew up? Of course, everyone spoke in the vernacular. I must have been a little vague, for the gardener's recommendation was quite definite: '*Go in't Höltken un schenge de Lule lut!*' ('Go into the pulpit and tell the people off!') or words to that effect. To the subsistence gardener the priesthood must have seemed a soft option of making a living.

I was never particularly suited to the religious life. Serving at mass was a very short and unremarkable interlude and holy smoke, or perhaps it was just standing in church, made me faint. Learning a little Latin, however, was welcome and began to give me an insight into language.

Below the tailors' parlour in my grandparents' old house was a low cellar that was entered down a few steps through a trap door in the thick-planked floor. In the autumn, the cellar would become the depository of potatoes and beets and in one corner would be the cemented trough that contained the salted meat. Smoking and salting and preserving in glass jars were ways to secure foodstuffs for the long winter months before the advent of freezers and fridges. Glass jars with glass lids were made air-tight and kept closed tight by rubber rings that allowed hot air to escape at the boiling stage and kept the lid under pressure from the cooling stage on. Meats, pigs' trotters in aspic, fruits, and vegetables would keep secure for the lean months on cellar shelves.

One day, I followed my grandmother down those steps under the floor of the parlour, where she had to bow her head under the low ceiling. She lifted the weighty stone and the wooden lid that fitted snugly into a large round straight-sided earthenware pot, keeping shredded and pickled white cabbage under pressure. Another kind of food preservation. Sauerkraut would be on the menu that day.

Grubenhaus or pit-house is an expression used by archaeologists at excavations to describe a Saxon hut or hall with a pit or space below what might have served as floorboards. I have oft been reminded when finding archaeological recreations that resembled my grandmother's dank cellar.

Up in the straw-filled attic, shelves of apples would keep for months, as well as apple slices dried on strings and plums dried into prunes.

During the weeks leading up to Christmas, my mother, like many women in the village, would book a specific day and time at the local bakers.

When I was old enough, I was allowed to come along, though with the strict proviso that I did not get in the way of proceedings. While the dough had to be prepared at home, the baker's table surfaces, forms, and cutting shapes were available for the making of biscuits of different shapes, of moons and stars, trees, and people and animals that were pressed with cutting-edged forms from the evenly rolled-out dough.

More labour intensive, but also more interesting, classic and traditional were *Spekulatius* (spiced biscuits) that came as all sorts of seasonal images. The dough, mixed with spices like cinnamon, cloves, nutmeg, and cardamom, had been left to chill overnight to allow the flavours to mingle and make the dough firm and manageable.

At the bakers, the dough was pressed into biscuit-size carved-out images in blocks of wood, then separated from the surplus dough with a fine taut wire that slid across the wooden surface. The dough-filled relief images would then be turned over and released by bashing the work surface. Several of these wooden forms, usually with five or six images each, all different, would be available. The biscuits were transferred on to large rectangular metal trays that could then be manhandled, usually by the baker or an assistant, into the large ovens until they turned into crisply browned favourites. We children loved them. As visually interesting specimens, they might even decorate the Christmas tree, though those pleasures never did last any length of time.

Factory-produced versions are still part of the Christmas scene today.

Recipe for *Spekulatius*

2 pound flour
1 pound sugar
300 gr best butter
3 eggs
1 teaspoon baking powder
1/2 teaspoon cinnamon
1/2 teaspoon crushed cloves
A dash of sweet cream

Mix the butter into the flour, adding sugar, eggs, and spices. Add just enough cream to bind the mixture during constant kneading. It must not be too wet. Leave to chill for some time. Press into lightly floured wooden forms, separating surplus dough with a taut wire and bash to free from forms. Bake in bake oven to a light brown.

The village church with chapels and outlying hamlets.

7

A Plague of Cousins

People were used to walking for miles and miles. In past remembered times local men had walked across the hills to work underground in silver mines several villages away, there and back on a daily basis. When cousins from another village to the north-west visited at the old house it had to be on Shanks's pony. Their mother, Aunt Therese, my mother's eldest sister, had married Uncle Engelbert, a balding, stocky man in a waistcoat who worked on the railways in Wennemen. This being wartime, there was little local transport, so that whole distance was covered on foot. A common tongue-in-cheek saying based on wishful thinking was 'We'll only step here and there occasionally and it won't be far'.

They were probably young teenagers then, innocent and fun loving and happy to escape the stern household at home. To a small boy in short trousers they were grown-up women, tall, with permed hair and the scents of a wider world about them. I remember the long plain overcoats that made the Becker sisters, Else and Mia, look even taller than they were.

We children were largely ignored in their adult games, but they loved to tease—mercilessly, it seemed to me, once they realised my shyness. When it came to 'kissing good bye', I could not escape their attention. No one helped me. To others, my struggles were amusing, nor would the earth open up and swallow me. Kissing? Yuck! I struggled and cried, but there was no escape. Under the open sky, on the front doorstep of the old house, near the linden tree and in view of the whole village, they held me fast and kissed me. With tears running, annoyed with myself and the world of grown-ups, my shame was complete. What use has a small boy for girls, certainly not for the grown-up kind? Kissing, at that age, was for cissies. How could anybody do that in public? The adults just laughed and thought it funny, and in the grip of such adversity, someone even caught the struggling moment on film for posterity with one of those new simple black box cameras from Agfa.

Shyness was an early affliction, though I am glad to say it did not remain a problem. Bathing was a performance necessitating tin baths that would be brought in from their hooks usually on outside walls, into the kitchen-living room at home or into the washroom at *Oma*'s. Heating sufficient water in kettles must have presented

Left: Cousins walked for many kilometres just to visit.

Below: Kissing girls? Oh, the everlasting shame. The aversion did not last.

a problem on a range that supplied all the room heat as well as facilitating cooking and baking, etc. Bath water was never very deep. Certainly in summer, bath time would have been more convenient at *Oma*'s. Whatever my reticence, the several children of my grandmother all must have had the same no-nonsense experiences.

The washroom, with its cemented floor and simple drainage and its covered cauldron supplying the pigswill, was also a crossroad between animal and human sections of the house, leading to the hall and entrance, the living rooms and parlour, the rear of the building, and the stables.

Apart from bath times, that room was a great part of my play area. Potatoes that made it into the cauldron with its mixture of vegetables like beet were boiled in their jackets. Hot and hollowed out for a dollop of butter after pulling off the skin, they counted among my favourite snacks. Alternatively, added to the glowing embers of a cooling fire—not too early or they would be burnt—potatoes would take on a special aroma, but then that process is little different from today's charcoal grilled efforts 'in jackets'.

Above the washroom at the front was Uncle August's room. I was forbidden to go to the far side of the floor area there as the joists had parted between the human and the animal part of the house to sag at the corner. That did not stop Uncle August, however, to admit visitors to that precarious room.

Shoes were handmade in the village by two families of cobblers who, as fortune would have it, lived across the main road from each other towards the north of the village. Understandably perhaps, as neighbours, they were said to be not the best of friends. My father being in business for everybody, we patronised both shoemakers, one for the girls and one for the boys.

Amid heaps of cut-offs and scraps of leather, men and boy apprentices sat around a room among heavy-duty sewing machines, machines to make and secure the eyelets with metal rims, and curious anvil-like objects that consisted of various sizes of iron feet on one base. At that time, shoes were repaired, resoled, and refitted with metal heel and toe caps and of course hobnails as long as the leather would allow. Even some shoelaces were made of leather.

In the absence of shops and off-the-peg clothes, the village coped with the help of seamstresses. One such lady would visit my mother. She found it preferable to actually sew in the home of a temporary employer when lots of fittings had to be taken into account. She must have owned a portable sewing machine, for I remember her working by the window in our home by the church.

She was a spinster, and the talk came around to the rarity of eligible bachelors with so many men away in the war. Hers, she suggested, was also out there somewhere. Even then I became sport, quite against my better judgement and not allowing for the adult passion for antagonising youngsters. She quite fancied me, it was said, but it might take too long to wait for me to grow up. I was cringing in my hobnailed boots. Later my mother confided the seamstress had meant my Uncle Jupp out there in the war as her intended, but my mother refused to believe Uncle Jupp had been similarly inclined towards the seamstress.

The pretend game. Visitors would invite me to play with their own children, as here with Dr Padberg's family, all pretending to help at farming. I am working the breaks at the back of the heifer-drawn wagon just behind the lady, summer 1939. The sturdy young man was to become one of the names on the war memorial.

Farmers with forest areas might also be hunters of deer and wild boar, assisted by their farm workers, *c.* 1920.

Hats, high collars, and ties, all part of the early wanderers, which would most likely enjoy nature on a Sunday.

A group of wanderers between the wars. Liquid sustenance was never far away.

8

Healing and Wheeling

Franz Heinemann (Lamberts), senior, farmer, and landlord at one of the village inns, was also an asthma sufferer. I remember him sitting in front of the large black-beamed building on a bench under the young linden (lime) trees that flanked the entrance steps to the inn, gasping for air. He was a typical landlord in braces, waistcoat, and rolled-up sleeves, sprouting a fashionable hairy upper lip.

As everybody knew everybody in the village, when someone heard of a doctor with a treatment specific for asthmatics, as a fellow sufferer, he suggested to my mother to make the journeys together. Nobody knew of any successes, but it was worth a try, except that the good doctor's practice was in Essen, in the industrial heartland called the '*Kohlenpott*'—the Coalbucket—between Dortmund and Duisburg to the west, where coal mines, smelting works, and factories abounded. It meant several trips to Essen, which like all the industrial towns was a frequent target of bombing raids.

At one time, Aunt Anna accompanied my mother, the publican, and me. The train journeys alone were adventures few village children would ever undertake. Destinations, connections, and the unfamiliar surroundings, combined with the ever-present threat of air attacks, made the journeys more than arduous for the adults. After all, were not the villages filling up with evacuees from the industrial towns, sharing houses and homes and every available room?

Large-spoked iron wheels on skeletal iron scaffold towers and conical black mountains marked mining areas. The depressing journeys through drab housing estates, past industrial complexes, camouflaged, sometimes devastated, ruined streets, and broken buildings, with drab people, uniformed soldiers, and police in under-lit joyless stations, black-outs everywhere, left the travellers grateful for their homes on the land.

Huge letters painted on rolling stock insisted that 'Wheels must turn for Victory!' The drabness and destruction all around us made talk of Victory sound strangely hollow.

Farmer and publican Heinemann (Lamberts), here standing on a wagon in front of the inn that went up in flames in 1945, was a fellow asthma sufferer.

The doctor administered calcium in large syringes—10 cubic centimetres in the veins of an arm. 'Tell me when it feels hot at the back of your throat and I'll slow down the injection.' If you are ill, you will try anything. I got used to his 10 ccm too, but 10 ccm of calcium means quite a large syringe full when you have only got a little arm.

Homeward bound on a strange rambling station in the middle of unaccustomed chaos, with echoing announcements one barely understood, confusing, trains passing through in different directions and to unfamiliar locations, people carriages or just open wagons, whistling and clanking, belching acrid smelling steam, the air raid sirens sounded the alarm. The publican was absent, possibly enquiring train and departure times, as the agile young Aunt Anna reached and boarded a train that was about to leave, expecting us to follow. It was the wrong train. As she disappeared, fretting and waving, in the distance, we could do little but call after her. We would wait for her return. Then we looked for an air raid shelter. We were lucky. The 'all-clear' sounded soon after. It had been a false alarm. Aunt Anna eventually returned on another train, none the worse for her private detour, but happy to see us.

To build up calcium levels, several such journeys were undertaken. On one occasion, my father happened to be on furlough and he accompanied the publican and me to the large conurbation with damp and draughty stations. In all the confusion, we could not find a convenience in time, and to my deep embarrassment, my father filled my trousers with all the paper and handkerchiefs he could find to prevent me catching cold in my wet pants.

Such furloughs were rare and not of sufficient length to bond a father-son relationship. A whole generation of children spent their formative years without their fathers.

There were occasions when I had to take my father's place and my mere presence and thus protection really amounted to something when soldiers, usually officers, while passing through or on manoeuvres near the village, were quartered out to private homes for want of suitable military accommodation. The well-worn *chaise longue* would be requisitioned and served at such times, even in the two-room house of kitchen/living room and bedroom of a small family. Men in uniform, away from home but not in front trench danger, might take advantage of the vulnerability of another serving soldier's wife or daughter.

As we children slept in the only bedroom with our mother, I would stay up late with her encouragement until she, too, retired on such occasions, discouraging even the most ardent of suitors. So I began a pattern of late retiring that was to stay with me throughout most of my life.

Furloughs were such rare occasions. It was a rainy day and we all stayed indoors in the small house by the churchyard. The radio of glossy veneer with its cloth-backed fretwork front was broadcasting light music—folk tunes, cheeky ditties

Essen with its important Krupp Works in the heart of the industrious Ruhr region was among the Allied bombers' favourite targets. (*Credit: Sergeant 619449 Cyril Moore, Wellington Bomber rear gunner*)

from Berlin, nostalgic songs, songs of separation, of longing and joyful reunions—and waltzes from Vienna. The little house was filled with bliss. Dad was on leave from the war front. Mother was happy, yet also a little embarrassed in front of the children by the sudden attention of an overactive husband who tried to compensate for months of separation and hardship in two short weeks.

To me, the soldier father was a stranger, a break in the familiar routine of our days, almost a threat. When the visitor grabbed my mother around the waist in a spontaneous waltz and danced a few steps on the lino floor, swinging her from the hip with his strong arms, she struggled and scolded him in mock outrage. I mistook her protestations and rushed to her defence.

Without hesitation, I kicked out at the stranger who seemed to hurt my mother. My kick happened to be high to a vulnerable central part of the anatomy. With a short yell of pain, my father clutched the affected part, dancing solo about the kitchen on one leg, convulsed with laughter.

His son was not so sickly after all. Perhaps he also realised that he and his son were growing apart, the longer the war went on.

The eldest son of my father's only sister, Robert Knitter, Fighter Pilot (*Jagdflieger*) in the Luftwaffe, suffered a dangerous accident when his aircraft hit the side of a mountain. The impact threw my cousin forward and through the cockpit cover of his plane, practically scalping him in the process, his scalp being attached still on one side only. Luck must have been with him, for he survived and later seemed none the worse for his misadventure, though for the rest of the war he flew larger—and slower—transport planes.

On one furlough, he managed to pass a message to my father with the chance of a lift back to the Russian front in his Ju 52 Luftwaffe troops and cargo transport, rather than relying on uncertain railway connections. It meant my father could stay home a couple of extra days and still make it back to his post in time, and, of course, he would be flying with his sister's son.

These details were filled in later. The Junkers plane was nicknamed '*Tante Ju*' ('Aunt Ju'), a standard transport airliner. Unaccustomed to flying, before take-off, my father had sought advice: would flying be preferable on a full stomach or on an empty one? A full stomach had been advised, which prompted my father to demolish most of his supply of home produce that had been lovingly packed for him by my mother.

On take-off, he had been provided with a bucket and it had been in use for most of the flight. My father, understandably, was not best pleased, as his precious provisions from home had been lost so pointlessly. Nor did they land anywhere near his destination and he was admonished for returning late to the front.

Later, in peacetime, cousin Robert Knitter took up politics, joined the Centre Party and became Mayor of his home area in Iserlohn, and the two Roberts became good friends.

Above left: *Jagdflieger* cousin Robert Knitter generously distributed his pictures among relatives.

Above right: Cousin Robert with '*Tante Ju*' ('Aunt Ju'), a Junkers Ju 52 transport aircraft, once thought of as the safest aircraft in the world.

9

Early School Days

When school started in September 1941, I received some new books, a wood-framed slate tablet with sponge and cleaning cloth attached, and slate pencils in a long thin wooden box with a sliding lid and a leather satchel made by or at least bought from the local saddler to mark the event. The saddlers were practically neighbours, living two doors along the main street and also backing on to the churchyard. Their youngest son joined school at the same time.

One of the new books carried pictures of children with huge pointed goody bags like upside-down witches hats, only colourful and filled with bonbons and confectionery. The images with such luxuries must have been from some past utopian time to sweeten that first and inevitable parting from apron strings and the start of endless school years spread before us.

My mother took me along to my first class in the New School, which had rooms larger and ceilings higher than I had ever seen and they made me feel small and insignificant. Because of my delicate health, I had been much protected.

Yet I was surprised there were others who watched with long sad faces that were close to tears when their mothers left. Even some who had made fun of me in the past with my warm clothes and scarf-covered face. A farmer's son arrived late and refused to stay without his mother on that first day. No way. To stop his crying, the kindly teacher allowed his mother to stay with him in the small benches. School suited me, as it allowed for talents and themes of interest other than physical prowess to shine and excel and improve.

Our first teacher and muse was *Fräulein* Fischer, small, dark, and dapper. Her brother was the priest in Eversberg, the mountain village or rather town as it was then still, of my father's birth. Eversberg (it literally means 'wild boar mountain'), with its imposing timbered buildings and its castle ruin on its ancient mountaintop, had its historically superior aspirations, and two of my father's brothers and families still lived there.

Miss Fischer, though, was a warm and kindly lady, and being quiet and artistic rather than boisterous, I had found a kindred soul and protector until, that is, the

First school day, September 1941. The stone behind me by the church was known as a 'Findling', a stone found, but not local, very likely deposited during an ice age.

To us, it was the new school, but then a newer school was built after the war. Just like the old school by the church, the grounds are now public open spaces.

occasion when she visited me at home in our small abode by the churchyard while I had been missing school. She delighted in the way I had amused myself by drawing and writing and the advances I had made in learning, until she found the cut-out heads of a man and a woman in profile that were stuck down and staring at each other on paper. Between the two faces I had written the grown-up word 'kiss'. The spinster's enthusiasm for the poorly child dampened considerably from that day on. Obviously my earlier aversion to kissing was on the wane.

Even with short trousers, full-length knitted stockings were the norms in those early years to keep warm. It is difficult to describe today, but they were held up by adjustable rubber garters attached to a '*Leibchen*', a kind of bra without the bumps, a linen band about the chest supported by shoulder straps. My bouts of asthma were especially frequent at spring and autumn times, usually the results of catching colds. Reading and learning filled much of my childhood.

Candles were at a premium, serving all sorts of uses, not least during power cuts and in the absence of torches. It was a long time since my grandfather had produced beeswax. My experiments with candle making were failures, first of all for the lack of tallow wax, though I collected every drop from Christmas trees and wreaths. To the rescue came neighbour Bernard, the saddler's son: 'I know where there is wax'. Bernard was a regular acolyte at mass and he returned with a fair quantity of bright white tallow. Altar candles tended to produce drips that were of little use to anyone. The tallow wax would be heated and liquefied in tin cans on the kitchen stove and then poured into straight-sided medicine phials I had collected. Still the production was doomed, for even if I had managed to secure a wick string centrally at the bottom, the phials had to be broken to release the cooled product because suction would not allow easy removal.

A large wooden chest stood in the foyer of the 'new' school, containing all we had on official sports equipment, some dumb bells, a couple of usually deflated footballs, clubs, a medicine ball, etc., though they rarely saw the light of day.

Sports were not particularly high on the list of priorities for our elderly teachers. Nor do I remember much obesity among students. There simply was not the food available to support such extravagance. Some children walked for miles mornings and afternoons in all weathers from the outlying hamlets. Of course, it meant starting out early in the mornings to be on time.

Once, during break time, the cry went up that a mouse had been seen scampering across the wide stone floor and was skulking behind the sports chest. Someone brought a long stick or a broom handle along and several arms proceeded to pull the heavy chest a few inches away from the wall. Trying not to be thought chicken, I occupied the opposing end with my hobnailed boot between chest and wall, moving the toes up and down from the heel. Somehow, I hoped the usually elusive creature would escape, while the stick prodded from the opposing end. It was a bad move on behalf of the mouse, as the chest rested directly on the floor without a space to hide underneath. Nothing was seen, so when eventually our operation was abandoned, we found a partially flattened mouse where my boot had been.

10

The Prolific Chicken

One fine summer's Sunday morning, a rally had been organised on the football pitch south of the village. It was then grandly named a sports ground. A small wooden aircraft had been deposited at one corner of the field as a rallying point exhibit and example of craftsmanship and pride.

The event would have been planned to coincide with and possibly detract from High Mass, but as the dour village community went their own traditional ways notwithstanding, there was a smaller audience than might have been expected lining the street or watching from windows. Among farmers, life revolved around animals and church, no less on a Sunday. Either family members would divide church attendance between early and High Mass, or they would attend High Mass together from the outlying farmsteads once the animals had been provided for.

Gran's old house stood in sunshine, the lime tree tall near the front door beside the footpath. Its branches had been lopped, but it was still taller than the house. The fence, which constituted the border between the front lawn and the farm next door, stopped at the stone path. From there to the road and up to the side of the house, the approach was open, allowing for access to the large barn doors and to the accumulation of the roadside midden at the corner of the house. That feature was an accepted part of village layout. Few houses were without, as most people kept domestic animals of some kind. Even in the middle of the village, the High Street was still lined with these necessary side products of animal husbandry, although their owners might be shopkeepers, saddlers, shoemakers, or factory workers in the nearby town.

With my asthma, I was excused church attendance more often than not and I was visiting at Gran's house when we heard the music. Snare drums and a small youth band, fanfares sounding ahead of the marching, banner-waving young people in brown shirts, short trousers, and knotted scarves, singing of their belief in a great and lasting future under one leader.

I ran outside to watch. Hitler Youth was on the march. It was also compulsory. The village had no such organisation and the visitors came from larger communities along the railway line or the nearby town—superior beings to set examples to village folk and encourage recruitment. '*Uns're Fahne flattert uns voraus*' ('Our flag flutters ahead of us'). Young voices sang the new songs and tried to stay vocal in spite of the uphill climb.

A handful of people had gathered and stopped to watch. One of the adults carried my little sister shoulder-high for a better view. Chickens and their rooster scratched around the house as usual, unconcerned by the commotion. In the last moment, someone ran to the open front door, into the hallway, and up the stairs to an upper front window for a better view.

Unfortunately, a chicken that had been peacefully scratching near the front door got caught up in the excitement and fleeing, entered the house ahead of the speedy human, and, as the only way forward was up, headed with flapping wings and considerable noise and cackling for the open window at the top passage. An old ironclad chest with a curved lid stood under that window, which led the chicken up and to the only exit available. Chickens over the millennia have lost the ability to fly any large distance, but when forced, can still put up a show, albeit with a remarkable velocity of accompanied sound that is not easy on the ears.

The window stood open, as the windowsill was also gran's place for air-drying small handmade caraway seed-speckled cheeses on a wooden platter that started out white like eggs but were at their best once they had matured to a golden yellow. The harassed chicken exited noisily and with frantically flapping wings from that upper window, astonishingly followed by up to a dozen cheeses roughly the size of eggs. Naturally, the fowl's noise drew the attention of the marching column, which then watched the perceived eggs following from on high. It was not funny from gran's point of view, though the poor youngsters in their impeccable uniforms could not help but lose their steps and their tune as they fell about with laughter at the sight. It took some time to restore order, but deliberate sabotage was not suspected.

11

The Green Arbour

If he ever became a great leader, I cannot say. Or perhaps a famous sea captain or a captain of industry? Perhaps he was looked on as leader only because he was the tallest and oldest in the small group of friends and playmates that met in the green arbour to consolidate their fears and dreams.

Hanni was one of those young people who shoot up quite suddenly, to look down on their contemporaries before their clothing has time to catch up. His trousers were set for high water—they did not reach down to meet his shoes any more, his sleeves were too short and his hands appeared larger and longer than they were. But he was friendly and good-natured and was not ashamed to play with those that were younger and smaller than he.

We had met in a Council of War and we had our problems. The goat-herders from the west side of the village were plotting belligerently and bragging to such an extent, that it could be expected they might appear in other areas with or without their curved horned charges at any moment. They had a lot of time to plan and egg each other on while their bleating livestock grazed along the edges of fields and roadsides outside school hours, and they were largely tall, weather-hardened boys.

As for the lower half of the village, there were so many children now, especially with the additional evacuees, that it could be expected to be overrun at any time. Maybe it was influenced by national events, but somehow one felt threatened.

We would have to do something, even if our plans were only defensive. In the green arbour most of the plotter-conspirators were weakly and delicate or small—except Hanni. But we made up for physical weaknesses by possessing reasonably useful heads.

Perhaps it was only because of the war that we saw danger around every corner. 'We need a cannon,' contributed little Otto, whose reluctantly unkempt hair kept falling over his eyes, 'then we could show 'em something.'

'And if they come from behind with their slings and catapults?' Norbert wanted to know. 'What do we do then, when we're not fast enough to turn such a heavy cannon 'round?' His shoulders heaved as he breathed until they almost touched his ears. Norbert and his smaller sister, Brigitte, were fellow asthma sufferers who with the rest of their siblings and family had been evacuated to a neighbouring farm.

'We could build a glider and bombard them.' Their brother, Karlchen, warmed to his idea, 'yes, with stones. Or hot ash.'

'How can you take hot ash into a glider?' Brigitte had her reservations. 'That would burn, wouldn't it?'

Norbert's ideas flew not quite so high: 'We could build a kite from wood and paper, with a mirror, and when it's high enough we could see when somebody's coming.' That sounded at least simpler.

Little Otto saw his first idea vindicated and stuck to his gun: 'And if we could see when they're coming, we could turn the cannon 'round'.

'I could knot together a long tail of bits of paper,' Brigitte offered, thus underlining her brother's argument, 'for the kite dragon.' But that still was no solution to actual defence.

I had a more down-to-earth idea: 'We could design a plan for something amazing. Outdoors somewhere. Best in the woods—where no one can find their way who doesn't know the plan'.

Hanni did not understand what I meant, but he did not laugh at me. 'What do you mean, something amazing?' he asked patiently.

'You know, we could plant hedges, thorny ones, with false exits and entrances and dead ends and when they're big enough, we could sit quietly in the middle and no-one could find us. No-one who doesn't know the way, I mean. And we wouldn't tell them.' I was proud of my idea, though none of the others had a clue what I was talking about.

At long last, a light lit up in Hanni's head: 'Ah, a maze, you mean?'

'Of course. That would be amazing, wouldn't it?' I felt expansive and vindicated and I breathed deeply, savouring the thought. Anyway, they had to listen to me; after all, I was at home. The green arbour and the meadow and the house that was maybe 15–20 metres away belonged to my grandmother. The arbour had been planted by earlier generations, formed and trimmed and shaped as a part of the hedge that followed the road, or rather the ditch beside the road that gave the only protection from eavesdroppers at the back. The green leafy ceiling and three green sides could be likened to an especially airy room or den, all grown naturally from hedge plants.

The knotty rough bench with backrest that stood against the middle 'wall' parallel to the road, fitted into its natural surroundings as if it, too, had grown from the gnarled roots, which here and there pushed through the earth floor, attempting to snag little feet. Not everyone had a seat. The small table I had found in a shed was too wobbly. And the bench was not long enough. It was not meant to cater for such a meeting of conspirators, rather more likely for clandestine trysts of lovers. The many carved and green overgrown hearts, arrows and initials were proof of that. Perhaps it had been my grandfather's in times past?

But that did not impress the small company yet anyway. Even so, I had difficulties in getting my ideas across.

'We could plant hedges in which one could get lost,' Hanni tried to help me.

'Thorn hedges,' suggested Norbert, who liked nature and was beginning to get the idea. 'Really thick and prickly.' His asthma made his shoulders rise and fall and thick veins stood out on his neck with the effort. 'That'd show them. A sort of garden with paths that go here and there and stop quite suddenly … with high hedges.' His asthma differed from mine in that he almost permanently laboured for breath.

Otto scratched his head.

'And only those in the know can find their way,' I repeated my point once more.

'Exactly,' coughed Norbert. His breathing was bad again. He would not be able to contribute much to the heavy work, but for that we had Hanni after all.

'What's a maze?' asked Otto, while rubbing his sleeve along below his leaking nose. 'I don't want to get lost.'

'But you'll know how to get in and out,' I explained patiently. I was a few years older than Otto.

'You dummy,' said Brigitte, if only to shield her own uncertainty.

Hanni had kept quiet. Deep in thought he had given the problem some serious consideration. 'We'd need a larger piece of land for that sort of thing. Or woodland,' he said at last, in order to move the project along. 'A secret piece of land that's easy to defend.'

I had no such problems: 'My grandma has land. Tons of it. Out near the little chapel and on the Hennebach and up on the Goldener Strauch. On the Hennebach it's soggy and there are trees and flowers that spring if you touch them'.

'Trees that spring?' asked Norbert with some enthusiasm.

'No, only the seeds of flowers.' There was no time to explain such minor phenomena.

'Robert, coffee time.' My mother stood by the back door of gran's house and called in a loud voice. She had to repeat the call before I could tear myself away. 'Now come along. The sooner you come in, the sooner you can be back out.'

Hanni proved his leadership as a true Führer: 'Why don't you bring it out here? Then we can carry on our discussions without interruption. But don't give away any secrets.' His voice followed me into the house.

A short time later, I was back, carrying a platter of open sandwiches, cut into quarters. Home-cured ham on dark slices of rye bread with hard crusts and rounds of marmalade, also on rye bread, all spread with fresh butter. A cup of 'Ersatz' also balanced among the display. Hanni helped me lower the tray safely. They all stood around me, eyes firmly fixed on the quarter slices: Norbert, Brigitte, and Karlchen, as evacuees would know at home only what could be purchased via the meagre ration books. Nor did Hanni's family have any agriculture at home. Such a veritable feast before their eyes would seem like a mirage.

'We need to find a large sheet of paper and draw that all up to start with,' I said, while chewing heartily with full cheeks. 'That's not so easy. I'll need to have help with that.'

'Yes,' said Hanni, thoughtfully, without taking his eyes off the sarnies feast. 'We'll have to stick together and help each other out. And share everything.'

'Hmmm,' said Norbert, 'one person can't eat all that—I mean, do all that alone,' he corrected himself.

'We'll need graph paper with ham on it … ah … millimetre paper, of course.' Hanni, too, showed signs of confusion and stress.

'Would anybody like a piece?' I asked at last, generously. When I looked back down, the platter was empty.

'That's better,' said Hanni, 'it's difficult to think on an empty stomach.' Then he added some praise: 'Robert, you're good at organising. Why don't we start right away with another round? The same again? You could say you are hungry from all that planning. But don't forget. All this has got to stay secret.'

I knew I would not be believed. I never ate that much. 'He hasn't got a bum in his trousers,' Aunt Minna had remarked often enough about my skinny physique.

'You're going to grow up strong and healthy, if you can eat that well,' commented my gran as she filled the platter once more. 'If it makes you that hungry, you ought to play with them more often. What are you doing?'

'Oh, that's a secret,' I said, mysteriously.

'Small wonder he is suddenly so popular,' commented Aunt Anna, who found the episode somewhat suspicious. My mother had left the house in the meantime.

'And another cup of coffee with the rations?' asked *Oma*. 'Or don't they like our coffee?' I am sure I went red in the face and I was glad she held open the door for me and I did not have to look her in the eyes.

In the arbour, I was a favoured organiser who collected much praise. Hanni promised to find a spade for the groundwork of our secret maze defences. Norbert discussed the planting procedures. Nobody gave any thought to the time it would take for such a natural construction to grow high and dense, so that prospective enemies could not simply squeeze through. Nor that by that time, childhood would be over and that grown-ups have quite different problems. Not when there was a chance of more such prospective planning stages in that nourishing arbour.

'How come you know so much about mazes and things?' I asked the heavily breathing Norbert the next time we were alone.

'I have leant you the book, remember?' was the disarming answer. 'The one with the maze diagrams?'

Hanni left the village soon after that. He was going to be adopted by relatives with a farm who had no children of their own. The war soon brought problems quite different from those we children had imagined in the green arbour.

Left: Behind the old house. *From left to right*: Uncle Franz (Aunt Anna's intended), Uncle Jupp, a visitor friend, me, Aunt Minna, and my sister Marianne.

Below: Uncle Jupp fashioned a paper hat for me.

Above and right: Uncle Jupp as soldier somewhere in the east (second from right in the horizontal picture and right in the upright one).

12

The Rye Harvest

The stubble field was rough on small feet and painful when one fell over, especially for a small boy in short trousers. The horses stood patiently by as sheaves were stacked on the wain, higher and higher. It was harvest time and one had to prepare for winter, even in wartime—especially in wartime. It was warm still and the men had turned up their sleeves and the backs of their shirts were damp with perspiration.

Occasionally, the horses neighed and shook their heads violently so that the manes flew and their chains rattled. Long tails swished constantly to dislodge the ever-present nuisance of flies. For all that, they stood patiently. Flies and horses seemed to be inseparable.

'Robert, don't go too near to the horses. They might kick out.'

'He'll know it when it happens,' came a voice from above. A neighbour accepted the sheaves from the tines of the fork reaching up to him. Skilfully, he distributed the un-threshed corn about and beneath himself, as he rose ever higher as in the story of the Tower of Babel.

'You know what I mean,' called my mother, without reacting to the hard-hearted joke. 'Don't go too close to the legs, particularly the hind legs.'

Mother and Aunt Anna collected the sheaves from all over the field and laid them down where Uncle August could stab them on to his pitchfork to lift them high to the waiting hands. Having been diagnosed with a shadow on his lungs, he coughed and wheezed, but no healthy men were available to take his place. The women would help out on the neighbouring farm in exchange for the help and the loan of horses and wagon. As he skewered the sheaves to lift them, it seemed a dangerous sport to me, as the neighbour, so high on the wain, might fall into the offered tines.

Suddenly, Uncle August jumped into the air, just as he lifted a sheaf above his head. Pitchfork and corn were thrown to the stubble, he cursed and carried on and danced like a puppet as his hands flew to his thigh and pressed as if he intended to wring out his kerchief in his pocket.

'It's a little late to start dancing about the maypole,' laughed the fellow on the harvest wain. 'And without music.'

'It's not funny,' countered Uncle August, standing on one leg, 'something jumped into my pocket. The devil, it's huge … and wild. Ahhh.' With that, he pulled his braces sideways and reached a hand deep into his waistband, before he pushed the contents of his pocket outwards. A drowsy little field mouse tumbled out. Staggering and reeling, it scrabbled under the nearest corn sheaves.

The women stood still, awaiting the outcome of the sudden interruption, but without actually laughing. At least not immediately. My mother pressed her hand over her mouth to suppress her giggles. Aunt Anna turned away.

The fellow on the wagon was still convulsed with laughter: 'Quick, shoot it, it can't be far'.

As Uncle August moved the sheaves about, the small giant mouse had disappeared from the face of the earth.

'You ought to sew up your trouser pockets in the autumn, you're a tailor, aren't you?'; 'You're lucky you had no holes in your pocket,' were the convulsed comments from on high, 'then the mouse would have had a fright'.

'You can laugh,' Uncle August protested: 'Up there nothing can jump into your pockets. I didn't know what it was, did I?'

'Something huge, you said. A hippopotamus, wasn't it?'

The sisters busied themselves with sheaves, reaching them up as best they could, to try and suppress their mirth. A light diversion was always appreciated in the monotony of the backbreaking work. The young neighbour would make certain Uncle August would not forget the episode in a hurry.

Their task was almost done when a more unwelcome interruption stopped work. Out of a blue sky came a not unfamiliar noise that quickly grew louder. They all stood up, hands supporting aching backs, wondering at the marvel in the sky. Hands shielded eyes that squinted upwards.

'Must have lost its way. Hope they're not in trouble. He's coming this way,' came a concerned voice from the wagon. The plane grew quickly in size and seemed to be making straight for us.

'No! It's an attack!' yelled Uncle August suddenly, while running to the edge of the field and throwing himself into the ditch beneath the overhanging hedge. 'Save yourself!'

My mother grabbed me by the hand and together we followed Uncle August under the hedge, pressing ourselves as deep into the earth as possible.

As the engine noise increased, so its tone altered and became almost a physical sensation, instilling a sudden and unexplainable, but tangible fright.

'Ratatatatat.' A machine gun rattled and then the shrill noise subsided as quickly as it had arrived as the plane gained height again and disappeared in a westerly direction.

Slowly heads lifted out of the ditch, blinking and looking about for the others.

Pale faces stared at each other in surprise and disbelief, but we were unhurt. Bits of straw and weeds stuck to hair and clothes. Uncle August had pulled his hat over his ears as if that could protect against bullets.

'Anton! Where is Anton?' The neighbour was missing.

Uncle August jumped up and ran towards the harvest wain, where the horses still tried to ward off the inevitable flies. They were more than just a little agitated. Alfred sat under the wagon, beating a few stalks of straw from his chest.

'I stayed under the wagon,' he said, with a shaking voice. 'I thought he can't see me through so much straw.'

'But the horses could have shied and taken off,' considered Uncle August.

'Nooo. They're Westphalians too, tough and thick-skinned, just like me.' Then he asked: 'Are you all in one piece?'

I had returned with the women, remembering a story I had learnt in school, about the first Westphalian: how, when Christ still walked this earth one day with St. Peter, the old fisherman stumbled over a particularly tough lump of clay. 'Damned Westphalians,' swore the veteran saint.

'What on earth did he want with us?' Aunt Anna asked, not expecting an answer.

'Damned Tommies,' said Anton. 'Perhaps he saw some beautiful women and fancied a closer look.' Then he wiped the perspiration from his face with his sleeve: 'I wasn't afraid. I stuck my tongue out at them'. Nobody believed that, but nobody contradicted him either.

'Robert,' my mother called me, 'fetch the food basket over, will you? There ought to be some coffee in there still.' Something to do. I skipped to the edge of the field and returned groaning with the rye bread sandwiches, the chipped enamelled cups and the '*Ersatzkaffee*'. I was proud to be of help, though I probably overacted as far as the weight was concerned.

We sat on the sheaves of corn and munched without speaking, each one in his or her own thoughts. Anton was the first to break the silence: 'With all this rye, you can roast a lot of coffee.' Then he added: 'Tastes best cold, I always think'.

'Hmmm,' said Uncle August, his cheeks bulging with brown rye bread and thin smoked ham slices. He had hardly listened. Normally, it was he who had a word or several to say for every occasion.

'What have we done to him?' asked my mother at last, saying what was foremost in everyone's mind, 'we are not making war.'

Uncle August spoke quietly: 'What had the French done to us? Even so our Robert went there. And your husband'. Perhaps he thought about his 'fallen' brother and about his older brother who was in Russia, where my father had now been drafted to as well. He had been in France at first. 'Or the Russians?' he added quizzically. Then he coughed and held his tongue, for to speak like that was dangerous. Everywhere in the village one could see the posters: '*Feind hört mit*!' ('Enemy listens in!'). People had disappeared for such talk.

'Such a madness,' said my mother. Then everyone fell silent again and thought of absent family members and friends. Aunt Minna's husband had been ordered out there somewhere, too. He had sent pictures of ancient ruins from the Mediterranean. Aunt Anna was sweet on a fellow in the village who had been pressed into uniform as well.

At last, Uncle August brought them back to the present: 'We better finish this. It's nearly done anyway'. With that, they stacked the rest of the sheaves silently on the wagon.

While they worked, I would try and amuse myself as best I could to while away the time. Something must have attracted my attention, for I made what I considered quite a discovery. Delighted, I ran back towards the grown-ups: 'Look what I found'. In my hand I clutched the casing of a machine-gun cartridge.

'Where did you find that?' fretted my mother and took the trophy from my hand. Instantly she handed it to Uncle August, who went pale.

'They were really firing at us,' he said breathless, only then realising the full reality of the attack. With that, he threw the unwelcome object as far away as he could into the hedge.

'But I found it,' I insisted.

'Never must you touch anything like that,' my mother protested, 'you never know if it's exploded or not. Do you hear? Never.'

I was quiet. It was my bullet they had thrown away. I could have taken it to school as proof that I had really been a target in the war. Personally. But that did not seem to matter.

The rye sheaves properly stacked, the men secured the slim beam that was a traditional part of the harvest wain, centrally along the top of the stacked sheaves. Ropes tied down to the corners of the wagon, front and back, would hold it in place under pressure.

'Do you all want to come up here to make it a real harvest wain?' asked the neighbour from above, where he sat right at the front, holding the reins of the horses.

'I'm staying at the brake,' added Uncle August, 'but Robert here, he'd quite like to travel on top, I'm sure.'

He wanted to help me up, but I struggled free: 'I can do that on my own'. Reaching for a rope at the back of the wagon, I nevertheless found it difficult to climb up, though breathing heavily, I made it and I seated myself on the central beam behind the driver.

'Stay in the centre and everything will be fine,' said the neighbour.

'Be careful,' my mother shouted up, 'you and your asthma.'

I did not have to be reminded, I had difficulty enough breathing.

'He's alright. I'm looking out for him,' the neighbour called down. Then he raised the reins and brought them back down quickly so that he sent waves along the leather straps that then slapped on the backs of the horses, waking them from their boredom. 'Now move you lazy beasts. Home. You ought to know the way.'

Even though the ride home atop the harvest wain belonged to the more interesting activities of the farming year, I was still unhappy because of the find that had been denied me.

'*Hoch auf dem gelben Wagen sitz' ich beim Schwager vorn*,' ('High on the yellow wagon I sit with my brother-in-law up front.' *Schwager* is actually an adaptation of the French word '*chevalier*', meaning the postilion at a mail coach) the neighbour attempted to sing a traditional folk tune with a dry and dusty voice.

'I'm not your brother-in-law.' I was still cross. 'And the wagon isn't yellow, either.'

The young fellow in front of me could or would not hear that as he concentrated on his song. He was still trying to forget just how close the bullets had fallen on the field. If his legs had grown straight and normal, he, too, would be cannon fodder somewhere in a uniform.

When we came to the spot where the road falls away more steeply, a red-faced Uncle August was turning the handle that operated the brake and pressed the blocks of wood against the iron rims of the rear wheels to slow them down and help the horses. Smoke came from the points of pressure as the wood could barely hold the strain.

A pedestrian, who just happened to come towards us on the road, threw his arms in the air and shouted: 'Have you heard? There has been an air attack in the village. They've shot the chimney clean off the Tuckelsburg'.

The harvesters were too busy and tired to stop and listen just then.

The 'Tuckelsburg' was a rather small house built lofty and castle-like on a rampart on a stone foundation near a crossroad in the middle of the village. A large family occupied the two elevated rooms above workshop and stable, somewhat similar to our own arrangement by the church.

On arrival at grandmother's house, the wagon was taken directly to the farm next door for threshing at a future date, after which the straw would be brought in through the large barn-like doors and raised internally up to the roof-space of the old house, the hayloft, for winter fodder and as floor covering for the cows below.

My mother called up to me: 'Now come down immediately. You have to go down the road and fetch a can of small beer [*Drüppelbier*—the cheapest of beers]. I'm going to make beer soup this evening. But don't hang around at the Tuckelsburg, do you hear?'

Harvest time on a larger farm.

A harvest festival occasion with young folk in country dress on a harvest wagon. Listen to the boy with a zither. Looks like Aunt Anna second from left.

Following the harvest wagon, farmers try to keep straight faces on such an official occasion.

All good efforts finish with a celebration.

The agricultural year could not be imagined without the diligent, patient horses.

13

The *Hambummel*

He had been a part of the landscape, like summer, winter, and autumn winds and lambs tails on hazel bushes, though perhaps not as regular. He must have had a name like other people, but in the old house on the hill, he was known only as 'the *Hambummel*'—the vagrant—though probably not to his face. He had visited as long as anyone could remember, but *Oma* was old now and younger people were in the house. Even so, it was almost tradition when the curious, over-dressed figure trundled up the road that he made directly for *Oma*'s house. He came to the village via the single house of market gardeners on an unmade road that was certainly no highway. Perhaps they had a welcoming tradition, too? There were large farms and bigger houses in the village he passed by.

It is only in my earliest memories that I can recall him. What I could not know was the wanderer's experience over the years. In earlier times, before the state would rather do without people that did not make a contribution, such peripatetic people who made their living by begging all knew where a good-natured heart could be found that did not turn them away or was protected by ferocious dogs. Even so, there was no welcome as with an old friend, more an 'oh, it's him again'. Times were too hard for that. In the past, a vagrant would have been a source of information, gossip from the wider world, now most everyone was informed by radio; and who wanted to hear more bad news, anyway?

But, of course, he would say, the lady of the house was one of the best he knew. Heaven would thank her, even if he could not.

Although there were no riches in the old house, there was always a round of sandwiches, some clothing cast-offs, an old pair of shoes that no one would wear or could wear that would be more useful to the living than the dead. In his long overcoat were torn and oft-mended pockets that contained most of what he owned, the rest was concealed in a brown paper parcel, held together with string, that he carried under his arm. How often would it serve as cushion on which to rest his head in some barn or attic?

Where would he take his baths? To a child, he was both to be avoided and admired. Where was he from? How much had he seen of the world? All those other places. Was there war everywhere? Was he too old for the war? His hair and beard were a dull colour grey and trimmed quite short, but was he really as old as he looked?

Was he the wandering Jew mentioned in one of my reading books? That man was doomed to wander the earth because of some unkindness he had done to Christ when he carried his cross. Windows had been smashed, slogans painted and people disappeared even in the nearby town just 5 km away. I do not remember mention of Jews at anytime, but then I was only a child. Country folk are survivors, they just kept their heads down and minded their stables, though today it is well known what happened in other places at that time, it would not feature in censored news.

Even so, in fact, in the early days, when such things were still possible, one local businessman and innkeeper helped a Jewish woman to escape, quite possibly for remuneration. With his lorry, he would make occasional forays to the River Mosel to restock his wine cellar. It is said he drove out to another village the evening before such a trip in 1938, collecting and hiding a Jewish woman at his home overnight. He managed to deliver her safely to the border before going about his genuine wine-trading business. When Donners' establishment fell victim to the fire-grenades in 1945, their well-stocked wine cellar was one of the less well-known tragedies.

Mother would not let us children get too close to the vagrant. In the evening, we were bathed and combed with a special comb with tough long and close-set tines that scratched and pulled the hair. Perhaps that was why he was not in the war? Perhaps in the war they did not want to worry about fleas?

There were lots of new people in the village, evacuees from towns that were bombed and burnt out. They were poor, too, but still they got their rations and a roof over their heads, even if that meant sharing with other people.

Where was he at home? To me, as settled in the village as I was, a village where everybody knew everybody, with aunts and uncles and family all around, however distantly related, the idea of not having a settled home seemed almost a punishment for some sin or other. It is perhaps ironic that I myself would turn my back on the village and '*Heimat*' and move away and make my home among strangers. Four of my sister's five children still live in close proximity to the parental home. Only one moved a few villages away.

The old house stood on the hill where it was then still called 'the Knippe'. In fact, as was the case with most old houses, the name went with the house, not the owners. In this case, it must have been named by its position on the road. The people who lived there, though their name was Schütteler, were known as '*Knippen*' and in the local vernacular that meant my uncles were Knippen August and Knippen Jupp, my mother, though her married name was Hallmann, still remained Knippen Maria to most people.

A document dated 12 January 1640 existed in the old house that marked the time when Hans Schomacher, who lived '*auff der Knippen*', was granted the land by

Long-distance merchant traveller with his dog-drawn supplies, buying up eggs and butter for town dwellers and selling haberdashery to householders.

the then owners of the big house that still exists on the edge of the village, Wilhelm Dietherich Kloidt and Anna von Schulteis (see image of document, page 20).

In recent days, when more roads had to be adapted and named, the name Knippe has been relegated to what used to formerly be a back lane nearby. The plot contained the house with two gardens, fruit trees, and a meadow, with a row of oak trees along one side and several tall fir trees near the house along the road. During a great storm, the fir trees were blown over, barely missing the house. Today, it has all been dissected into building plots.

Uncle August had a story of such a wanderer, though it was years later that I learnt it. In his version, it was a peripatetic Capuchin monk who called at a big house one cold winter's evening, begging for a bite to eat and a cot for the bitter night. He was offered welcome as behoves such a religious personage and he was invited to share their servants' table and afterwards a warming seat by the fire. Once he had passed on the latest news from his travels and it came to bedtime, he was offered what seemed to him extreme luxury, the best and softest bed in the house in a well-appointed room. He could not believe his luck, and he was soon ensconced warm and cosy in his featherbed slumbers, when the maid entered and apologised demurely. She had made a mistake. The saintly man could not do otherwise, and piously, he followed the maid to a slightly less salubrious room and bed, yet still quite above the monk's expectations. No sooner was he warm and snug again and the maid entered, again apologising and again leading him to a slightly less well-appointed bed. This happened several times, whenever he had made himself comfortable, he was taken to a smaller, harder cot until he ended up in a cramped attic room on straw and a blanket. Finally, the meek and pious man found the courage and asked why had he not been led to this spot in the first place?

'Well, I cannot lie,' said the maid haltingly, 'but that first bed was in the mistress's bedchamber and the next one was her daughter's. The last one was mine and I, too, thank you for pre-warming my bed on a night such as this.'

On my father's side in the hill town of Eversberg, the Wenks-Wiesehöfers family tree is illustrated with ears of corn, a plough, hammer, pen and brush, and a spinning wheel. Research reaches back to Rutger *v.* Wennickusin, the first date found is 1330 with early names like Gotfridus, Eckard, Vrederich, etc. Even a witch is part of our past.

Grave marker of Jost Hennecke, behind it the home of the verger (where he lived) and the church in which he was active.

Jost Hennecke

I never met our local feted poet and author, factory worker, verger, and musician Jost Hennecke, though his writings, poems, and prose in both High German and in the now almost forgotten vernacular were still well remembered and often quoted. He had published a number of books that were appreciated over a wide area, especially by those who cherished tradition and heritage. Locality and homeland were favourite and innocent enough subjects, even under a Nazi regime. 'Platt duitsk', in the Low German vernacular, was spoken by our parents and grandparents, but not to us children.

In the First World War, Jost Hennecke served as stretcher-bearer under fire at the front in Flanders, Belgium, keeping up his notes, writings, and making sketches whenever possible.

Der Krankenträger
Zeichnung Jost Henneckes aus dem Weltkriege 1916.

Above left: 'Carrier of the wounded'. A sketch by Jost Hennecke, 1916.

Above right: Shepherds still moved about the landscape, especially in autumn and spring.

14

Prisoners on the Land

With almost every able-bodied man called up to the war effort, the most constant male population left were old men, invalids, and, of course, the stalwarts of land work allocated to farms all over the area—prisoners of war from France, the Low Countries, and Russia, but especially Poland (on one of the outlying farms, an Italian prisoner from the previous war had stayed on). Being themselves largely of farming stock—at least they usually pretended to be—they were treated variously, depending on the humanity of the individual farm or artisan folk. Stories of maltreatment were whispered, as well as tales of prisoners displaying talents beyond their professed backgrounds.

Some fifty of them had arrived on foot, marching with backpacks from the nearest railway station 5 km away in the autumn of 1939. Later there would be about eighty.

Mornings they were marched out and distributed to their allocated workplaces—farms, shoemakers, smithies, saddlers—and evenings they were collected and marched up to the village hall (the *Schützenhalle*) where a smaller annexe had been added to the large festive hall for more intimate meetings and festivities. Rows of double-bunks meant the prisoners spent their nights together under watch, windows secured with barbed wire.

In their long and ungainly ex-military greatcoats, baggy and unshaven appearance, they made themselves useful by taking over the absent males' jobs. At least there was always food available on a farm and there were warm straw and warm creatures that did not make distinctions of nationality or creed.

Although apparently we were not meant to interact with them, to us children they were strangers just like the soldiers that passed through, only usually friendlier. Some of the 'Polaks' even became our friends, though mixing with them was 'not allowed'. They themselves spoke a curious and often funny kind of German, though to us, trying to speak their languages became a kind of game, knowing the rudest swear words a kind of dare.

Likely anything they said might be regarded as swear words. Whole sentences strung together of unknown but rude-sounding words became familiar jargon among the young—sentences in foreign tongues that made strange sounds and therefore carried a risqué element. It was not until a considerable number of years had passed did I realise I had been taught the sentiments 'I love you' and similar endearments in several languages and obscure accents.

We boys knew several languages anyway. Our parents and other grown-ups, though they might address their children in High German, always spoke the traditional Low German vernacular among themselves. At religious studies, in our service as altar boys, we learnt a fair sprinkling of Latin. Though Poland, just like our village, was predominantly Catholic, the prisoners were not allowed to mingle, not even at mass.

There was an incident in 1944 when the Poles refused to leave for work one morning. In the ensuing standoff, something was thrown at a guard and the young guard shot back, killing the prisoner. The unfortunate man was buried in the village cemetery.

Good Friday 1945 was a day of near calamity. A '*Sonderkommando*', a detachment possibly of the SS, had been ordered to blow up the small hall with its Polish prisoners. The orderly in charge, having prior knowledge, is said to have avoided a catastrophe and stopped the village from becoming a byword for brutality when he ordered his foreign charges to disperse to their various places of work,

Some of the Polish prisoners of war by their nightly quarters at the *Schützenhalle*. Being forbidden to mingle with the civilian population apart from work, of course, they would have provided their own entertainment as prisoners of war have done through the ages. Highest ranking officer is standing far left.

while he himself hid out at a lonely farm some distance away until the arrival of the Americans a few days later.

Jan was a blond young Dutchman in glasses, who had been forced from his native country to work in the village bakery. He spent some of his free time at the old house, glad perhaps of the informal normality, where grandmother would welcome without politics or fear, as her children happily returned and everybody 'mucked in'. Cousins like Aunt Therese's daughters might walk for miles and miles for a visit. It was not only the girls, Jan used to bother with us children as well. His own curious accent had more in common with the Low German language spoken in the old house, than with normal High German, as I was to find out years later. Sometimes he would conjure bakery products from the folds of his Dutch jacket.

It seems his enthusiasm became his undoing and apparently he got into bad company. One day he had left, it was said to join the SS. Many years later in conversation with people who had known him, it emerged that after the war, on his return to Holland, he had languished many years in prison for his change of allegiance.

Dutch forced-labourer Jan, a baker, with my little sister Marianne.

The Wild Man of the Woods

Rumours had been spreading about the area for some time. A Russian prisoner from an isolated farm in one of the outlying hamlets had absconded. He would be hiding in the woods somewhere, living rough off the land. Drip by drip, the story grew of disappearing foodstuffs and clothing. Then it was said that a young overconfident farmer's son had taken a gun and disappeared into the woods to make an end to the thefts. He had not returned.

That news was followed by the arrival of a detachment of soldiers who had been seconded to comb the woods. Eventually they returned to the village with a quiet man, dirty and dressed in what were no more than rags. On his back he carried a rough sack of what were said to be stones. The soldiers congregated at Lamberts inn, one of the three hostelries in the village. It was also a farm with a large farmyard right by the road in the village centre.

Locals stood around, talking and trying to find out what had happened, or just gawping at the fellow all the fuss was about. The soldiers had their man. It was unusual to see them not actually marching or standing to attention, but relaxing where they could, many preferring the cooler and hospitable confines of the pub.

All this was going on between my grandmother's and my mother's home and I stopped to watch along the way. The wild man of the woods was no Grimm's Fairy Tale, but for him the day was grim enough. He was real. I can see him still in my mind's eye, tough, stocky, dishevelled, stubble-faced, and a haircut that reminded me of a hedgehog.

How far had he carried that sack? It was a very hot day and someone attempted to offer a drink to the prisoner who visibly wilted under the sun. Slowly his sack of stones slid to the ground. Almost instantly, it seemed, someone in a smart uniform, probably an officer, exited from the inn, down the few steps between the two lime trees and barking orders, forced him to take the sack up again, not sparing the butt of a rifle. Then followed a prolonged exercise with knees bend and up, down and up, down and up movements, all the while stubbornly clutching that incongruous heavy sack. The stubborn human, it seemed to me, tried hard not to show weakness, but to grin at his torturer, which did not help his cause. He took the rifle butts when his body slackened, but he did not utter a word, at least not within my hearing. Then again, I was not all that close.

Somehow it seemed unworthy of the glorious German soldier one knew from propaganda, even to a small boy who was torn between a human instinct of compassion and the just desserts of someone who might have killed the farmer's boy. That was the problem—the maybe. Everyone was certain that our men from the village would never behave in such a way and that these were not frontline troops facing the enemy, but shirkers who stayed away from 'the front'.

Years later, when I enquired about what had happened to the Russian prisoner from that day, I was told he had died, but he had confessed to the boy's murder before that. I also found out that for Russian prisoners disappearing into the woods was a way of avoiding problems, but they might have been helpful in return for the odd cigarette or two.

Other Russians hid out, even after the end of hostilities, armed with handguns, rifles, and ammunition that could be found in woods, discarded by absconding soldiers. They would raid farms for food and clothing and slaughter cattle in quiet meadows. One farmer was shot through his closed front door as he went to open it.

Part of the old road between Remblinghausen and the administrative town of Meschede.

16

Visitors and Bombs

Behind the village, on the long walk back from the woods, we passed a small chapel with a small barred window in the door and a statue of Our Lady inside, right opposite the sports field. Next to it stands a large cross with the carved and contorted figure of Christ upon it, but overshadowing both is a majestic lime tree of great age and with a trunk of considerable girth. How many children have climbed in its branches? Tough gnarled roots spread outwards even above ground to snag unwary feet. It is believed that witches were burnt there in the Middle Ages and that later generations tried to sanctify and mark the spot.

I was shooting stones with a sling cut from a wooden branch in the shape of a 'Y', with an old rubber band fixed to each of the top ends of the gavel.

My attempts at shooting my slingshots over the top of that tree had not been particularly successful, largely because I was torn between that feat and keeping up with the wanderers while appearing not to listen to their lurid grown-up conversations.

A herd of brown and white cows trundled slowly towards the village. There was no speeding them up, in spite of the herdsman's attempts to hurry them along with his threatening stick and his rude flow of curses. The soft juicy grass of the Long Meadow was transformed into fat-rich milk even as they walked, awaiting the hands of the milkers. Udders full to burst were swinging obstacles to speedy progress.

The cowherd was well aware he would be looked upon as a country bumpkin in his oft-mended trousers and grubby overall that also had seen better days. Holidaymakers loved the village and he felt there were too many eyes focused on him. It gave him inhibitions. The feet that had so far protected him from being called up added a comical accent to his behaviour. But what else could he do? The cows still had to be milked.

'Now move it, you damn bovines,' he called out in a mixture of High and Low German as his stick landed without much conviction on the tail of the nearest of his charges. The tail twitched and rose without further ado as the so singled out

Aunt Minna's friends arrive in the village. It still is a magnet for visitors today.

recipient of his attentions declared her lack of interest by ignoring him totally. She could, after all, move no faster than her sisters ahead of her would allow.

The small group of people, who could afford the rarity of taking time off and perambulate on a normal working day, kept their distance. After wandering in the hills above the village, there was no reason to hurry anyway. The near liquid results of mastication by the unperturbed beasts who had no qualms but to cover the rough road in their slithery emissions, kept the wanderers well back and especially watchful not to step into and slither about in fresh deposits.

Aunt Minna was in her element. She had a soulmate with whom she could converse in the knowledge that their conversations would not be repeated throughout the village. Not only their views and their humour matched, their statures, too, had their similarities.

'That's how men think of us,' Aunt Minna was saying, nodding in the direction of the cows.

'How so?' asked her friend, as she followed the direction of her glance.

'Whatever do you mean?'

'Well, the fertility, the full … We're neither of us neglected in that direction.'

'Oh, Wilhelmina, don't let my man hear that. He has such sweaty little hands.' The cosy comfortable little lady laughed wholeheartedly.

'At least there aren't too many calluses on them with his job,' Aunt Minna joked in return. Her husband was in the war and she reminisced. All the same, the two women shook with laughter and what they had been discussing shook in unison. Only their tough stays kept them in control.

'Yes, the Lords of creation appreciate a soft spot when they find them to rest their weary heads.'

'Before and after they kill each other off.'

'Well, after all that ruling and yelling orders and putting the world to rights they need to recharge their energies somewhere.'

I had moved close enough to hear snatches of their interesting conversation, though I might not understand everything. I fell back a little, but very soon I was close enough again to listen in.

Still the two well-favoured ladies failed to suppress their giggles and everything about them shook as if at sea. *Frau* Muteng had difficulty telling her story: 'My younger sister is a doctor in a rather large factory. She says that the men all stand to attention and greet her like little soldiers during health-control, when she hammers their knees and tells them to cough. My sister has a similar figure to mine'. Then she added, a little quieter, 'Lords of Creation without their trousers on are pathetic creatures.'

Her husband had walked ahead a few steps with their son. Now he stopped, concerned, and waited for them to catch up. Even so, the two women insisted they had been laughing about the antics of a cow or two.

Herr Muteng only shook his wise head. He was a short, well-set, and dapper man with dark wavy hear and a friendly face, wearing a neat suit and tie. As a family, they liked visiting Aunt Minna and the still very traditional village, not only because there were more chances of a meal than in a town. There were also fewer chances of bombings (am I spelling their name correctly? It might well have been Muteng or Moutain or similar, as I never saw it written down). They had met at one of the government sponsored holiday and recuperation resorts and found they had much in common, not least their sense of humour.

Only the Muteng's son was a little above it all, as someone from a town and obviously from a better background, but quite probably it was simply the fact that he was older than me that he preferred his parents' company. I was happily amusing myself, dawdling and catching up again as I followed the grown-ups, close enough to listen, yet seemingly otherwise occupied.

Aunt Minna had suffered a stiff unbending knee ever since an accidental fall from a neighbouring hayloft at the young age of fifteen. Following the long walk, she was beginning to feel the effect of the knee problem combined with her weight and admitted to being tired: 'Oh,' she sighed, 'I'm glad I'll be able to sit down soon. Even laughter is beginning to hurt.'

Only a few days later, as the evening wind blew softly through the docked branches of the old lime tree in front of gran's cottage and swallows made the last

In front of the old house, *c.* 1942. From left *to right*: *Herr* Muteng, mother, my sister and I, *Oma*, a neighbour, Aunt Minna, and *Frau* Muteng.

dives of the day after insects on the wing, we stood watching the sunset in front of the old house. Aunt Anna was there, my mother and my grandmother and passing neighbours had stopped to watch. Aunt Minna and her friends had paused on their way to or from a pleasant after-dinner walk. Over across the road and the meadow of the neighbourly farm the horizon was glowing, not as at an ordinary sunset but more sinister.

Conversations were hushed, as if noise would make the matter worse. The sky glowed long after the sun had set, unevenly, sometimes stronger in places, then dying down again. The eerie display was made more sinister by the absence of sound. Sound does not travel as well as light reflected under clouds.

An air raid. There would be an air raid over there in the distance. People were speculating. Where could that be? Some places were mentioned, but it was impossible to guess how far away the bombing took place, only that it must be terrible and that it must be a large town considering the breadth of the glow, as if the earth had caught fire. The sound of intake of everyone's breath could be heard whenever a spot glowed brighter than others, and a whispered: 'There, over there now'.

Nobody said it, but it was on everyone's mind—people would be suffering over there. People would be crouching together in cellars under burning buildings. Collapsing buildings. Scared. Wounded. Frightened. We were safe and grateful to be where we were. There was nothing we could do, except pray for those under that glowing sky. I stood quiet, too. In the event, I had been forgotten and not sent to bed.

'Oh, God,' *Frau* Muteng whispered and pressed her husband's hand. Was that where they lived? Where they would have to return to? In the gloaming, the others could not see her tears in which the unusual distant light reflected. If I recollect correctly, it was the last time the family came visiting Aunt Minna.

On another occasion, strips of silver foil had been dropped down from enemy aircraft like bands of shimmering rain—to confuse the radar during bombing raids, it was said. I considered collecting any strips to cut into even narrower strips and save them for the Christmas tree, though I could not find them. There were stories about items found, like pens that exploded when handled, though if there was truth in such warnings or if it was simply propaganda, I never found out for certain.

Night of the Dambusters

One morning in the old house, the adults were quiet and subdued, barely speaking. When they did speak at *Oma*'s, it was whispered amid sighs of resignation. A disaster had happened that night, but such news had to be treated with caution, or it might be misinterpreted as subversion. It took some effort on my behalf to find out what it was. Even then I did not quite fathom all that they were saying. Many people had died, but most of them had been women workers from Russia or Poland.

The large towns and industrial area lower down on the River Ruhr, the *Ruhrgebiet* or *Kohlenpott*, also known as the 'armoury of the Third Reich', required water to power industry and at that time that meant largely war machinery. Our hills and mountains produced many clear streams. Several reservoirs had been built and valleys flooded. The Möhne dam was opened in 1913, when it supported the largest reservoir in Europe. In wartime that made it a target.

Today, in hindsight, we know what had happened: several reservoirs were attacked on the night of 16–17 May 1943 by British bombers with specially designed rotating bombs that skipped over the water surface towards the wall, avoiding the anti-torpedo nets. The bombs were designed to sink down by the wall before exploding.

RAF 617 Squadron of Lancaster Bombers (The Dambusters) had flown at such low levels, people running for cover reported seeing the faces of the pilots. Of course, hiding in cellars downstream was the wrong action to take when the holed Möhne dam poured around 330 million tons of water downriver. Survivors reported the water flooding in with a gushing sound that rapidly reached its crescendo up to 12 metres in height to devastating effect. Twenty-seven people died in one village nearby, including six members of one family.

At least 1,579 people died that night, 1,026 of them foreign forced-labourers held in camps in the water's path, the majority of them female Russian workers.

The spinning bomb's inventor, Barnes Wallis, is said to have been devastated by the heavy loss of life by the aircrews. Eight of the nineteen attacking Lancaster aircraft did not return and fifty-three out of 133 aircrew were killed, three captured.

The 230-foot-wide gap in the Möhne dam was repaired by 23 September the same year. A replica of the Barnes Wallis bomb is kept there as a public reminder. Of the three reservoirs attacked, the largest, the Sorpe dam, did have a hole, but it was above the water line. Another destroyed dam, the Edersee dam, did not supply water to the Ruhr. The resulting damage to German infrastructure did not reach its hoped-for effect.

The dams were left in peace after that as Bomber Command under Air Chief Marshal Sir Arthur Harris concentrated on levelling urban centres in Germany, even after Germany was all but beaten.

No doubt the greatest effect of the raid was in the field of propaganda as it evolved into legend, especially aided by the 1955 film *The Dam Busters*, starring Michael Redgrave as inventor Barnes Wallis and Richard Todd as Wing Commander Guy Gibson, leader of the operation, underpinned in no small measure by Eric Coates' *The Dam Busters March*. On discussing the Lancaster raid and the closeness of my home then to the Möhne location, I was asked once: 'Did you hear the music, that night when the Lancasters approached?' (In 1977, the Geneva Convention outlawed attacks on dams if it meant civilian casualties).

We often heard the heavy droning sound of Lancasters as they passed overhead to drop their deadly cargo at some more important destinations. The closest we came

After the attack. Möhne dam breached. Photo by Flying Officer Jerry Fray of No. 542 Squadron from his Spitfire. Notice the barrage balloons above the dam.

to actual bombardment was the nearby town of Meschede, 5 km away, where the large Honsel works manufactured light metal aircraft parts, giving work to many people in the area. The company had begun in 1908, making aluminium cutlery, but had opened a larger works in the town in 1917, smelting aluminium. Meschede did become a magnet for Lancasters, but chance would have it that the flares set by reconnaissance aircraft identifying a specific target would drift in the wind and bombs were discharged largely over countryside. In 1945, however, shortly before the end of the war the works were completely destroyed. It took three years to bring it back into production.

So distributed were bombs about the countryside that even today, more than seventy years later, bombs are still being found and diffused every thirty-six hours in North Rhine–Westphalia alone.

Many years later in England, one fine day, a quite unexplainable fear gripped my chest, like bands tightening about the heart. I soon realised it was the rhythmic droning or throbbing sound of a Lancaster in the sky somewhere above me that had to be the reason. Checking the news later, I understood that one of the last of the Lancaster bombers had been flown to its place at a museum. I had been close to its flight path.

In the early years, while all went well and Hitler's military fire roller moved outwards, soldiers were sent on holidays, to the Alps for instance, but so were the wives of soldiers. Like Aunt Minna, my mother, too, was sent away on a fortnight's recuperation. Her destination was the health spa of Baden-Baden in the foothills of the Black Forest. It must have been a welcome break and a change of atmosphere for my mother with all that was happening and the death of my first sister. At the same time, I, too, was to enjoy a 'change of air' to improve my asthma in a children's home in a place some distance away from home called Schwelm. Aunt Minna was to look after my sister, but she promised to make the journey to come and see me every so often.

The woman in charge at the home was a lady we called Aunt Herta. She must have replaced Aunt Minna very soon in my affections, for when I fell ill and was sent from the home to a hospital, it was not Aunt Minna I called for, but Aunt Herta, making a thorough nuisance of myself so I was told. Aunt Herta had a holiday home for children to run and she could make it even less often than Aunt Minna. Somehow the message was passed on and 'Aunt Herta must come! Aunt Herta must come!' was a phrase that was used to tease me for a long time afterwards. I still remember the ward in that hospital where I shared a large room with rather old men who would go walk about and then, forgetting which bed they had left, started arguments when the bed they tried to return to was already occupied.

Did it do me any good? It is difficult to say, but in a time before adequate asthma medication, a change of air was thought of as a remedial treatment. My mother on the other hand came away refreshed and with good memories from her stay in a health spa.

17

The Snow Princess

One entrepreneur had started a bus or coach service mainly as connection to the nearest town, cars were rare in the village unless they were official or military and that usually meant the latter. If only out of necessity, people clung to the old ways. Horse-drawn coaches and Landauers, mostly single-span, but sometimes double harnessed, that had been languishing in dark barn corners especially on the larger farms, were recovered, mended, and polished for trips to the village or even for longer journeys. When bells announced the Angelus, they called out from the sky-piercing tower of the church and the familiar sound carried far across the landscape. For High Mass on Sundays, horse-drawn carriages converged on the village from all directions, reminiscent of nineteenth-century images. Elegant or practical, they were a heart-warming sight.

Winters were especially exciting. Sleighs would be brought out and some coaches could be transformed into sleighs with their wheels removed and runners added instead. Small bells were usually attached to the horses' harnesses, so they could be heard even in snowstorms or in the dark.

Especially on Sunday mornings, I would be pressed to the windowpanes at my grandmother's house when the coaches arrived and left. It was rare that I was allowed to join into services in the unheated church. I was a spectator to life for too many of my early years.

The farm next door had in the grey and distant past been the vicarage and there was room for several horses to be tied up, freed of their sleighs or coaches, and fed from strap-on feedbags, while their owners visited the church and afterwards caught up on gossip with family and friends.

Womenfolk like darkly attired farmers' wives with dark flowery hats, shawls, and muffs for their hands might then return to the homesteads to oversee or arrange lunch and the care of animals. Their sombre-suited menfolk might retire to their traditional tables in one of the three public houses in close proximity to the church. There they would meet with relatives and friends, and sustained by the congenial

In one of the outlying hamlets, Bonacker, the Angelus bell on the barn on left is still rang regularly today.

Young people 'hanging out' in an old coach.

At the 750 Year Celebrations of the village's existence on 4 July 1992, old farm tools, sleds, and coaches were again on display.

smokes and litres of frothy beer with Schnapps chasers, the weather was discussed and the state of the fields and the sons that were fighting or missing.

For children, the lack of traffic, especially on weekdays, turned the whole village into their play area after school. Standing on undulating terrain, dipping down to the church or away from it, the village streets and lanes became sleigh tracks. When I was older, I tried to join others whenever my health would allow. It was with great delight to be able to run and slide and build snowmen like others did. Winters were particularly fierce and snowbound in those years.

The dip in the main road past my grandmother's house to the centre of the village was particularly pronounced. While on bad days the walk up the incline might present an asthmatic obstacle, on good days in snow, it served as a track for sleigh races. Iron strips curved as runners under wooden sleighs that were expertly made with sturdy struts were passed on from generation to generation if they survived— treasures in attics and cobwebbed sheds.

Ungritted street surfaces of hardened, frozen snow were ideally suited. Some of the larger sleighs featured specially movable front sections to facilitate steering, which otherwise had to be effected with boots that acted as brakes, turning to whichever side such pressure was applied.

Tightly packed with young bodies, the weight of the larger sleighs might produce considerable velocity, though the greatest pleasure for many was the final tumble when a sleigh ran out of street or when a slide had to be aborted for lack of steering control. Grazes and bruises were received and with gritted teeth carried as trophies.

Older children and teenagers got their kicks after dark, so it was whispered, when the necessity of close proximity on the sleighs made physical contact almost inevitable in spite of the multi-layered protection against the freezing weather and the final groping at the inevitable tumble in the dark gave excuses for many a normally taboo adventure.

The real experts, however, would have their own sleighs all to themselves. They could be pushed to a running start in the obligatory iron-shod and hobnailed boots. Then the driver/pusher would leap forward in the manner of today's bobsleigh teams and flat on his or her belly, head first, improve steering with gloved hands as well as boots.

Naturally, such operations turned the streets into mirror surfaces. It also meant that sloping roads became almost impassable for other traffic, except perhaps well-shod horses. This also meant the law had to step in.

The law in the village was the rotund policeman complete with slate-blue uniform, shiny buttons, and Kaiser Wilhelm-style pith helmet. *Herr* Knoppick, who by no stretch of the imagination could be described as in the full flush of youth, lived at the top end of the village, higher than Grandmother's house even, before the road takes a sharp dip down to the Sägemühle.

The inevitable confrontation meant a slow-moving upholder of the law, hopelessly outnumbered by cruelly nimble-footed taunters and teasers made almost unrecognisable by winter clothes, which sometimes covered everything but their eyes. He would appear wheezing at the top of the road, wielding his truncheon. They simply started lower down the slope.

When he went in pursuit, they disappeared up a back street and continued their fun. The triangular road system that made this possible, guarded by spies, favoured the children. Policeman and children alternated in the occupation of the high and low ground, while he stood shouting and threatening and slamming his hands to his sides to keep out the cold. 'He doesn't need a sleigh. His belly will do.' Children can be cruel and insensitive and finally truthful.

The children were more persistent when he called out the parish employees to grit the streets. Often ash might be used in the absence of sand. A few farmyard brooms would soon remove such spoilers ineffectively to the roadsides. The law was invariably the first to throw in the towel, blaming the parents.

Nor was taunting reserved for authority. A slow-thinking, if good-natured farmhand had been sent into the village from one of the outlying farmsteads on some errand or other on a dray. The simple, one-horse-drawn, low-farm conveyance, new and unsullied, had been provided with a front bench seat and backrest, from whence to steer the horse with rein and whip.

Unfortunately, the slow trotting speed meant that the children were able to run alongside, calling on him to stop and supply lifts. While the young man was able to topple off unwelcome boarders from his front seat, the rest of the low sledge offered easy enough access to persistent youngsters. Amid the taunting and name-calling, it did not take the cruel swarm long to realise the driver's reluctance to use his whip with any serious intent. It resulted in the dray being occupied by a heap of arms and legs and small bodies, which dispersed taunting and teasing whenever he stopped.

A few days later, that same driver and simple conveyance again passed through the village, only this time he was not alone. Beside him on the raised bench seat travelled a vision of beauty and elegance—a stranger to the parish—somehow strangers seemed to be of more interest than local girls. Age was difficult to determine under the travelling rugs. She may have been a little older than I was, but what age are angels anyway? The strange girl seemed to be amused by our village-boy antics.

I was one of the boarders, hitching a ride, as we had done before. When we realised that this time the driver was not going to stop for long in the village but carry on past the church, most jumped off again one by one—all except I. I seemed to be rooted to the wooden dray, even when the trip was not confined to the village.

'You were one of the hooligans that called me names the other day. I recognise you,' said the driver. 'I don't know why I don't throw you off. Well, perhaps you weren't one of the worst.' He had noticed the girl's amusement and being no great conversationalist himself, he must have decided that perhaps company of her own age might be interesting for her.

Perhaps the girl had indicated her approval? I simply stayed put. Eventually the driver said, 'It's a few kilometres, but we'll be coming back this way later. You can stay if you want. It will be a cold wait outside when we're visiting, though.'

I did not mind. Perhaps the strange girl was the magnet, perhaps I simply tried to show off to the other lads. I certainly enjoyed the idea of doing something unexpected. An adventure. There was little conversation during the journey.

We followed a narrow road out of the village to the north, little more than a lane, a track in the snow that wound up on to higher ground, past a small wayside chapel where the angular white fields and meadows resembled a patchwork of winter quilts under the crisp clear sky. To one side, the road to the village from the nearest town curved up through the trees in the valley below, on the other, the land spread out until it dipped down to the level surface of a frozen reservoir that covered most of that valley (it was a lesser of the reservoirs saving water for the industrial Ruhr district, too small to be attacked by the 617 Squadron with their famous bouncing bombs in May 1943).

Ahead lay two farmsteads that made up Vellinghausen, the hamlet we were heading towards, while all around in the distance, beyond the road and the lake, white hilltops were patched largely with different sizes of fast-growing evergreens like regimented Christmas trees.

In my imagination, I was travelling through a magical Alpine scenery, or the wild open spaces of Russia from one of my books. The heavy farm horse became a prancing steed, high-stepping, pulling the delicate sleigh with a beautiful princess, her half-tamed coachman, and me as protector companions. Just to be there with them was quite enough. I could hear the music of the wind, the bells of the harness, feel the endless road sliding, gliding, crunching under the runners, and smell the musky steam that rose off the fast trotting horse.

When we arrived at the large farmyard, which was surrounded on three sides by house, stables, and barns, the girl was received with warmth and affection. A relative's child visiting from a town somewhere with an unpronounceable name. The princess visiting one of her castles.

The horse was fed and watered while I considered the long walk back, then prepared instead to wait on the dray outside for the return journey. But I, too, was invited in. I felt foolish. What was I doing there? You cannot explain that you followed to protect a fairy-tale princess. The driver had explained my ride-hitching accurately enough. Of course, they knew my family.

I must have been well behaved among the strangers. The large room, the large fire, the traditional furniture, especially the huge table, everything was larger than at my Grandmother's and certainly no comparison to our own small dwelling. The girl may have been puzzled and flattered by a country boy's behaviour, but lionised by grownups, she paid me little attention.

The greatest part of the adventure was to be invited to share their table and this being a real farm there was no discernible food rationing, even in wartime. I declined the offer of cake and cream, but the rounds of open smoked ham sandwiches served up on black bread with real butter and the warm coffee made from roasted corn like my gran did, made up for the cold journey. Only shyness prevented me from overeating.

When I jumped off the sled as we passed back through the village on the return journey, I thanked the driver and the girl, realising that my reasons for the journey were so difficult to explain, I had better not attempt to tell about it.

In the depth of winter, special forestry trips might be undertaken to help wild game populations surivive with extra feeds.

The village in winter. In the distance (top right), we see Meschede.

A farm in Vellinghausen. Was this the farm of my sleigh-ride visit?

18

The Old School by
the Churchyard

Of the two school buildings in the village, one was a fairly new, lofty brick-built building, while the far older wattle-and-daub school, long and low by the churchyard, opposite the church entrance, was the building where village forebears had been educated. In fact, a school had been there at least since 1656, though the building we called 'the Old School' with two schoolrooms and a teacher's flat had been built in 1811. Primitive toilets were placed on the ends with a basic urinal on the side nearest to the inn on the approach to the church.

Attached at the back were the living quarters for one teacher included in the cramped space. *Fräulein* Michel was a spinster of middle years, who, with *Fräulein* Fischer in the newer school, complemented our two male and married teachers, one of whom was the head teacher; the other was a fine musician who doubled as organist in the large church with its colourful baroque interior.

Of the two classrooms by the churchyard, one usually accommodated the older girls and one the older boys. Our desks with angled lids came in rows for three pupils and had depressions for pens and circular openings at the top with metal lids for inkpots. Perhaps it was due to the privations of wartime, but even there we were still issued with slate tablets, ruled on one side and crosshatched for maths on the other. Of course, a small cloth and a sponge went with that—a practical and reusable arrangement.

While there was the obligatory portrait of the Führer framed under glass on a wall at the back of the class, our teachers were non-political. As far as I can remember, we never had political instructions, certainly not modern history. We did learn about the Romans—there had been a decisive historical battle in Westphalia, in the Teutoburg Forest a little to the east, where the local tribes under Hermann the Cherusker (Arminius of the Cherusci tribe) were successful in falling upon and annihilating three Roman legions under the command of Publius Quinctilius Varus in AD 9. Emperor Augustus is said to have torn his clothes, refused to cut his hair for months, and, for a long time afterwards, was heard upon occasion to moan:

The old school by the churchyard.

'Quinctilius Varus, give me back my Legions!' Alas, the loser Quinctilius Varus had done the Roman thing and fallen on his own sword.

We did learn about Wotan, Thor, Baldur, and Vikings and Valkyries and all the exciting stories that made up the old faith, as well as the Holy Roman Empire and Charlemagne. There were knights and jousts and troubadours, and the plague. Once a year, on Ash Wednesday, I believe, one of the older boys was sent up into the attic of the old school to retrieve some old posters that would be unrolled for our instruction and contemplation with the grave seriousness the day demanded, as part of our religious instructions. Catechism was a part of the curriculum.

I particularly remember an image of medieval war machines attacking a burning walled town and Albrecht Dürer's *Four Horsemen of the Apocalypse* in full hue and cry making us think of man's short span of life. We did not need too much reminding. Death and destruction were the undercurrents of daily conversations. Making up the four riders apart from the skeletal Grim Reaper are also Famine, War, and Pestilence.

In the last years of school, our German poets, authors, and playwrights Friedrich Schiller and Johann Wolfgang von Goethe, as well as more local writers, were discussed and explored. Large tracts of Schiller's poem *'Das Lied von der Glocke'* ('Song of the Bell') with its poetic portrayal of work, life, storm, and fire were practically learnt by heart.

As well as Germanic and Roman history, we embraced Greek Mythology, the Gods, Homer's *Odyssey*, and the *Iliad*—anything but recent German endeavours.

Our head teacher, *Herr* Bolte, who limped with one unbendable knee, had seen service as a Prussian Hussar earlier in the century.

He had two serving sons, one a *Jagdflieger* (fighter pilot) in the Luftwaffe. It was on one sunny but ordinary day that the sound of aircraft intruded into the drab lessons in our school. It subsided, but returned even louder. *Lehrer* Bolte bade us remain seated while he carefully investigated. It was one of ours. One by one, we left our seats to stand outside, between school and church with the tall tower-raised steeple, craning our necks skywards while a pilot in a small aircraft repeatedly circled and dived, always managing to avoid the steeple with its staunch weathervane cockerel.

Children ran for cover with hands over their ears when it approached and shouted with joy when the daredevil revved up again. One could see him waving.

'It's a Stuka.'

'Don't be daft. It's a Fieseler Storch.'

Someone cried out, then others. Something had been thrown from the plane, something bright and not very heavy. Pupils ran off to find it and eventually it was retrieved—a letter or a note in an envelope. It was addressed to *Hauptlehrer* Bolte. Our teacher went indoors and read the letter quietly. It was a while before lessons continued. A message from his eldest son, we learnt later. We never knew the actual words. Neither of head teacher Bolte's sons survived the war, only his daughter did.

Some years ago, I am told, an American Jew arrived in the village with a story that would direct him to our former headmaster's house on its hillside. On approach, he easily recognised the house as he told his story. *Herr* Bolte's fifteen-year-old son, also named Karl, had on 10 November 1938 brought home with him from his *Rektoratsschule* (Stiftsgymnasium) in the nearby town of Meschede a Jewish boy to protect him. The boy had survived the war, but alas, neither his protector nor his younger brother had.

Hauptlehrer Bolte did not shy away from using the rod, should that be required in order to elicit some sense, some reaction or some effort from any of us. I do remember the rod being used to punish, but not by which teacher. We called him '*der Alte*', (the old one) in a mixture of respect and dread. Anyway, a sharp swipe to an open hand usually would suffice. But the fact that it might happen made the actual event practically unnecessary.

Homework was usually the last thing on our minds. In my case, I always left it as the last task of the day, though it had to be done and then bedtime would be delayed with some justification. Depending on the subject or task, our efforts usually had to be read out in the mornings.

One particular day stands out while we were reading our latest homework essays to the class.

Norbert was an evacuee from the Rhineland. He was one of the newcomers who swelled the usual village scholar community considerably, coming from different backgrounds and different stages of education and lodging in various usually cramped conditions and with greatly varying distances from school. Some pupils walked for miles there and back. I was one of a few exceptions, living just a few doors away across the churchyard. The homework theme was one to which Norbert was still trying to adjust, although it was a farm on which their family had been settled: '*Der Bauernhof*' ('The Farm').

'Come now,' *Herr* Bolte tried to encourage the quiet boy who had difficulty breathing, 'now show these dullards how to put together an excellent essay.' Then he added, 'and stand up straight.'

With his asthma, Norbert stooped a little while his shoulders heaved, but he shot up another centimetre or two, while staring at the slate tablet in his hands.

'Louder!' The teacher was getting impatient.

'Ahem,' started Norbert. 'The Farm. On a farm are many animals. They live on one end and the people on the other. We live in the middle.'

'Are you quite sure?' interrupted the teacher.

Norbert kept reading as if nothing had happened. 'When I entered the parlour for the first time my eyes fell upon a large glass cabinet.'

'Quiet!' ordered *Herr* Bolte, to end the sniggering that followed. 'Perhaps that was painful. I suspect an optician has put everything back again painlessly?'

On another occasion, the tall Hännes who later left the village to pursue a life on the high seas enjoyed his favourite subject as theme for his essay. He had made a special effort. Not everybody could write about the high seas with some authority. He was the youngest of several brothers, some of whom had been to sea: 'The Ocean. On the oceans are many ships, staffed with seamen. They're called seamen because the water is so large, they've got to see over great distances'.

'I think I see what you're getting at,' echoed the teacher. It was enough to lose one's composure.

Sometimes there just was not a chance to complete the homework, if one had to help out at home, as at harvest time for instance. Karl was a year older than I, and like most of his large family, he had a rather useful brain that put him at the head of his class. Even so he made a mistake that almost cost him the top position among his peers. When he read out his essay one day all went well, content, sentence construction, composition, expression, clarity were as one would expect from someone of his intellect.

'Now why don't you move your eye balls occasionally?' interrupted the teacher presently. 'Everything can't be written on the same spot, surely? Why don't you come down here and let us share that miracle!'

Karl hesitated. Being top of the class meant he was furthest away from the teacher. This was a turn of events he had not anticipated, but no face-saving idea came to mind. In the end, he walked to the front, a little sheepish, expecting the worst as he handed his clean slate to the teacher. The teacher lifted up the bare exhibit and praised the skill and dexterity of the author/reader who had composed his essay on the spur of the moment. Nevertheless, Karl realised his audacity could not be repeated.

My embarrassing mistake, probably around Mothers' Day, was in an essay with the title 'My mother'. I had my own idea of beauty, and my mother in her wartime dark clothes and with all her worries did not fit my ideas. With the honesty of a child, but a complete lack of tact, I had written or my mother had observed me writing 'On the outside my mother is not especially beautiful'. She never forgot that sentence. What I went on to write, or what I meant, was that her beauty was on the inside, her nature, her love, her stoic and unswerving loyalties were a beauty that transcended such transitional aspects as perceived physical looks. It never got said. Now, far too late, I am sorry I missed the opportunity of setting the record straight.

As stated, my walk to the old school was a very short one. On one particular day, during a break in lessons, two brothers who lived next door to us, but were several years older than myself, had taken it into their head to teach me a lesson. I cannot think what the reason was, but they attacked me within sight of the school. Perhaps it was simply because they were bigger? Or maybe I appeared to them a clever little know-all? I certainly do not remember any particular animosity, and I have never had any problems with attracting bother, usually having been able to talk my way out. But I have my limits, as the two brothers found. Instead of giving in or begging them to stop, I gave as good as I got. Bullies seem to respect that. I never had problems with them again.

It so happened that the bell was rung at the end of break time and looking up I noticed *Herr* Bolte standing by the school door watching us. I really thought I was in for a lecture at least for fighting. I dusted myself down and ran back. The teacher just grinned as I rushed past him into class.

I found that essays and composition presented no great problems for me. Even spelling, art, and handwriting were passable. My difficulties came down to mathematics. At school report time, it was a case of mathematical dexterity. School places and seating were allocated according to a grading system from six to one, from 'unsatisfactory' to 'very good'. The marks for the varying subjects, attendance, etc. were added together, then divided by the number of subjects taken. Results would determine your position in the classroom. Low was right in front of the teacher and high was right at the back where all sorts of privileges could be worked.

In earlier years, I had become lax and indifferent to schooling. I do not remember any specific event or time that brought it about, but there came a change when I felt I was wasting my time if I did not try and learn and improve myself. I had become hungry for advancement and knowledge.

So when results were handed out, it was a case of mathematics deciding whether one moved up or down. Knowing my aversion to maths, my near friend and neighbour Bernhard offered to help me out. Out of the kindness of his heart. I was about to accept my place a seat below him when something felt not right. I had had better results than he had. I did my own maths and as if by magic our positions were reversed.

Herr Bolte grinned: 'I've been wondering when you'd wake up and improve your maths'. I was left with the distinct feeling he would not have interfered had I accepted the lesser result.

On several occasions (in later school years), *Lehrer* Bolte arranged special outings to beech woods for the collection of beechnuts. The small triangular hard-cased nuts were especially sought for oil and margarine production. On other occasions, we would be helping farmers gather flax that had to be pulled out in bushels by hand. Being shorter than grown-ups in stature, children were particularly suited to certain tasks, though the pulling of flax also demanded a prerequisite of muscle. As one of *Lehrer* Bolte's legs would not bend at the knee, it made walking more difficult and it cannot have been an easy task to direct such events in undulating terrain, especially as children make no allowance for the comfort or otherwise of teachers (very likely, such outings would have been ordered by official directives, though among us children there were no end of speculations as to what the teacher's gain was in such operations).

In the spring, several classes might be descending on potato fields in an effort to scour the plants and remove from the budding foliage the little pests responsible for much destruction, the striped American Colorado beetle, before their greedy larvae could begin their leaf devouring habits. Such outings afforded great opportunities to show off to the girls, who might take flight head-over-heels at the offer in hand of the odd frog that was languishing in its present form and would improve greatly when kissed by a nubile maiden. Somehow that kind of wooing never quite caught on. Not even the chance of a husband in the form of a handsome young prince could impress some girls.

Winter fodder drying in small fields and meadows that belonged to different families, as did the patches of varying forestry.

Aunt Minna's class, early last century. Aunt Minna is in the front row, fifth from left.

Teacher Anna Bolte, the head teacher's wife, and her class, 1920s.

Above: *Fräulein* Fischer was my first teacher. Here in the 1920s, Aunt Anna (second row, third from left) is in front of the girl in white. Elaborate bows to hold up hair seem to have been the latest fashion accessories.

Below: *Fräulein* Michel and her class. A wood-framed slate and a slate pencil would require an attached sponge and/or a cloth like the nearest boy's in the aisle to the left to keep the slate clean.

Above: Teacher Heinrich Kortenkamp with a mixed class at the end of the 1920s or early 1930s.

Below: Head teacher Karl Bolte (back row, left side) with a musical generation of village boys, some of them in the uniform of the Hitler Youth, 1935–38, at the east end of the parish church.

19

The Brazen Trout

Above me, pastel-coloured clouds sailed across the clear blue sky—clouds that bubbled upwards yet were flat like compressed wool underneath. Clouds with faces, bulging eyes, thick lips, projecting pear-shaped chins, and cleft bulbous noses. Some had blown-out cheeks and warts that grew larger by the watching until everything changed and took on different forms again, ahead of the breeze that pushed them along. Flying cathedrals with onion-shaped domes drifted by. Strange fish. A huge lion's head yawned soundlessly. Clouds coasted along like sailing ships, one large cloud or perhaps several towering smaller ones bunched together, their upper parts separated like the sails of a giant aerial windjammer, a galleon manned by invisible pirates.

The ripe golden cornfields below played their part by imitating waves on water as the wind like invisible giants' hands stroked them in ripples. My imagination raced ahead of the wind, as my thin, bony legs felt the sun's warmth where they protruded from my short trousers.

The clear sound of the noon bell from the small tower of the village church brought me back to the present and reality. Lying on my back, hands folded under my head on the slope of one of the hills in the chain that guard the village to the south, it was easy to dream. The splendid view takes in fields and meadows, the village and various outlying farms and settlements. Soft, forest-dark hills mark the horizon in almost all directions.

My limbs were stiff at first, but the long march down and back towards the village soon forced life back into them. I had chosen a roundabout way via the long meadow that runs along the bottom of grandmother's fields, when I met Walter.

'I have been looking for you,' said Walter accusingly, as if it were my lot to be found easily, 'where have you been?'

'Oh, not far,' my answer was evasive, which did not reveal a great deal, but sufficed for Walter. He was older and taller than I, but equally thin and gawky—the son of a child-rich family who lived on the slope of a hill to the east in a small house, the walls of which could barely contain its members when they were all at home.

Walter was no professor and he had no great liking for school, but on the subject of flora and fauna, he knew his way around and was more cunning than many of his contemporaries. If he wandered alone through the landscape some people might be suspicious, but with me for company, nobody would take much notice. Maybe he was simply friendly and liked company and I was impressed that someone older would bother with me. Even though the age difference was only a year or two, Walter was certainly more streetwise.

'How are your trout?' I asked, before Walter could bring up the subject, perhaps still being suspicious of my companion's reasons for his friendship.

'They're not my trout,' Walter sounded hurt. 'They're everybody's, not just the fat farmer's.'

'Have you looked in the kettles yet?'

'No, that's why I was looking for you. It's time to have a look-see.'

My interest was awakened. We jumped down an incline towards the small stream that snakes through the Long Meadow, looping around a soggy damp spot marked by tall hemlock and pretty swamp orchids. The grass was juicy and green. Hazel shrubs reached across the gurgling water, giving shade and marking its passage. Here and there the stream had washed out the soil and ran under green overhangs where dandelion and buttercups balanced precariously.

Walter lay on his belly, sleeves turned up to their maximum, while his hands felt the dark hidden places under roots and driftwood. He had no luck. The secret hiding

Early view of Remblinghausen from behind the big house. Front centre is the Parsonage and the timbered tithe barn beside it. To the right of the church, we see the cluster of the original medieval village. From this side, American GIs and tanks would arrive.

places were empty. A little further along, an old bucket, dented and full of holes, was quite suddenly jerked from the water. But not fast enough. Like a silver arrow, a small fish escaped as the handle caught on a root just for a fraction of a second. Water escaped like small fountains in all directions before the trap was carefully replaced.

'Out of interest,' I asked, a little doubtful, 'have you ever had any luck with this sort of thing?'

Walter sounded hurt again: 'Do you think I'm lying? Trout always hide under something, overhangs or the like. And when a bucket lies on its side…. If you can do any better, you can have a try next time.' We wandered a little further to where a kettle would be waiting innocently on its side. Perhaps we would have better luck there?

'We need more kettles and buckets,' said Walter, always the practical one, as we came to a bend in the stream. I offered to look out for some. The moment we jumped across the water at a narrow spot, we were no longer shielded by the hazel bushes and quite unexpectedly we were confronted by the presence of a girl. Or rather a young woman. It was too late. She had seen us. Cows were grazing peacefully about her on the lush grass and she seemed glad of the company, even if at first that did not appear so.

'What are you doing here?' the maiden asked snootily, equally surprised. 'Don't you disturb our cows.'

'Good day,' I said politely and without thinking. 'We only wanted…'

Walter's elbow found my side, seemingly by accident, 'we only wanted to study nature a little closer. It's for an essay in school.'

'Oh,' said the maiden with disdain, 'Writing essays? You poor boys.' She was older than Walter even and had left school already and by her attitude was much more grown-up and exalted. But smaller and rounder.

Walter coughed inelegantly and just managing a nod and a 'G'day!' wanted to pass on. He had not reckoned with her mood and the fact that she had time on her hands. I believe all three of us realised that normally she would not have given either of us the time of day, even though she was from the village—she had said 'our' cows. Girls are so much ahead of the male sex at that age. The meadow probably belonged to her family, she being a farmer's daughter.

We were all the more surprised when she started a conversation, which neither of us could duck out of without being rude. She seemed to know Walter, because she addressed me: 'And who are you then?'

'I am from *Knippen*. Maria's son.' My grandmother's fields nearby would give me a reason to be in the vicinity.

'Oh, yes,' mused the young lady, 'the tailors. You have some fields hereabouts somewhere? Yes?' In tough lace-up boots, pinafore, knee-length dress, and empowered by a stout cowherd's crook, the term 'lady' was perhaps a little generous. She did not await an answer. 'That has to be a great help to feed all those mouths. Are you looking after the cows there?'

'No, they're in another meadow.' It felt good to be able to show off.

She did not react to the extra piece of land: 'I often wonder how the little people manage with only a cow or two and then all those children as well. I don't do this usually, but when the men are ill'. She sighed deeply at her sacrifice, but if she had hoped for sympathy, she had met the wrong two adversaries, so she continued: 'One has to help out nowadays with this war. My brother is supposed to be called up, too—and he with his weak back, and his feet. Of course the eldest one can't go at all. Heaven knows how we'll manage'.

I wondered silently how her brother's feet could win or lose 'the war?' As for managing, nobody had asked my father how he could manage his business in his absence before they sent him to the front.

'I only have one sister,' I said quietly.

We did not want to win the war. We wanted to get back to the trout. But I could not think of an excuse to leave. She spoke to Walter now, but without as much as looking at him. Walter's parents might have owned a few goats, but from her point of view, they were definitely *kleine Leute*—'little people'.

'You're going to school, you must know long John in the village near us? He really ought not to be in school anymore. It's just because of a few days. And now they're giving him such a bad name. He isn't at all like that. I know him. We used to play together when we were smaller. A neighbour of ours. He's only too grown-up for his age. Even if he is a little wild now and then. Many a person would be glad to know such a fine young man.'

We had kept silent during her pontifications, being quite uninterested in her 'long John' and quite unconcerned as to whatever he had done or was supposed to have done. Anyway, he came from a more well-to-do family. Though the girl had not introduced herself, I now began to get a notion of who she was, or at least from what family—farmer neighbours of 'long John' in the lower village. There were many 'little people' in the lower village, too. I could only think of one farmer that fitted the description. Not a large farmer, mind, and not exactly a small family either. Long John was the eldest of three, born in a public house, but his father also owned a shop and a mill. Obviously they did not count as being 'little people'.

Her admiring tirade seemed to speak of more than neighbourly acquaintance. 'The tall fellow is bound to have more taste,' I thought, trying to keep a blank expression on my face.

'You can tell that to your teacher. Somebody has to speak up for him,' the maiden continued. A handful of cows had taken advantage of her distraction and had wandered out of her sight. 'Wait a moment, will you, I'm coming back. Now don't go away!'

As soon as she turned to scamper after the unconcerned bovines, we hurried in the opposite direction back to the stream.

'Do you want to?'

'No, go on, hurry.'

Walter lifted the dented old kettle from the clear water with unexpected alacrity and to both our surprise it contained a medium sized trout. At the same time, we could hear the herdswoman shout: 'Come here you stupid cow … and stay here!'

There was not much time.

'Quick,' said Walter, and the slippery prize smoothly disappeared down his trouser pocket, ere both of us, whistling innocently, wandered back before the girl could come looking for us.

'Oh, there you are,' sighed she, a little out of breath, 'it's so rare that one meets anyone down here, let alone have a conversation with. I mean, anyone one can trust, so alone in the open. There are so many strangers about, soldiers and Poles in the village, one never knows. The stories one hears…' She shook her head as though she constantly expected the worst.

Perhaps she realised that we had not contributed to her 'conversation'. We were just waiting for an opportunity to flee her company.

The breathless trout in Walter's trouser pocket had spawned a small damp patch and chose that moment to make one last effort to lurch for air and freedom. In its confined space, that was not easy, but understandable. Or perhaps it had only lost its balance.

Unfortunately, the unexpected movement had not escaped the concerned young woman. Her eyes grew larger and her cheeks coloured rouge in a mixture of horror and rage. 'You unashamed … louts.' Words failed her as she raised the knotty cowherd's staff and trained it down on Walter's back, just as he jumped off, ahead of me, to escape her wrath. He was lucky. The aim had found its mark, but only in glancing. Walter was surprisingly agile when it counted. Behind us we heard words a lady of such tender years should not have known.

'Whatever's the matter with her?' asked Walter when at last we stopped and he tried to reach and rub the affected shoulder with the opposing hand. He said a lot more, but 'fat farmers' was the main theme I could understand. '*Die dicken Bauern.*'

'I bet she thought you fancied her,' I said at last, trying to sound grown-up and finding it difficult to stop laughing, in spite of my difficulties in breathing.

Walter understood what had happened well enough and he, too, broke into spasms of mirth: 'What, and all that because of an old trout?'

'Only when she suspects what's in your pocket.'

'Well,' said Walter when we had calmed down, and he pulled the dead trout from his pocket. 'I think I've earned this. It's died in my pocket. Just as well I'd mended it, the pocket, I mean.'

I had to agree with him. Walter had earned it. It was far too small to divide, and I did not want to know what else had shared the poor creature's final moments in that fathomless pocket.

Having left the narrow valley, we felt the wind pulling at hair and clothes. We were still laughing as we reached the cross-roads where Walter would be turning off.

For long moments, we stood baffled in our hobnailed boots, hands in pockets and not quite certain if we could trust our eyes. On a recently mowed meadow close by, an unusual act of nature was taking its toll. Of the newly raised haystacks that covered the area in reasonably straight lines, some were wholly or partly empty and swathes of hay played ring-o-roses in the air. Between them leapt grown-ups and children in a comical, un-choreographed dance as in a film sequence that is being presented at the wrong speed.

There were sound effects, too—curses and wheezing from the grown-ups and the tinkling laughter of children—as they threw themselves with outstretched arms over the moving hay or jumped high after hay clouds that rose spiralling to the heavens as if God were collecting his tithes, before the bunches disintegrated and fell back to earth over a wide area. A summer whirlwind.

My mouth must have fallen open. There were brown arms that reached out of turned-up sleeves and straining blouses, wide skirts, and plenty of underwear, and here and there rubber band-secured panties and white knees, as they rolled about in their determined efforts to hold on to the flighty hay. Braces lost their buttons from torn and mended trousers and pink-white skin glistened on bald heads when the whirlwind caught and dislodged a felt hat, sailed it some distance through the air, and dropped it again out of the range of its power.

Walter, too, found it difficult to remain straight-faced.

'Take your hands out of your pockets and come and help,' called a breathless voice between amazing acrobatics. We looked at each other quizzically.

'Do you fancy dancing with hay?' asked Walter.

'Me with my asthma?' said I.

Walter played with his well-hidden fish. 'Those fat farmers, they can lick my … they're welcome,' he said, as he turned away and still grinning broadly, walked towards home and his small fish supper.

20

Uncle Engelbert and the Allies

We may have had a lift, my mother and I. Perhaps my small sister was with us as well, but more likely she would have stayed with Aunt Minna. In a village where everybody knew everybody it was usually known when anyone with transport had to travel any distance and sometimes there would be the possibility of a spare seat or seats. People would help each other. A chance to visit Aunt Theresa, my mother's elder sister, the only one who had moved and married a few villages away to Wennemen on the railway line. The older daughters were not present, but a late addition to the family, a boy younger than myself, was there and so was Uncle Engelbert, a typical employee of the railway company, braces and waistcoat, fob watch and chain, and a walrus moustache, thick set, and set in his ways.

Uncle Engelbert had it all figured out. In spite of all his efforts, the war was not going well and it seemed inevitable that we would be overrun by the Allies from the west. It would be the end of the world and just too much to bear. Uncle Engelbert confided to all who would care to listen, that he would not be there to witness the final humiliation. He would kill himself before the Americans forced their way into the town.

It must have been a holiday or a Sunday when we visited and while the sisters caught up on gossip and with the extra hand at his disposal, his son and I were to accompany Uncle Engelbert on a fuel gathering expedition. In Uncle Engelbert's view, inherited privilege should have been done away with years ago. The National Socialists were going to change all that and now the Americans were about to stop them bringing in the reforms to help the common man. To start with, Uncle Engelbert was going to strike a blow for the common man and collect his winter fuel from the privileged woods.

We all three travelled out on his bicycle, his son on the handlebars and I on the parcel rack behind him. He hid the bicycle at the edge of the stately forest, then wandered out among the trees that were the property of the family of the Graf von Westphalen. Uncle Engelbert seemed familiar in the terrain, so it probably was not his first such outing.

I do not remember how far we walked. I remember the wild woods being remarkably tidy and we had to cover some distance to find any naturally dropped dead branches or some that could with a little effort be encouraged to drop.

Uncle Engelbert had collected a fair bundle of faggots, some taller than himself and secured them with string, a load which he carried red-faced and snorting aloft on his shoulder. My bundle was more modest, but I, too, carried my load and his younger son's would have been proportionally smaller still, but I distinctly remember the change in attitude and confidence as Uncle Engelbert suddenly stopped on our way back.

'Oh, no! That's all I need. Damn!' or words to that effect, added to a string of mumbled curses. 'What's he doing here?' On a rough forest track curving among the trees on the flat terrain, a man and a woman casually sauntered towards us, quite possibly on their Sunday constitutional. It was too late. We had been seen by the Graf and his companion, perhaps his wife? After all he had said and done, Uncle Engelbert could not avoid his fate. I did not quite grasp what was happening at the time, but I did realise we had been rumbled. At the same time, I could not see the significance of the bundles of dry branches that were of little use to anyone else. I can still see Uncle Engelbert, though, standing to attention among the tall trees, straight as his body would allow, bare-headed as in a church with his hat clasped to his chest as in homage, while hiding behind his bundle of faggots that, stood on end, shielded most of his person.

We must have presented a curious sight to the Count and the Lady—a red-faced man hiding behind a bundle of faggots and two small boys with a few sticks of wood on either side, standing stock-still and upright in line as they walked past. The well-dressed couple paid no attention to us, at least, I do not remember any conversation. Perhaps a nod? When they had passed, Uncle Engelbert sighed a sigh of relief and let fly a few more curses about his bad luck, being caught out by the influential Count, hoping he had not been recognised so that he could not be held to account. His position at the local railway station was at stake and it was important. After all, there were banners along roads and railways and anywhere they might be needed to remind citizens: '*Räder müssen rollen für den Sieg!*' ('Wheels must turn for Victory!').

We loaded and tied the bounty on his bicycle and walked back all the way to his home. It was the nearest I ever came to someone of note in my younger years—the Graf von Westphalen himself in his own park, Schloß Laer—I have never been especially impressed by title or rank.

Late in 1944, the noble premises of Schloß Laer came under military command with the establishment of a V-2 rocket base that, because of the rapid advance of the Allies, was never completed.

Uncle Engelbert did not 'top himself'. He survived the arrival of the Americans and lived for many years after the end of the war. He died a natural death, not a violent one, and certainly not a self-inflicted one.

Years later, as a teenager, I once attended an equestrian event in the stately grounds of Schloß Laer with a contingent from my home village. As a young male, my lasting impression was made by a youngish lady who seemed quite at home at such events and who at specific opportunities, like prize-giving, would bow to the appreciative crowd. Her loose fitting dress and generous *décolleté* on such occasions meant that her unfettered person was quite generously displayed during her forward movements. Later, back in our village and in a less formal environment, a local wag was heard to comment on just how the young lady's naval had been displayed as a broach beneath it all!

Schloß Laer, a moated castle near Meschede, the stately home of the Grafen von Westphalen, and proposed site for a doodlebug station.

21

Messages from the Front

I was playing close by the churchyard when my mother returned and called me at the bottom of the stairs to our small rented home. There was an air of seriousness about her—more serious than usual.

She had called me on previous occasions when there had been a letter from my father or a postcard from my favourite uncle. Uncle Jupp's mail was special. He would send postcards from the Eastern Front, addressed directly to me with just a few words of humour or encouragement. On one occasion, he had sketched a donkey, seen from the rear, its hind quarters high in the air and kicking, in a way that seemed peculiar to the stubborn character of mules, but funny as a cartoon to a small boy. At Christmas, he had drawn a fir twig with a bauble and a candle, with just a Christmas greeting.

There had also been little space for writing on a postcard that carried a drawing of a swallow. A swallow in flight. Swallows were a familiar sight in our village where they built their grey nests on ceiling beams in stables and barns where ticks and flies were plentiful about cattle and horses. Farmers welcomed them because they helped reduce the swarms of insect pests that troubled the animals. In autumn, the swallows would congregate on telegraph wires like musical notes in a simple composition before sensibly taking flight to warmer climes for the winter.

The friendly tailor must have been sitting out there, far from home, in the unfamiliar vastness of Russia, bidding the elegant free spirits that know no boundaries to carry his greetings, perhaps his wishes, back to the hills and fields and woods that were his home and that he loved. A man who had not seen much of life, a gentleman, torn from the family and everything he knew to make up numbers.

One day, a letter arrived at the old house on the hill, addressed to all the family. It had been written in pencil on both sides of a piece of paper. It was his testament. The last will and testament of a man who knew his fate.

Some of the words have stuck in my mind, as my mother oft repeated them in later years: 'Our Company has been attached to the SS' it read. 'I shall not return.

My brother August will be the head of the family now, but as the oldest I wish every one of my siblings to have a plot to build their own house'.

'I shall not return'. Such simple words. Such finality. Much of this I did not understand until much later. Uncle Jupp's division had been attached to the dreaded SS. SS meant '*Schutzstaffel*' (Protection Squadron), but it had grown into an insatiable monster, carrying out the state's most depraved orders. The organisation had started as bodyguard, protecting the hall entrances at party meetings—'bouncers' they would be called today—but their later actions of infamy had destroyed their humanity. The dreaded runic 'SS' insignia resembled lightning flashes. Russian people might feel compassion for the ordinary conscripted soldier, but there was no sympathy for the SS.

At an earlier time, Uncle Jupp had confided how he stood on watch and lorry loads of people were driven past, the vehicles always returning empty. He had drawn his own conclusions. That is why Uncle Jupp had written: 'I shall not return.'

Some time later, another letter arrived at the old house on the hill, an official letter, typed, but also quite simple: 'Josef Schütteler is reported missing in action, presumed dead'. His whereabouts were not known, was the gist of the information. The family strongly suspected that he took his own life.

This time, when my mother called me to her, she held another letter in her shaking hands. She tried to read it out to me, but her eyes kept filling with tears. It, too, was an official notification, typed and standard issue. This letter concerned my father, just as the previous one had mentioned Uncle Jupp. It, too, was a simple official notification.

It read: '*Obergefreiter* Robert Hallmann is missing in action on the Russian front'. Or words to that effect. The difference between that message and a notification of death was that it replaced certainty with hope. My father had been a dispatch rider. Horseback was obviously the most reliable way to get about cross-country on Russian roads and byways. He had never advanced further than his two stripes, though. He had, however, fallen off his horse and damaged his knee.

I could not cry. Why could I not cry? I was ashamed of the fact that tears would not flow, though all our future was in jeopardy with that message. My father was missing. He might be a prisoner of war? I hid my face from my mother. Maybe he was a prisoner? Maybe he was still alive? Death had become an everyday companion, but here was at least just a glimmer of hope.

Not all mail from the front brought bad tidings. If memory serves me right, it was a neighbour, Josef Nelle, but others may also have sent seeds in their mail, loosely added in envelopes together with their letters. The following year, the colourful erect spikes of lupins (*lupinus*) flowered in village gardens and I remember lupins spread all about verges and waysides in the years that followed. His lupins flourished, but Josef Nelle did not return.

Orders, Just Orders

Up at *Oma*'s house I found Uncle August in an argument with a soldier in uniform who had been quartered there overnight. He was the driver of a rather large military truck that had been driven in through the wide doors of the 'Deele' at the street-side end of the house that was traditionally the gateway for hay wains and harvest wagons to enter. I could not see whether the lorry was laden or what its contents were, but it had been determined that such interior spaces offered good camouflage and hide it from aerial reconnaissance. Having opened the parallel doors at the back of the 'Deele', the soldier was about to drive his noisy vehicle out that way, rather than attempt the tricky manoeuvre of reversing past the midden he had negotiated on the way in.

Uncle August tried to stop him with considerable alarm in his voice and demeanour, 'No, no, not this way.' Standing in front of the heavy vehicle, he tried with his bare hands to stop its advance. He had recently installed drainage pipes at the back of the house and was in fear of their destruction by the vehicle's weight.

Purposefully, the uniformed driver stepped down from the vehicle, undoing his holster. 'You know,' he said earnestly, looking Uncle August straight in the eyes, 'I am supposed to shoot you dead right now. Anyone who hampers the war effort is to be dealt with on the spot. Such are my orders.'

Uncle August stood aside without further uttering another word. He did not know it then, of course, but the end of the war also spelled the end of the old house.

22

Grandmother's Death

Oma's death left a large void. Her life had not been an easy one and she had been little more than skin and bones. Of her children, seven had made it into adulthood. There had been hard times. A photograph shows my grandparents behind the old house with their collection of beehives. They both look smart and well dressed, gran especially, but my mother later confided that her pristine white overall was borrowed for the occasion of the photograph.

Remembering times when honey spread on dark-crusted rye bread toast had been all there was at mealtimes to such an extent that my mother would not eat honey for the rest of her life, a natural product I count among my favourites.

There had been a special bond between my *Oma* and me. *Oma* would take my side unreservedly; she would protect me and make excuses on my behalf whenever some shortcoming might get me into trouble.

That is why I could not understand that my grandmother of all people would return after her death to haunt my dreams and turn them into nightmares—frightening, chasing me with large bulging eyes about the old house. In the end, I found myself praying that she should not return. Not in the guise of a nightmare, please, God. I hated to think such thoughts, but that was not the way I wanted to remember her. My *Oma*. My beloved *Oma*.

There had been so many deaths, two of her sons had been lost to the war, but my mother hinted at other siblings, still-born children and one boy, young Willibald, who had suffered from meningitis. Doctors could not help him and he knew he would die. The unlucky teenager had looked after a pair of geese as his favourite hobby. The geese had spent their noisy days at the back of the cottage, where pigs also had their special wallowing outdoors enclosure, foraging, chattering, and protecting their space, attacking intruders and strangers better than any dog could. This had been before my time, when my mother was young. The saddest moments she described were when he prayed that he could see his geese just one more spring.

Maybe it was just as well gran died before the theatre of war settled in and around the village and destroyed her world.

There was a family secret that only late in life my mother could talk about. 'Her from the smithy,' she would say in a very dismissive tone when we looked at old photographs of Adam and Maria Schütteler's wedding. 'Her from the smithy' was her father's mother. 'I'm not letting you go,' she had insisted when it came to marrying my grandmother. After the wedding, she had turned against her daughter-in-law to the point that following a miscarriage, she had pronounced her guilty: 'You are doomed now. There is no point of your going to the sacraments. You have killed your child'.

To the quiet and utterly selfless woman, that must have sounded like eternal damnation.

The author in 1943 at a neighbouring farm that in years gone by had been the Vicarage. Long stockings and short trousers.

23

My Window on the World

My mother often commented in later life how my nose used to be pressed against the windowpanes. Whenever weather and health disallowed the outdoors, I watched village activities from my vantage point in our home in the centre of the village. Sometimes I would disobey and open the window of our small home that was a wooden addition to a larger brick-built house—one of two general stores in the village as I remember. That did not, however, prevent our landlords from raising their own pigs like most people.

The difference in height between the churchyard at the back and the main street at the front of the house meant that the pigsty was below us at ground level two storeys down, with my father's storeroom between.

When my father first started up his roofing business in the village, it had given him a central base to store his tools, slates, scaffolding, planks, etc., though he also kept a storage space for the longest planks and scaffolding poles near my grandmother's house and some very long ladders between two houses in the neighbourhood.

Almost opposite our home, a side street rose uphill, flanked on one side by a large lawn and garden of a farmhouse of wattle and daub, the first farm of several. Opposite on the right-hand side of the road stood the butcher's shop of modern rendering. Head teacher Bolte's modern house, the highest on the side of the hill and visible from most parts of the village, stood foursquare above them all, the four corners marking the points of the compass.

One of my favourite sights was a pair of proud and formidable stallions that rippled with muscles and were stabled up at the Kamphof farm for short periods each year. They were known as Wallachen after their place of origin, Wallachia, better known today as the former kingdom of Vlad the Impaler—or Vlad Dracula.

The super studs were brought in to the village at a certain time of the year to improve the stock of our own local heavy horses and they would be led through the village with chains clanking, visiting the various farms in rotation. Every farm of a reasonable size still kept its own horses. I was especially impressed by the fact that these magnificently good-natured beasts could be handled by just one small man. But then theirs was a life of privilege and grooming without the burden of normal farm work, at least during the time they spent in the village. I do not think they ever returned after the war.

I witnessed the gentleness of large horses one day when an altercation in the street sent me rushing to the window. A farmer's son clung on for dear life, not on the galloping horse's back, but under its belly. He had got himself into difficulty, very likely because it got spooked when a harness had not been secured properly. The heavy horse had taken off along the main road in its panic, dragging the young man along underneath. People in its path jumped out of harm's way, while the young man yelled for someone to grab the horse and stop it. He survived the ordeal without serious damage. In its blind panic and confusion, the horse had not been able to avoid treading on his chest, though even then it had avoided putting pressure on the weighty iron-shod hoof.

Horses were still the main suppliers of power on farms, very important with the shortage of oil and petrol. Horses need no spare parts, just feed, water, and regular shoeing at the smithy. I loved watching the blacksmith at the forge in his heavy leather apron, forming the red-hot irons on the anvil like Thor the God of Thunder in the wood-cuts of my picture books, trying them on while the bored beasts stood by with endless patience, continually fly-swatting with restless tails. Several times, the farrier would be reworking the glowing shoes until they fitted perfectly. The distinctive smell of seared hooves was a part of that traditional experience.

There used to be two smithies in the village, but even in my earliest memories, one of them was winding down. That left Hanses to the northeast of the church, distant relatives like so many families in the village. The smithy was a separate building in an area that saw a number of houses clustered rather closely together and where people and animals lived cheek-by-jowl. That had been the original village when it was still a small collection of cottages surrounded by a protective ditch and maybe a wall.

One of the houses was the home of a boy from my class, and I remember on one visit hitting a white-washed wall with the flat of my hand. The pattern of my hand remained like a dark mark on the wall, composed of dead flies. Because of the proximity of animals and people, flies were a problem, especially in summertime. There was hardly a home without the sticky brown flypaper curling down from its ceiling in kitchens and living rooms.

When our landlords' daughter was to be married, we children were invited. I found myself in a conundrum. What would it be like, going to a Protestant wedding? Would God allow that? Our landlords were, I believe, the only Protestants in a Catholic village—except perhaps for newcomers and evacuees. The ceremony took place in the nearby town. All I remember of the actual event in its wartime privation is that all sorts of delicatessen were on the menu.

Above: Horses were still the main source of power on the land. An ever-friendly farmer and his environment.

Left: His home, Schmittmanns, the oldest house in the centre of the village reaches back to 1669.

There is something traditional and legendary about an old-fashioned smithy.

Geheimwaffen—Secret Wonder Weapons

It must have been during that last desperate winter in the war that I was watching the village activities from my usual vantage point at the window of our small house. A fair part of the street was visible from there, and the spectacle passing below was a very impressionable sight for a nine-year-old. The news had been bad for a long time, however much the state machinery tried to put a gloss on the fortunes of the nation.

News came from the little dark brown radio with its fretsaw sunrays front, and the news broadcasts were wedged between classical or military music and schmaltzy Viennese waltzes, traditional folk songs, and '*Schlagers*' (popular songs) with the voices of Zarah Leander with her Swedish accent or Lale Andersen. It took a good few years and my move to Britain before I realised that 'Lili Marlene' had been popular on both sides in the conflict. Zarah Leander seems to have sung it for General Erwin Rommel's Africa Corps in 1939 and later another version was broadcast to British forces in North Africa.

Zarah Leander's '*Ich weiß es wird einmal ein Wunder gescheh'n und ich weiß daß wir uns wiederseh'n*' ('I know one day a miracle will happen and I know we shall see each other again') seemed to touch a raw nerve in many a separated heart.

Some news used to come in the form of what had been a very informative illustrated magazine issued by our insurers, but that publication had shrunk to little more than a newssheet.

I particularly remember a poem accompanied by images of mud-covered soldiers, horses up to their bellies in mire, and machinery stuck axel-deep in what might have been dirt roads or fields. The last stanza read: '*Trotz Rußland's Straßen haben wir's geschafft*' ('We made it in spite of Russia's roads'). It puzzled me. What had we achieved in spite of the obstacle of Russian soil? We were in retreat.

There were images of ruins, lots of ruins, and rows of huge concrete blocks that snaked along countryside and were supposed to halt any advance on to German soil, promises of yet another secret weapon the Führer had up his sleeve and pictures of an enormous cannon called 'Big Bertha'. For all its possible veracity, would an enemy not simply walk around such a huge object at a safe distance, even if it could be moved by rail?

We had attacked Britain with bombs and what the English called the Doodlebugs and the V-2 rockets, and we were being bombed in return. Now there had been the Normandy landings of a large force of 'Tommies' and 'Ammies', though what we had done to the Ammies a nine-year-old found difficult to fathom. They were pushing back our troops from the west. We had mourned the news of the disaster of Stalingrad and the Russians were approaching ever closer from the east, driving our forces back before them.

I had a small tin globe, angled on a stand. Looking at the tiny area of Germany, it seemed that the entire world was fighting against us.

Our glorious victorious forces had come down to this? My mother wanted me to close the window, but I could not tear myself away. Below me snaked the last remnants of our defences, not in exacting goose-steps as we had seen in pictures, but as disgruntled, weary individuals in patched-up and mostly civilian clothes, poor shoes, carrying an assortment of weapons. Some were pushing or pulling carts, some pushed prams or bicycles to carry their burdens of guns and hand grenades. The most surprising observation of the passing section of our no-longer-victorious army was the ages of the men. Some were old men, limping along, some were mere boys, only a few years older than myself.

This was *Volkssturm* (People's assault units)—the people's storm. The last of the fighting force? Old men and boys? Bicycles and prams with anti-tank grenades?

Someone shouted to the caravan of misery: 'Why do you bother, when the Führer has a secret weapon that will take care of everything?'

One of the geriatrics in the column lifted a '*Panzerfaust*' from his pram (a stick with a club-like widening on one end, which contained the explosive that was meant to stop tanks in their tracks). Unsmiling, the veteran shouted back: 'This is our secret weapon'.

I later heard they were supposed to be outfitted with uniforms at our school. It never happened.

24

Casualties of Our War

It was the afternoon before my first Holy Communion, myself and all the other ten-year-olds from my class, on Saturday 7 April 1945, when the shelling began. I had been to confession and I was still conscious that my thoughts were not always pure enough to welcome the Lord. Holy Communion is one of the Seven Sacraments of the Catholic Church. But where I actually was when it started is difficult to say. Reports of much of what happened had to be pieced together afterwards.

The village grapevine carried the news: the war was coming our way. First casualty in the village was a mother at the back door of her house on the edge of the village to the northeast. Surrounded by her children, she was engaged at some very ordinary task like cleaning shoes in preparation for the following Sunday. Out of a blue sky, a missile exploded close by, killing her instantly.

There had been no warning, though I believe people had heard the sound of distant fighting and of course cellars had long been strengthened in case of bombardment. An explosion under a blue sky. One family's children suddenly orphaned. They would be taken in by relatives in the sweetshop not two doors away from our home on the churchyard.

We went down into the cellars as had been practiced when heavy bombers had droned overhead in the past.

First material casualty was the parsonage some time later, also on that same edge of the village to the east of the church, standing slightly apart in its large gardens with a large traditional tithe barn at its side. The wooden barn received a hit and caught fire, in its fury destroying the parsonage, too. The village fire brigade and the fire engine were called out and attempted to save the building known for its large collection of books.

Nearby stood the church caretaker's house and next to that the vicarage for the assisting priest. By the roadside between them and the parsonage was a small rectangular pond, a water container with iron railing surrounds, just a few metres deep. It was known as the fire brigade's pond, though it was woefully inadequate.

The explosions resumed again. Two local men as well as two passing soldiers who had stopped to help were killed as they attempted to douse the fire and the firemen's task was abandoned, the house left to the flames. It was the only attempt at fighting the infernos that were to follow. In later conversations, it was not the loss of the priest's abode that loomed large in people's sorrow, it was the loss of 'all the beautiful books' and historical documents that were remembered. Another house nearby in the densely built up medieval origins of the village was also turned into a pile of rubble.

Our largely wood-built home would be no protection against grenades, bombs, or cannon shot, and we had joined our landlords in their cellars in what was usually called the '*Waschküche*' (the laundry room), a large space with stone or concrete floor, where the family wash would be boiled and dried and the pigs' feed was prepared; the ceiling had been reinforced with wooden props. It was not a cellar in the real sense as the front was at street level and the house and shop above were reached via stairs from the road.

We had our own cellar at the back of that room under the main house, where our small coal supply was kept and where at least one wall was lined with shelves

The priest's house with its large tithe barn in foreground on the road from the east.

Right: View to the front of the *Pastorat* (the priest's house), with attached tithe barn, the first to fall prey to the firestorm.

Below: Earliest part of the village where houses still crowded together. Two houses centre front were among the first to burn in 1945.

containing the inevitable glass jars with their preserved foodstuffs (all sorts of meat, vegetables, fruit, and berries would be heated in glass jars with glass lids. Held airtight with circular rubber bands that fitted snugly between jar and lid, they would stay airtight when cooled by pressure thanks to the escaped air when hot).

A cake to celebrate my first Communion was among the deposits, as well as a few other items of value and a rack of clothes my mother had grabbed when the call came to take to the cellars. Because of the disparity in height between the churchyard at the back and the road in front, our cellar room was largely underground with just a small horizontal window high on the wall. A single metal bedstead had been placed against that wall.

People from around the neighbourhood joined us in the cellars, from a shoemaker and family to one side and *Fräulein* Michel, one of our school mistresses who lived in the old school nearby, to the other. Six or seven children slept or rested on the bed like sardines, but sideways on. Shelling came in bouts, interspersed with quiet periods. At one time, shells exploded in the churchyard, close enough for the small window above the bedstead to be shattered. We were lucky. The bed was not occupied—as it would have been at night-time—and the falling glass left no major injuries.

This was not everywhere the case, as we found out later. The new school, in theory, should have been one of the safest shelters in the village, with cellar ceilings also strengthened by wooden supports. It, too, was crowded with people cowering from the grenades and artillery when it received a hit that shattered a ceiling, passed through and exploded against an outside wall that was pushed in, falling on families and leaving it open to the elements. Several children and grown-ups were wounded, some severely.

The eldest son of teacher Kortenkamp went out to find the doctor, though the man could not be persuaded to leave his family and the relative safety of the cellar in which they sheltered. Finally, it was the paramedic-trained vicar who was contacted at the large farm a little outside the village by that same older boy of the teacher. One young woman was so badly wounded she died of the injuries she received, in spite of being rushed to an American military hospital once that was possible.

It was observed that information of movement in the village was gathered and passed on to Patton's Army some safe distance and mountains away by a circling reconnaissance aircraft that prudently disappeared before salvos of artillery fire rained down on the village again. Even the boy who risked running outside, dodging along the hedgerows to find the doctor, became a target and triggered a barrage, shattering trees behind him as he ran.

While shells exploded seemingly all around us, in our cellar, *Fräulein* Michel (the teacher) sat bowed with her mouth open and her hands pressed over her ears, a posture that had been recommended to save eardrums during the loud explosions. All of us probably did that, but perhaps I watched her more than others for that memory to remain.

Some recollections may have dulled or blurred over the years, but there was one overriding emotion I have never forgotten from that time in the cellar. When I watched the teacher, my age, or rather the lack of it, was my biggest concern. At least she had lived what seemed to me then some considerable time, but I had not. I wanted to live. I very much wanted to live. I had seen little of life and there was a big world out there I had not seen and I was not going to finish here before I had seen it. It would not have been unique to harbour such sentiments, but I can only speak for myself and that overriding emotion.

In lulls between the shelling, the old men would go upstairs or maybe outside and check on things. There was not much good news.

We heard how someone had hissed a white flag out of a dormer window in a house close to the church, but a struggler from the retreating army passing through had threatened the owner with instant execution according to his orders and the offending sign of capitulation had been withdrawn. Talk was of a '*Funker*' or signaller who was stationed up in the church tower. He had been the target of the devices that rained down on us, though by some chance, most of the missiles had fallen to our side of that tower.

There was structural damage to the tower itself, as became obvious afterwards.

Rumours circulated that the village had been a target for both sides at the time, though that seems unlikely, as little opposition had been left in the area apart from stragglers or small groups of stragglers moving away from enemy fire.

Our landlord and the shoemaker, roused by some suspicion, had ventured upstairs again to check before they hastily returned with the devastating news: 'The house is on fire above us. We need to get out. Everyone, save yourself!'

I do not remember much of the panic and the cries or what happened to others. Luckily there was the door to the street at ground level. My mother's instinctive move was to take us to her birthplace, to the old house on the hill, a child on each hand.

Outside, in the bewildering confusion, it seemed as if the world was burning. All around us flames leapt to the sky, though it emerged afterwards that not every house had been hit by the phosphor grenades.

While running, I looked back up to the house where I was born. Curtains were blowing out of the windows from where I had watched the war and my little world roll by, but the blowing curtains were burning. Fire seemed to be running down walls below which we had been hiding. At a glance, most of the village behind us seemed to be alight, too. Such memories sear into ones subconscious so that it still seems like yesterday.

My little sister got caught in the tangled traps of downed telephone masts and wires that coiled and snaked around the street, snagging at feet.

The sound of shelling must have stopped us.

Three doors along, the slate-clad public house and post office Kotthoff (Schäpers) was still intact and we were accepted in, though that cellar was already overcrowded among barrels and bottles.

It was standing room only, there were so many people. In the pandemonium, soldiers mixed in with civilians. A serving son of the family and comrades had stayed behind from the retreating troops, discussing the best action to take. Should they simply change into civilian clothes? I believe they did, but handed themselves in to the Americans eventually, when just for a short time they became prisoners of war.

We could not stay. During a lull between exploding grenades, my mother made the decision we would have to risk moving on, running up the road to my grandmother's house. From the street, we could see the old house on the hill ahead of us. Just a short run further, past another burning farm and tavern and shelling started up again. Mother turned to the nearest house.

It became a bank later, but it was the home then of distant relatives (the teenage daughter, blackened with shoe polish, had visited us children once as Knecht Ruprecht to Uncle August's St Nicholas).

Again, the cellars were crowded, but we found or were found places to sit. This was a modern house without agriculture or animal husbandry. There were no provisions, but some of the people sheltering had animals to tend at home. Pigs, cattle, goats, and chickens, even dogs, needed feed and water. People would wait for a lull in the explosions and slip out, back to their own homes, if only to check they were still standing. One kind lady returned with extra tasty sandwiches: 'At least something for the children'. My sister, Marianne, remembers those sandwiches especially for their tasty and generous filling of liver sausage.

That evening, Vicar Moog, a trained paramedic as well as priest, ventured from cellar to cellar offering general absolution from sin to all present. Would we make it through the night, this weekend of my first Holy Communion? The communal attendance had been out of the question for me.

There were more children and their mother had said: 'Where there is room for five, there will be room for two more'. We were squeezed in to lie down for the night, though my head was so close to the bottom of a staircase, my mother had kept watch so I was not trodden on.

I must have slept through most of the night. Something was wrong. Mother was crying, though she tried not to show it. '*Oma's Haus ist abgebrannt.*' ('*Oma's* house is burnt to the ground.') She had heard whispers some time about midnight and as all was still she had slipped out into the street.

The friendly old wattle-and-daub house where she was born, so full of memories, had taken about half an hour to burn down to its foundations. All that wood, straw, hay, and corn, all flammable under a slate roof, it had one last moment of glory as it lit up the night sky, watched only by my mother at a distance.

What we did not know then was that we would have found the house empty, had we not been stopped by another round of shelling by the American 3rd Army. People from the upper part of the village had taken to the woods and camped out with some of their belongings, building 'wigwams like native Indians', provisional shelters and hides, looking back on the inferno that was the village below.

Had we reached the house, very likely I would not be here to write my story. The cellar was simply a dug-out space beneath the tailors' parlour, to be reached through a trap door and down a few wooden steps to where potatoes, etc., were kept dry through the winter. I had been down there with my grandmother, collecting Sauerkraut, when I had been able to walk freely, but grandmother had to bend down under the low ceiling. Only wooden beams and floorboards made up that ceiling. It is questionable that we would have escaped such a firetrap and survived had we actually reached that unsafe haven.

I cannot say if the cows and pigs perished or if they had been released as precaution. It was never talked about in my presence and I never asked, but Aunt Anna, her husband, and Uncle August later built their new house in the old traditional style with space for animals and a large opening to facilitate the storing of hay and straw, etc., so maybe…

In the morning, with the possibility of shelter at the old house no longer an option and my mother with nothing left but two children, we went down a side street to seek out Aunt Minna in the Vicarage. Up the road, a black scar trailing smoke was all that was left of my grandmother's house and its memories.

It was the only option, my mother's older sister, Aunt Minna in her flat upstairs in the Vicarage, which was just down the road on the south-eastern side of the churchyard.

We had barely started down that road when we were stopped by an unlikely obstacle, a familiar donkey, the one that had regularly pulled a small wagon to deliver milk churns into the centre of the village for collection. On occasions, its braying could be heard all over the village at particularly bored or frustrating times, usually at eventide. Distraught and upset or perhaps frightened, now the freaked-out obstacle occupied the centre of the road, kicking out with its hind legs and braying like something possessed. We could not know that it's stable and farm had been destroyed by fire. Not only humans suffer in wars. Nobody counts the animals that endure pain and death in their bewilderment.

Pressing against an opposing wall, we did eventually manage to edge past.

At Aunt Minna's, we children were bedded down in the cellar on top of the coal supply. There were more children from the family who shared the Vicarage on the first floor beneath Aunt Minna's flat. The eldest son was just a year younger than myself.

25

The Ruhr Pocket and the Wider View in Hindsight

The Battle for Oberkirchen

Oberkirchen is a picturesque half-timbered village south of Remblinghausen in the Sauerland. On the night of 3–4 April, few German troops were left behind. Most of the Panzers had withdrawn in the morning. American troops and tanks were approaching.

It must have seemed a lost cause to many by then. German soldiers were noticed to ditch their weapons and some changed into civilian clothing, but an order from *Generalfeldmarschall* Model decreed that Oberkirchen was to be held until Thursday 5 April. The village was to be retaken. Two Panzers were destroyed, three American tanks also were burnt out. That resulted in the calling up of air support, and bombing and machine-gunning damage. Also phosphor grenades were employed.

By early evening, American troops were in charge at Oberkirchen. Then, in the small hours, there came another German attempt to retake the village. An American tank was destroyed by a *Panzerfaust* for which a contingent of the elderly *Volkssturm* claimed responsibility. Germans retook a few houses, but were again repulsed in one of the rare occurrences in our experience at least, when the two sides actually met. More German tanks returned from another direction, and according to reports, the night was filled with close combat encounters of Sherman tanks against Panzers and man against man, in hand-to-hand and house-to-house combat.

'Pools of blood in the streets, wounded and dying were taken into cellars, dead lay in streets and tanks rolled over them,' someone remembered.

At lulls in the fighting, any remaining villagers joined others and French POWs who already sheltered in a slate quarry.

'Oberkirchen lies in flames. The battle moves back and forth.'

Eventually, on 4 April, Oberkirchen fell.

Sherman tank of the 31st Tank Battalion, 7th Armored Division, destroyed during the fighting for Oberkirchen, Sauerland, 5 April 1945.

This image of the battle for Oberkirchen truly recalls the barbarity of war.

Historical note: Today, Oberkirchen is again a village of picturesque timber-framed houses, but between AD 1598 and 1685, a total of seventy-five people were burnt to death there as witches, not only women but men and children, too, in a series of seven witch processes.

An unhealthy place to live in those times, but in the Second World War, it was a rather lucky place for at least one American airman. In more recent times in the village, a friend happened to meet the visiting former airman who happily shared his story: his aircraft had received a hit and burst into flames while on a bombing raid mission. The raging fire prevented him from reaching his parachute and in desperation at the very last minute he simply jumped clear of the burning machine. Dropping on to a dense fir tree forest near Oberkirchen, his fall was saved by the trees' generous and pliable branches that had cushioned the impact and deposited him to the ground with little damage.

Artillery fire supported by aerial bombardment and machine-gun fire as well as phosphor grenades prepared the way forward, village by village, farm by farm, as it did in Remblinghausen a few days later. With German aerial activities no longer an option, the skies were free to observing aircraft that reported any movements on the ground and instantly barrages of shelling would eliminate the movement from a distance. That kind of warring certainly saved lives among the advancing troops, whatever the damage ahead. Very few villages escaped the shelling and destruction. Usually, infantry would move in first and tanks would follow when all was secured but occasionally there would still be actual contact.

In Nichtinghausen, artillery fire began on 7 April about 9.30 p.m. The first hit killed nine—eight soldiers and an evacuee from the Rheinland. A child was badly wounded. On the River Henne, a German battery was hit and annihilated, as dead horses, ditched artillery pieces, and several wounded soldiers that were transported to the nearest farm were witness to. They had been preparing to retreat when they were hit.

On 3 April on a road exiting Remblinghausen to the west, a vehicle park column was attacked by low-flying aircraft with on-board machine guns and a soldier was killed. An anti-aircraft battery in a nearby wood took up fire, attracting aerial reprisals that set a large farm on fire and resulted in the death of the farmer.

Our village was machine-gunned at that time, though to little effect. Woodland, it was said, would carry the reminders of those times for decades as shrapnel was embedded in the fibre of trees.

Remblinghausen was approached via the settlements of Ramsbeck and Bödefeld and via Frielinghausen and Höringhausen, where the fire barrage was temporarily halted. The village had seen little activity until then, apart from a contingent of bicycle-transported *Volkssturm* from Düsseldorf that had arrived in the old school to be kitted out for resistance warfare. It never happened. There was, however, the unfortunate passing through of retreating columns of troops in those final days, which attracted the sustained fire and caused so many buildings to be destroyed.

I have received information though not confirmation that German High Command, in an effort to escape the bombing and fighting in Meschede, escaped to Remblinghausen and that that was the reason for our village's special attention by the mortar crews.

As previously mentioned, the first grenade fell on 7 April at about 10.30 a.m., after which a German contingent left the village, leaving behind only telephone and radio operators. Attack fire proper resumed at 6 p.m. in the evening and continued with breaks until the morning of 10 April. One German battery on the side of a hill that had held up the American advance had left the day before. After that, the baker and an evacuee raised a white flag from the church tower and the guns quietened down.

Comments from the Diary of Edgar Van Hooten Bell (Lt-Col. Edgar V. H. Bell)

I had always imagined that large American cannon had been shooting at us from across the mountains in April 1945, so the actual reality of puny chemical mortars doing all that damage comes as a surprise. Most likely we were bombarded with 'Phosphorus Smoke', classified as smoke shells. When fired at a solid object—i.e. an armoured vehicle or house—they would ignite and stick to the object obscuring the opponent's vision in a tank or set fire to a house. Nevertheless, those muzzle-loaded devices managed to cover great distances.

The War Diary of Lt-Col. Edgar Van Hooten Bell, Commanding Officer of the 90th Chemical Mortar Battalion, left behind an insight into the American way of waging war. They had moved from Oulton Park in Cheshire, England, and were

The Honsel Works in Meschede from an earlier publicity leaflet.

Above and below: Honsel, the town's main employer before and during the war.

Above and below: The centre of Meschede in spring 1945. Not even the church (on left) was spared.

engaged in combat as a unit of the US First Army, crossing the Rhine at the railway bridge at Remagen before it finally collapsed.

Van Hooten Bell's notes give a precise record of his movements with just the sporadic succinct comment that tells of a mobile warrior's concentration on his duties and orders, caring for his men with the occasional side swipe at superiors that do not match his standards.

On 4 April 1945, he noted: 'This attack looks tough. Mission—clean out all Krauts to the Ruhr'. Three days later at Hesborn and Siedlinghausen, we find a simple note: '104 prisoners, 60 dead Krauts, counterattack smashed. Captured 4 healthy Krauts in a camp near Winterberg'.

Almost constantly on the move, on 9 April, he reported from Meschede, 5 km from my village: '… sniping in town, still cleaning up'.

From 11 April, he settled down in Niedersorpe for five nights, 'quartered in local inn' while supervising the war effort. Again he passed through Meschede: 'I went 130 miles today'.

Leaving Niedersorpe on 12 April via Elspe and Kalle, he ordered: '1st platoon Rumbeck, 2nd Westenfeld, Siedlinghausen, 1st platoon Ramsbeck, 3rd Remblinghausen'.

On 14 April, he wrote: 'What a day. Saw Gen. Van Fleet. Very pleasant. Great praise for the 90th. "Splendid troops". Took Brig. Gen. Roane, Col's. Power, Scott and Gearheart on tour of the 'front'. Said they wanted to see mortars in action. Told them the war was over here. Sorpe Staubecken dam. Steak for the brass, cold K rations for my drivers. This is the dumbest bunch of real bastards in the Army. Thousands of prisoners everywhere'.

On 17 April, Van Hooten Bell took time off from the war and availed himself of the local wildlife: 'Ramsbeck. Ostwig. Winterberg. With Hall to spot along creek near Brunskappel. We got 18 trout with grenades. Zickfeld made FF potatoes. I dipped trout in egg and K ration cracker crumbs. Whole staff in to supper. Boy, were they good fish. Bath and clean shirt, first since February. Clean pants, too'.

The next day, he did not feel too well, but the war machine rolled on. On 27 April, he reported from Hexanagger for the River Danube crossing: 'No opposition at all to crossing, but lead BN got hell knocked out of them in Eining on E bank. They pulled out and ABLE Co., in position at Arresting, blew Eining right out of existence. It was beautiful. The town burned like hell all night'.

Unlucky Eining! On 7 May 1945, Germany signed an unconditional surrender to the Allies at Reims.

Edgar Van Hooten Bell finally left the Army as a brigadier-general. He had served in the First and Second World War and later in Korea.

I just vaguely remember hearing the story at the time of Americans killing fish in a stream or lake with explosives, an act of vandalism that would rankle with country folk for its devastating effect on everything else living in such water.

26

An Early End to a Reich Supposed to Last 'A Thousand Years'

A strange air of trepidation heightened the atmosphere in the cellar of the Vicarage. After all the propaganda of the previous years, what would happen? The house stood on the edge of the village to the east, from where 'the Ammies' were coming, though we were not aware of that. The shelling had stopped. What would happen? The war was lost, but that was like an Act of God and beyond anybody's intervention. It was 10 April.

My abiding memory is the view up the stone cellar steps to daylight near the open front door. Behind me, people whispered anxiously in anticipation of the unknown. All I could see was dirty high-laced boots and above them khaki gaiters fastened below combat trousers. There were voices in their strange language but the boots walked on, not even bothering with us down below. The 'Ammies' had arrived, but they moved on into the village.

Generally, General Patton's 3rd Army combatants were well behaved in those first days, quite better than one had imagined or been led to believe. Watching from Aunt Minna's high window, I later noticed a single tank lumbering over the ridge of that steep country road towards the village from the east, the direction of Löllinghausen. It is the only tank I remember seeing in the village, though there would have been more. On the high ground, the clumsy vehicle stopped, turret swivelling sideways to a hay or straw stack in fields on the slope of the opposing hillside and destroying it with a noisy salvo. It seemed quite unnecessary, like a frustrated whim at the lack of action or opposition? Or had something moved up there?

One GI got his kicks shooting up chickens in the backyard of a house in the neighbourhood, the noise of the shots and the frantically clucking fowl echoing around the neighbourhood, at first alarming and then raising eyebrows when the truth was realised.

There were so many uncertainties. Grown-ups were unsure how to behave. Not to upset or offend. One surprise to me was that some of our conquerors admitted to being German, or at least their ancestors had been.

The road from the east towards the junction with the main road.

At Aunt Minna's, all was not normal. There were plenty of rumours, but I was pretty well left to my own devices.

My mother, on returning to our old home, found that while our house was but a smouldering pile of rubble and the houses to either side were burnt-out shells, too, the fire had not actually reached our cellar below the main house. Most of the conserving glass jars had popped and the clothes on a rack nearest to the door had been singed in the heat, but as by a miracle, some could still be worn. The cake to celebrate my First Communion was baked rock hard, but was still edible and among the few things my mother had managed to grab and take into the cellar when the shelling started, or maybe earlier—my father's Agfa box camera had also survived. Later I stood by the ruins considering searching for the gold rings that had perished and should have survived, I thought, even if only as molten droplets. I soon gave up on that idea.

It was a curious surprise and a deft reminder of an end to an era, finding our large framed portrait of the Führer, that had been obligatory on school walls, pinned down on the gravel between church and school with a ceremonial sword or sabre thrust through the broken glass, the hilt swaying above it. The token end of the most powerful man in my young life, the man who had promised a glorious reign of a thousand years, who had been admired by millions, and had caused millions to be killed and much of the land to be in ruins, had become a mere bagatelle in the dirt of our playground. For one mad moment, I thought, as someone had abandoned the shiny weapon there, I ought to collect it, but only for a moment. Someone was bound to come back for it.

The Agfa box camera survived
the firebrand.

The unfortunate *Volkssturm* contingent from Düsseldorf that had been sent to be kitted out in Remblinghausen is said to have surrendered there, but as I do not remember any sight of them once American troops arrived, I can only presume they were moved back earlier.

One inebriated GI had spied a school friend's elder sister and apparently taken a fancy to her. She lived at the house of the saddler by the churchyard next to the tavern and post office that also had escaped the fire. Later that night, the lovelorn GI scoured the still-standing houses in the neighbourhood, looking for the girl who was hiding at the foot-end of her parents' feather bed.

The following day, the would-be amorous soldier apologised for his behaviour the previous night and the nuisance he had caused, by setting up a large cauldron of pea soup on our schoolyard near Hitler's pierced portrait, where people could come with their pots and pans and get used to a different kind of taste—a generous helping of American Army pea soup. A not unwelcome gesture for many of us, who had, gingerly at first, begun to get out and about again.

Many people came with Army-issue containers, the deep curved kind that would be carried on soldiers' belts with a metal clasp that allowed the lid to be a separate container with handle. Spoon and fork were joined aluminium utensils that could be collapsed and folded together.

Direct results of the indiscriminate shelling of the village besides the human fatalities were the domestic animals that were killed or wounded in the attacks. Many had to be simply buried.

The butcher's house and shop had been destroyed by flames, so a narrow passage from the main road with stairs to the saddler's house and its front entrance by the raised churchyard served as the venue for the sale of cheap meat in the days following the arrival of the Americans. In spite of the reason for its availability, it was very welcome. Of course, the glut did not last. One dare not think how many domestic animals had perished in the flames and explosions.

Of the three inns in the village, two had perished—only the most central one, Kotthoff (Schäpers), where we had temporarily sheltered during the shelling, remained intact. Heinemann (Lamberts) would be rebuilt with a wooden frame on the original stone base, tavern, and farm, though in more recent years, it has seen a metamorphosis into a bank.

Donners, known as Lex, also distant relatives on my mother's side, owned a large brick-built house on the north side of the churchyard. It must have been the most versatile business in the village with three separate undertakings. On the churchyard side of the main entrance had been a shop where wall-shelves held large bales of cloth that could be selected and bought by the metre before a tailor or seamstress would turn it into new garments. The contents of that shop may well have provided most of the raw material my grandfather and uncles and others fashioned into clothes in their artisan trade. I had been shopping there with my mother, probably for my communion suit not long before the fire.

To the right of the main entrance was the room of the inn, but there was also an L-shaped annex where agricultural supplies like corn, flour, seed, and animal feed were stored and sold. Those premises could be reached from the back lane and the yard, which was faced on the opposing side by a farm and the blacksmith. Even the blacksmiths were distantly related to my mother's family.

By a stream in another hamlet nearer to the town of Meschede stood one more asset of the Donner family, a corn mill.

Looking up from the churchyard through the stark blackened shell of the burnt-out Donner building, framed in silhouette against the sky without a roof or an upper ceiling, stood the outline of a sewing machine on what would have been a windowsill before the fire. It was a sombre witness to what had been. Today, the rebuilt and grandly enlarged 'Landhotel Donner' is the foremost hotel and eatery in the village and the wider neighbourhood.

A flight of stairs still leads down to the yard and the back lane from the churchyard between an entrance to the inn and one of the oldest houses in the village, Hanses, the picturesque black-and-white timbered building that would later become a template for our homemade stable for the figures of the Christmas Nativity scene in the church.

27

The Grown-Up's View

The Battle of the Ruhr Pocket, 5–18 April 1945

The first grenade in the village had fallen at about 10.30 a.m. on 7 April, when most of the German military had moved out, leaving only signallers and observers. The actual bombardment proper commenced that same day at about 6 p.m. and continued with pauses until early on 10 April.

I understand that five times as many Dutch people were killed by the bombs of the liberators than by those of the subjugators. Rotterdam, The Hague, and Nijmegen burned and bled to death from aerial bombardments. The attack on our village was against civilians, not combatants, but then who was to know?

Quite probably, the mortars that rained fiery destruction down on us were the US Army's M2 mortars, which managed a range of 4,400 yards (4,000 metres)—i.e. mountains away. Infantry divisions were supported by one or two chemical mortar battalions. The mortar had proven to be an especially useful weapon in areas of rough terrain such as jungle and mountains. They would fire white phosphorus-based smoke shells at tanks and buildings and the phosphorus would adhere to its target, generating smoke and fire. Even Sherman tanks used them.

Following the D-Day offensive by the Allies, the push east, and the subsequent lucky establishment of a bridgehead at Remagen when a Rhine bridge was taken almost intact, the US 1st Army managed to break out on 25 March 1945. The Rhine should have been a major obstacle to an advancing army, but at Remagen, the Americans arrived so fast and German communications stuttered to the point that the railway bridge was taken before it could be blown.

Known as the armoury of the Third Reich, the Ruhr area had been a major destination from the outset, but to attack it head-on would have meant a bloodbath, probably on both sides. Defending the 'Ruhr pocket', the industrial heart of Germany, were an estimated 320,000 to 400,000 German soldiers of Army Group 'B' as well as some 4 million civilians.

Left: Finding out that there were no mighty cannons that caused to set our village alight, these simple mortar devices, came as quite a surprise.

Below: Mortar teams could be remarkably accurate and reach great distances.

A mortar team in action on the Rhine in 1945.

Supreme Commander Dwight D. Eisenhower was in charge of 4½ million men and he was well aware of that. The plan was encirclement. His forces in the north consisted of British, Canadian, and American forces under Field Marshal Bernard Law Montgomery who would move towards the Elbe River and Northern Germany. In the centre fought the American 12th Army and in the south the 6th Army of American and French forces.

Against them on the German side stood Army Group 'B', under *Generalfeldmarschall* Otto Moritz Walter Model with the 5th Panzer Army on the right and the Fifteenth Army on the left. The 5th Panzer division was defending the industrial centres of the Ruhr, which included the massive Krupp Steel Works at Essen.

Model was known by his men as the 'Führer's *Feuerwehrmann*' (Hitler's fireman), one of the most determined and able fighters left on the German side. He had earned a reputation as a defensive genius on the eastern front in 1941–43, commanding the Ninth Army. So ruthless was he, the Russians wanted to charge him as a war criminal. In the First World War, he had fought on the Western Front, in the Second World War at first on the Eastern Front and then on the Western Front from the invasion of Normandy until he was finally trapped in the Ruhr pocket.

One arm of the American Army moved on at the northern part of the Ruhr Pocket, while another pushed south and then north over the Siegerland and the Sauerland regions in the direction of the Ruhr district. In our immediate area, they came from the east. Although basically rural, Meschede, 5 km away, with the only factory of any consequence, lies on the upper reaches of the Ruhr River.

On 1 April 1945, the Ruhr area was encircled by the US 1st and 9th Armies who met up at Lippstadt. Another move cut the encircled area in two at Iserlohn. The smaller easterly part in that area of Iserlohn capitulated on 15 April 1945. The Fifth Panzer Army simply had to give up. Hitler had ordered the physical economic infrastructure of the industrial Ruhr area to be destroyed by Army Group 'B', an order Model disregarded.

The partial pocket in the area of Düsseldorf only stopped fighting on 21 April. Even in the face of obvious defeat, Model remained stubbornly loyal to the Führer, no matter what the sacrifices of soldiers and civilians, but eventually, even to him, it must have dawned that his task was impossible.

Finally on 21 April, when his men had run out of everything—weapons, ammunition, fuel, and even food—he is reported to have said when asked for new orders: 'Tell the men there are no orders, it's every man for himself'. He dismissed the older and younger soldiers from military service and told the rest to either surrender or break out of the kettle and find their way home.

Outside Duisburg, Model left his aides, walked into a traditional copse of tall oak trees, and shot himself. Ultimately, there is always the bully's way out, though they themselves may think of it as heroism—the loser falls on his own sword.

The Führer Adolf Hitler shot himself and his newly-wedded wife Eva Braun in his Berlin Bunker on 30 April. Paul Joseph Goebbels, his fanatical Propaganda Minister, committed suicide the following day, including in his final act his wife and six children. On 7 May 1945, Germany surrendered unconditionally. *Reichsmarschall* Hermann Wilhelm Göring was taken prisoner, but bit on a potassium cyanide capsule the night before he was about to be hanged following the Nuremberg Trials of war crimes on 15 October 1946.

So fast was the American advance across Germany that local people might be surprised at their sudden appearance. From Gesseln near Paderborn comes the story of a priest holding a service in a barn or church on Tuesday 3 April, when one of his parishioners, disturbed by the sounds of treads clanking and wheels crunching, approached the reverend, whispering, '*Herr* Vicar, they are here.' The muzzle of a Sherman's gun pointed through the wide door directly at the makeshift altar. GIs, it is said, dismounted, entered the nave, knelt, and joined the congregation in their worship.

In the Ruhr pocket, leaflets rained from the sky and loudspeakers called for the German military to surrender and thousands, then tens of thousands did. Mass surrenders began. Numbers of POWs reached far in excess of what US Army intelligence had estimated and more than could be coped with and catered for. The

Right: Dwight D. Eisenhower's ultimatum, urging the people of the '*wichtigstes Kriegsindustriegebiet Deutschlands*' ('the most important industrial war industry area in Germany') to leave. A merciless bombardment was threatened. The Allies were not fighting the German people, only the German war machine, it said.

Below: Ruhr Pocket situation, 5–14 April 1945. A pincer movement with British and Canadian forces to the north and Americans approaching from the south and east aimed and succeeded in encircling and isolating Germany's industrial heartland by cutting off fighting troops from supplies, eventually splitting the remaining troops in two. The strategy probably succeeded in saving lives on both sides.

ALLIIERTES OBERKOMMANDO
Supreme Headquarters, Allied Expeditionary Force

AN DIE ZIVILBEVÖLKERUNG DES RUHRGEBIETS!

IHR wohnt in dem wichtigsten Kriegsindustriegebiet Deutschlands. Jahrelang haben Eure Hochöfen, Werke und Werkstätten die Waffen für den Eroberungskrieg geschmiedet. Heute aber bewirken diese Betriebe lediglich eine Verzögerung des endgültigen militärischen Zusammenbruchs.

Um eine Verlängerung des bereits verlorenen Krieges zu verhindern, wird daher die gesamte Kriegsindustrie des Ruhrgebiets einem erbarmungslosen Bombardement ausgesetzt werden.

Die Alliierten sind aber entschlossen, nicht das deutsche Volk, sondern nur die deutsche Kriegsmaschine zu vernichten.

Der alliierte Oberbefehlshaber erlässt daher folgende Bekanntmachung:

1. Diese Bekanntmachung betrifft sämtliche Personen, die im Bereich der folgenden Stadtkreise wohnhaft sind: DUISBURG, MÜHLHEIM, OBERHAUSEN, ESSEN, GELSENKIRCHEN, BOTTROP, GLADBECK, RECKLINGHAUSEN, WATTENSCHEID, WANNE-EICKEL, HERNE, CASTROP-RAUXEL, BOCHUM, WITTEN, DORTMUND, LÜNEN, HAGEN.

2. Der Bereich dieser Stadtkreise gilt von nun an als Kampfzone. Alle Einwohner der obengenannten Stadtkreise werden hiermit aufgefordert, sich und ihre Familien sofort in eine sichere Gegend ausserhalb des Ruhrgebiets zu begeben.

3. Es wird ausdrücklich darauf hingewiesen, dass in den obengenannten Gegenden des Ruhrgebiets von nun an weder Bunker noch Unterstände Sicherheit gewähren können.

4. Einwohner des Ruhrgebiets! Euer Leben hängt von der sofortigen Ausführung der obigen Anweisungen ab. Handelt sofort! Heraus aus der Ruhr! Heraus aus dem Krieg!

Dwight D. Eisenhower

DWIGHT D. EISENHOWER
General,
Oberbefehlshaber der Alliierten Streitkräfte

S.H.A.E.F. März 1945

DEUTSCHE ARBEITER! Gebt diese Bekanntmachung des alliierten Oberbefehlshabers sofort an Eure ausländischen Arbeitskollegen weiter!

WG 47

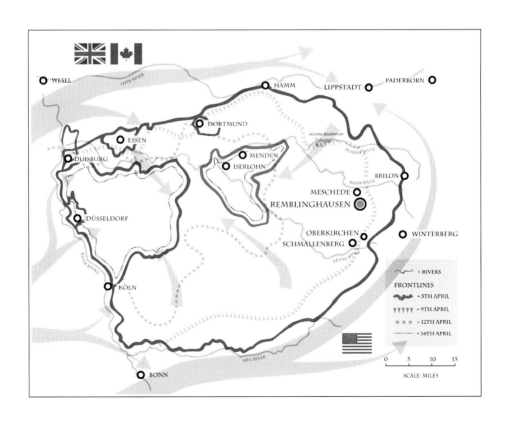

The infamous Rhine Meadow Camps where captured German troops were concentrated.

infamous Rhine meadow camps 'stretched as far as the eye could see' in barely fenced fields.

One thing I have learnt in a long life is that there is no such organisation as a Glorious Army. There are only good and bad people and even those are seldom 'all good' or 'all bad'. People react differently to situations. Some will rise to it and become heroes, others are out of their depth and they behave at their worst. Not everybody retains their humanity in a situation of unrestricted power and he or she is likely to take advantage. In hindsight, we have learnt much about such people, about atrocities committed and inhuman commands given. Does that excuse similar treatment by others?

There were rumours of horrible conditions, hunger, and deaths brought back by returning soldiers from the west, from the *Rheinwiesenlagers* (Rhine meadow camps) where millions of German POWs were collected in transit camps. Was it thousands or tens of thousands who died of deprivation and exposure as has been claimed? No records have survived or are available, but I remember watching a survivor when he found it difficult if not impossible to tell his story and people with our benign experience of American treatment found it difficult to believe him.

GERMANY – MAP OF THE OCCUPATION AREAS AFTER 1945

The village of Remblinghausen was situated in the British zone, close to the American zone.

General Dwight Eisenhower (a very German sounding surname) at Supreme Headquarters, Allied Expeditionary Force (SHAEF), had created a new kind of prisoner—DEFs—Disarmed Enemy Forces as opposed to prisoners of war who were covered by the Geneva Convention. They would not be fed by the army after Germany's surrender. The order was approved by the Combined Chiefs on 26 April 1945, except by the British, who refused to adopt that plan for their own prisoners.

As happened in my own village in those last weeks and days before the arrival of US troops, there were orders given by local Gestapo, SS, or Security Police in many cities and villages for the murder of prisoners and forced labourers, war crimes condoned by or on the orders of *Gauleiters* and Reich Defence Commissars. Some former leaders committed suicide. Top National Socialists in our region might have urged the population to 'fight to the last man', yet when it came to standing up themselves, they quickly disappeared, even assuming false identities in their quest for self-preservation. Some were recognised and exposed, others managed to successfully avoid retribution. Federal German justice spared many former leaders and war criminals following their release from internment and penal camps, and they lived out their lives in a new, different and democratic Germany.

28

The Handcart Funeral

A curious observation in those first days from Aunt Minna's home window, which had a good view of the firemen's pond by the roadside below, was the furtive way people came to the pond like thieves, not taking but deposited objects in its green algae-covered stagnant depth. Items appeared and disappeared from folds in clothing or aprons. In hindsight, it reminds of ancients making offerings to river or water gods, only without the due signs of reverence.

All became clear later when GIs arrived with the fire hose and firemen's equipment and emptied the pond. Daggers with Nazi insignia were found and medals like military Iron Crosses and Mothering Crosses, which the state had awarded to mothers of large families, were 'liberated'. Very likely, those finds today grace the collections or memorabilia of former combatants or their sons and families in the USA.

One of the saddest observations from Aunt Minna's window was the cheapness of life once it is spent at such times. There had been stories of heroism and duty even during the fighting, if those are the correct words. To us, it was simply aimless firing into the village by an invisible foe. Our own disillusioned troops were in retreat and the Americans were in the advance, but the pretence of war had to be kept up.

In the cellar of a timbered house by a crossroads above *Oma*'s house, two young soldiers had been sheltering among the civilians during continued shelling. Their task was to reconnect severed telecommunications. The young men had been scared, but they had their orders. They had to do their duty. In the end, that duty had made them go out into the road. We never knew whether they had been successful in their task, only that both were found dead and shattered by that crossroads when people dared to go outside again.

As I watched at Aunt Minna's, the fully dressed corpse of a German soldier was taken past the Vicarage in a '*Bollerwagen*'. The conveyance was a small four-wheeled all-purpose handcart—a miniature version of a farmer's wagon with iron-rimmed, wooden spoked wheels—that was very popular and served to move anything from garden produce to wood or milk churns. The front wheels could be steered and via an extended handle could be pulled by one or two people or even a child.

Bollerwagens were not, I think, ever intended for the movement of corpses. It certainly lacked dignity as it was too short and the dead soldier's heels scraped along the pitted road behind. There were dark stains on the uniform I could see even from my window. As I watched the sad spectacle of one man pulling another in the direction of the cemetery, something fell off and remained behind in the road. When no one claimed it, I went down to investigate. I found a peeked cap stained with blood and a tough leather belt with a metal clasp. A name was written on the inside of the belt.

Had I been older, I should have made my way to the cemetery, which was just around the corner. Instead, I resolved the belt would make excellent shoelaces if cut into narrow strips. I soon found out it was far too tough for a kitchen knife. What happened to the finds? I wager they were confiscated by adults and destroyed to ensure I did not hang on to such grisly trophies? In hindsight, one might possibly have found a family somewhere to put to that name, but in the chaos that was Germany at the time, it would have been an impossible task, even had I been older. The war lasted for little more than another month, ending officially on 7 May, though that meant little to us. For us, the war was over.

At that time, there still stood a number of cast-iron crosses as grave markers in the lawn about the church, they have all been taken away now and the church surroundings turned into a pleasant park. About 1882, a new plot had been acquired at the edge of the village. At the end of hostilities in 1945, some fifty-three soldiers were added to the locals under their white wooden crosses. There were no coffins or formal services for the hurriedly interred soldiers. Later, all non-local combatants were reburied in a special war cemetery close by the administrative town of Meschede.

Spring and life were interrupted that year. My first Holy Communion should have taken place on the Sunday after Easter. Instead, two of us attended just a few days later, in the church that was still covered in fallen masonry and debris from splinter damage and smashed shards of the once beautifully coloured stained glass windows. Air pressure of exploding shells had pushed in most of the old windows with their scenes from the Bible, with saints and allegories (they have been replaced by plain glass only).

The sky could be seen through the vaulted ceiling and roof, luckily a blue and dry sky. Few people attended the service other than myself and my mother and perhaps two of her sisters and a friend and neighbour, Bernard the saddler's son, supported by his family. A few of our classmates had actually attended mass on the Sunday morning in spite of the artillery bombardment and received the Sacrament as planned—brave souls—while we hid in our cellars. A new date was arranged a little later, when all the class and the community came together.

In Remblinghausen, life carried on.

Another Experience

In a school essay written later by an older girl, the days of the end to hostilities for us were described as starting bright and peaceful. The artillery bombardment had almost fallen silenced, only intermittent distant explosions could be heard. The young lady had not experienced the previous days in dank cellars, but out in the open in a forest where also Uncle August and Aunt Anna had been hiding out, trusting nature rather than relying on the inadequate protection of buildings:

> Everyone ran to the edge of the trees. A man from the village arrived and said: 'The enemy is already here'. We collected our things and joined the queue leaving the woods. Only now did we realise just how many people had spent days hiding out. The white flag was carried up front. Allied infantry men came single file through the meadows to comb through the woods. They did not bother with us. Now we could see the many shell craters everywhere. As we got closer to our home we saw the first American tanks. At home all was chaos. Doors had been forced, windows shattered, everything torn off walls. Roofing tiles were missing, but the house was still standing.

A little later new troops were quartered in the house, not the familiar Germans in grey this time, but Americans. They searched the house for German soldiers. How surprised we were when several Negroes came to the house. At first we were scared, but we soon got used to them. Three families were moved into one room, but we were happy to be back at home, even though it meant sleeping on the floor. It did not last. The following morning we were given one hour to leave the house. We found shelter next door in a washroom. Our things were packed and we made ourselves at home for several days.

The next day we found out there had been five deaths in the village and several wounded. One of the wounded died some time later. Many animals had been killed and buried by the men of the village. After three days we saw the American soldiers assembling and moving away. Our home was a mess, but we were only too happy to move back in. For us the war was over.

American troops moved on to the north-west, clearing the way with tanks, but relying more and more on calling up air support ahead. At Schüren, a village with a small glider airfield, a commandant was killed in his car and a group of Russian workers were hit by the first grenade to fall on the village. The top brass, including *Generalfeldmarschall* Model had spent the night of 9–10 April in Schüren, where a special effort had been made to halt the advance of American tanks at the cost of many fine mature trees that were toppled across roads to little effect. Even a mighty old beech tree that stood under nature protection was packed about with explosives that alas only managed to split the trunk lengthwise. German soldiers gave up the constant move away from the enemy by giving themselves up as prisoners of war in large groups now, rather than in isolation. Several hundred were reported taken in Schüren.

Remblinghausen picked up its traditional activities. Animal husbandry alone demanded to be kept up and life carried on. Now it must be said in all honesty that people in my village had never seen a black person in their lives, or were aware of them apart from the usual black-faced Knecht Ruprecht who accompanied St Nicholas in the weeks before Christmas. Also one of the Three Wise Men at Epiphany was usually portrayed as black as they came from various directions to Bethlehem. That must go some way to explain the episode, which was later told and embroidered with relish in the village, but the basic story I believe to be true.

Two milkmaids, young local women returned from meadows where they had been milking cows outdoors rather than trundle the animals home to their stalls and back out again. Cows are notoriously slow road users, especially when their udders are full. Villagers might be used to slow-moving traffic, but Americans and their jeeps tended to be in more of a hurry, apart from the unavoidable and rather slippery cow flans that decorated the road surface in the wake of such drives. Horse droppings, by comparison, might be eagerly collected by owners of gardens.

Thus returning with milk-slopping pails in the days after the arrival of the American 3rd Army, the two maids are said to have encountered their first black GI

It must have been rather a special occasion where milkmaids turned out in pristine aprons, stockings, and best shoes.

casually leaning against his vehicle by the roadside. Maybe he had looked at them or tried a greeting, but it was said that the two innocents grabbed their skirts and took to headlong flight, proclaiming to all and sundry that they had encountered the devil himself.

While most interaction between military and locals was benign or even helpful, there were exceptions.

To one farm in the village, a family of mother and several children had been evacuated. The mother was a black-eyed beauty, even to my childish eyes, while their father was also away in the war somewhere. It was her undoing. Following the arrival in the village of Patton's 3rd Army, some of its personnel were billeted in private homes. The mother was taken to one of the bedrooms by a GI, but managed to appeal to his nature, having expected better from the victorious army of the Allies.

She was released unharmed that time, but no such sentiments were listened to when later that evening another GI, somewhat inebriated, took her from her children and forced her into a bedroom. Her eldest son clung to his mother's apron, crying. He was brushed aside and his head hit the banister on top of the stairs. There was no help. The mother was raped and in the months to follow, before her husband could return to them, there was an abortion, something quite unheard of in the village. I understand it was not the only rape at the time.

The Rich GIs

The 'Ammies' were rich and well provisioned in our eyes. Cigars were usually smoked to about half their length and then discarded. Youngsters would pounce on them and puff away like the 'Churchill' they had seen in so many caricatures. Cigarettes also were plentiful. I am not quite certain just how they had got hold of them, but some older boys had 'acquired' several cartons of 'Camel' or 'Old Joe' cigarettes and taken to the woods with their loot to one of the hunters' look-outs that were raised on stilts at the edges of clearings to allow the observation and culling of deer and boar by those who owned the hunting rights.

They were perhaps slightly larger than traditional privies and could be accessed by rustic ladders, allowing reasonable privacy. There the enterprising lads chain-smoked until, it was said with no small amount of glee, they turned yellow and sickly and barely made it crawling back to their respective homes. I have to admit that, probably because of my asthma, I was never tempted and to this day I have not smoked a whole cigarette—a puff or two served me for a lifetime.

In earlier times, I had been sent out to buy cigarettes in the village for my father who used to smoke 'R6'.

The kind of hunter's hideaway on clearings that would lend itself to clandestine smoking sessions.

Finding a New Home

The village hall had been commandeered and taken over by military command to store secret equipment, quite possibly in connection with the planned resiting of a V-2 rocket base to Schloß Laer near Meschede in the final stages of the war. Unfortunately, during the attack on the village, one corner of the out-of-bounds hall had collapsed and was no longer secure.

In the general chaos and with nobody in command, village children found their way in to explore the highly technical items, specialist radio sets, and Morse apparatus. Much or all of it may have been connected to signalling and communication, fitted with mysterious glass bulbs, delicate valves like those in radios. Someone had found that if such glass bulbs with their silvery filaments were thrown in the air they would pop at a certain height. I heard about the unusual toys and joined in the destruction, in awe at the strange artefacts. While we were busy dismantling and busting the bulbs, a uniformed man arrived, ordering to stop our destruction as what we were doing was stealing. He spoke good German, though to our minds the dark hoard could not belong to the Americans and our own soldiers no longer had any use for it, so I am afraid the warnings fell on deaf ears.

Uncle Emil was one of the first to return from the war. Some people whispered he had actually returned before the Americans arrived and hidden out.

Of all the unlikely yet more familiar things I had 'found' in the village hall was a blow lamp, the type used for soldering; to this day, I wonder what I intended to do with it? It can only be explained that, when you have lost everything, even something as useless to me as a blowlamp takes on its significance.

Uncle Emil simply took charge of my blowlamp as of the right of an adult. I complained to my mother, she mentioned it to Aunt Minna, and thus my objections reached Uncle Emil. He ignored me, having bigger issues on his mind and quite rightly doubting its usefulness to a child. I would not let it rest and I insisted. I had found it. It was mine. Uncle Emil threw the object down the stairs after me.

Apart from an arm full of singed clothing and a box camera, there was nothing left. I learnt only later that my mother in her desperation had walked out to the seclusion of the family fields, darkly wrestling with thoughts of suicide. Only a mother's love for her children had stopped her in her darkest hour and she decided she had to carry on.

A miller-farmer in one of the outlying hamlets was said to have flour available for those who were celebrating their First Communion that year. The following Sunday after mass, my mother, not normally the most garrulous of people, gathered up her courage and approached the man, explaining that her son was one of the new communicants and that she understood he had flour for sale. It must have taken all her courage, but I was told the miller-farmer simply turned his back to her.

Still, somehow we managed, but we could not stay on at Aunt Minna's and mother found short-term accommodation at a flat where the owners were absent, but within a couple of weeks, the husband returned and they moved back to the village.

As a child, one never considers where the bread comes from that you are eating or that others may go without so you can eat. With grandmother's house gone, there was nowhere to turn, though in hindsight, we were still among people we knew, unlike the many evacuees and displaced persons in other parts.

Of two attic rooms in the large farm house across the road from *Oma*'s land, one was occupied by a Polish couple who must have met as prisoners of war and now decided to marry. The other room was spoken for by Aunt Anna, who had at last managed to get her long-time confirmed bachelor friend Franz to marry. Eventually, Aunt Anna relented. The wedding had to be postponed while we moved in, though not for long. There is one surviving memory from the time in the attic at the farm. The Polish couple next door invited my sister and me to their wedding as pageboy and girl. Having been liberated, they found living somewhat easier. It was the first time I tasted venison and there were puddings and cream.

Still, Aunt Anna was waiting to move in. I cannot remember where she and Uncle August were staying after the old house had gone. Eventually, we found rooms in a house just down the road. There, too, the husband had not returned from the war, leaving a wife and a small daughter. Our living room/kitchen was on the second floor, our bedroom on the first, and the toilet on the ground floor among the stables and sties. The rooms were a fair size and they became our home for several years. There were three doors off the top of the stairs, one to our living room, one to the hayloft, and one across the landing leading to a smaller room that was occupied by a single young lady. Her male visitor was hardly ever mentioned. By compensation, we had a grand view to the church and over much of the village and I remember how easily mice could run up and along vertical walls in the hayloft.

Uncle Anton, my father's eldest brother, visited from Eversberg (some 12 km away as the crow flies) in those early days. It must have been by bicycle. We stood by the ruins of our former home when he promised to send a kitchen cabinet that was no longer used or could be spared, and maybe a table as well. He had, of course, inherited the parental home. It was not a rich house (my father's family were known as '*Huierduierkes*'. It meant 'animal herders'. Previous generations would have collected the town's cattle, goats, etc., driven and chaperoned them for the day on common land, and returned them in the evenings or maybe even for milking during the day).

Cabinet and table, possibly chairs, and what was euphemistically called a '*chaise longue*'—an upholstered flatbed that was raised on one end as a head rest for relaxation purposes—duly arrived by lorry, the cabinet stained brown and in the traditional two parts, the lower with doors, the upper a display cabinet with glass windows. They were our first sticks of furniture for our new home.

My father had been thirteen when his father died. Uncle Anton had practically raised him as a surrogate parent. When he married, my father had been placed into an apprenticeship, which happened to be with a roofer. There were two other brothers and a sister.

Prisoners Turned Victors

In past times, the more prosperous farmers as the providers of work if not wealth had ruled local administration. There was a social divide topped by the '*dicke Bauern*' ('fat farmers'). Under the new 'Socialist' regime, the '*kleine Leute*' ('little people') got their say and workers and artisans became political leaders in the NSDAP.

Earlier in my memory, that office was taken up by a local builder at the lower part of the village. By the end of the war, the unlikely leaders were two brothers, one married with a plethora of children and one a bachelor who lived together in a small timbered house.

One story remembered is that immediately following the arrival of the American troops, a former Russian POW 'arrested' the brothers and took them to the back of the house to be shot, only to be thwarted by the timely intervention of the American commandant in charge. Another report adds that the brothers were sent away for a while for re-education.

I cannot think that the unlikely pair actually had been particularly politically active, though the regime rewarded and favoured large families. Perhaps later just the name of the office was enough to condemn them.

Almost every house had pigsties. The old police station near my grandmother's plot was not different, except that those sties were no longer in use and it was there for security my father had stored his pre-war motorbike. The police station survived and so had the bike. A young Russian had found it, as well as some petrol, and with that, he transported himself about the village—without bothering to inflate the tyres. My mother recognised the bike as my father's and promptly went to the American officer in charge with her tale of a missing husband whose last possession was thus being ruined.

Apparently in the ensuing confrontation, the young Russian was slapped about the face by the officer, the bike confiscated and restored to the police station pigsty, though when eventually the time came for its resurrection on my father's return, it was found to be beyond repair.

Very soon, a notice appeared in the centre of the village that tried to improve colloquial references to the victors: 'It's not Ammi, it's *Amerikaner*!' and 'It's not Tommi, it's *Engländer*!' insisted the directive. Underneath someone had clandestinely scribbled: 'It's not Nazi, it's *National Sozialist*!'

29

Dangerous Games

For about six months, we were left to our own devices. Schools were closed until a new administration had been arranged.

Retreating or returning soldiers had abandoned their vehicles in woods, then simply gone home. I remember cutting solid rubber balls from solid rubber tyres found on a vehicle in a dark fir tree thicket. Those balls were heavy and did not bounce well.

Other, more sinister finds also became toys in small hands. Munitions, even hand grenades, could be found about the countryside. Rifle cartridges, when the front bullet was wrenched off, contained some very flammable powder that could be made to explode by pouring in little heaps with a fine trail leading away from them. As they did in films, those trails could then be lit like fuses while the little experimenters tried to run for safety. Usually, this kind of activity took place well away from adult eyes and accidents did happen. My way of dealing with such cartridges was to wedge them into fence posts and then hitting the back with something like a hammer. The bullet would shoot into the wooden post.

There were no health and safety regulations and for almost six glorious months that summer there were no school lessons, either.

One intrepid group of scholars had made a game of throwing hand grenades at each other and catching them. A game of chicken, perhaps. Of course, the inevitable happened, a pin was pulled or lost and in the ensuing explosion one boy from my class was hit in the stomach. Wounded and bleeding and with shrapnel in his belly, they ran back to Walter's home, having to climb up a mountain and down the other side to reach it, before a doctor could be called. The wounded boy spent so much time in hospitals, his schooling was set back a year when he eventually returned.

Children will be children whatever the colour of their leadership.

Defending the Tuckelsburg

It was a labourer's cottage across the large yard of Lamberts (Heinemanns) farm and inn, though its situation on a knoll by the main crossroads in the village centre and its high, if compact aspect, had earned it the name 'Tuckelsburg'. I never found out just what the first part of the name stood for. It did not matter. To us children, it was a castle, and castles need to be defended against all comers.

With GIs buzzing around in jeeps, discarding half-smoked cigars, and handing out chocolate bars, we were still fighting our own wars. I was on the side of the defenders. Siegfried, a tall lad, the eldest son of the resident family, was in my class, as was his smaller cousin, also a Siegfried. The smaller cousins had elder sisters, though one of them had died and I had been to see her lying still in her coffin, all dressed in white. The surviving sister, probably about eleven or twelve years old, but definitely older, had been allocated the grand name of nurse or nursing sister and she had cotton wool at her disposal, as I was to find out.

Our castle was stone-built at ground-floor level, but timbered on the next, the human part, adding a feeling of height, as did the stone staircase that wound openly up around its side into a covered entrance like a lofty porch. There were two rooms upstairs, with benches around the living room/kitchen wall on two sides to save space. Beside the parents, there were at least five children to accommodate. The running water, as in the entire village, came directly from a small reservoir in the hills above the village.

Toilet, at the downstairs ground-floor level, was a barrel with a suitable opening in the covering planks. It meant that even the hallowed chamber pot had to be carried down the outside staircase. Chickens and I believe at least one goat shared the rumble and provisions downstairs. On one occasion, a chicken had been caught out in the downstairs space and, in the cackling manner of chickens when roused and forced to attempt to fly, managed to dive into the circular opening of the barrel. With a sigh of resignation that suggested it had not been the first time this happened, Siegfried retrieved the noisy complainant from the dark recesses and released it out into the surrounding cottage garden to more fowl complaints. Knights of old had to turn their hands at what we would consider all sorts of unpleasant tasks.

On the occasion of the attack by forces from other parts of the village, in that long summer without school, we the defenders of the castle had to imagine most of our armour and weaponry, unless one counted old pots, bucket helmets, and gardening implements. Siegfried vetoed the use of the chicken-prone privy cover as a protective oaken shield.

The cowardly attackers would use the high wall at street level that supported the cottage garden up to the castle as shelter and regrouping station from which to surprise the defenders in sorties of undisciplined timing. The battle moved to and fro, with us retaliating and breaking out from behind the downstairs storeroom door, chasing down the bailey, and retreating back up to base. Some of the smaller members of our tribe preferred the higher safety at the top of the outside staircase.

At the height of the battle, I was struck in the face by a missile, later determined to have been a stone, fired from a small hand at street level. Or maybe from a sling?

I was bleeding and I felt shrapnel in my mouth, though that turned out to be bits of a tooth that had sheared off under the impact. It could have been worse. We had to retreat up the stairs and into the provisional field hospital, where I was stretched out on a rough bench in the castle kitchen/living room. Instantly, the nurse took over. She was, after all, the oldest. Following a short inspection and a little prodding about the cavity, my mouth was stuffed with what may have been cotton wool to stop the bleeding. It did its job amicably and I lived.

The Tuckelsburg had survived the war and I believe was occupied once more by another large household when Siegfried's family moved out, though when living conditions improved and everyone built their own houses, it became a neglected symbol of the past. Around 2000, the old house had become an embarrassment and was pulled down. With its sixteenth-century history, it might have become a lovely little local museum.

At the time of our imaginative games, it was more of an adventure than a calamity. The galling bit came later on occasions when I had to suffer the ignominy of being expected to smile happily while several young villagers claimed the honour of having knocked my tooth out.

The Tuckelsburg, historical relic turned into a dwelling in the centre of the village. When it was finally demolished, we were not there to defend it. Is that machine-gun damage on the chimney?

'Tuckelsburg' may have been a name given to a less than salubrious abode in its elevated position set back from a road junction with access to the upstairs living quarters in full view via an outside stone staircase, but none of us realised the actual history of the place. Research found that it was named in documents of 1586 as 'Hoge Wardt', a lookout tower on the edge of the then much smaller village. The stone foundations, if not the wattle and daub upper parts, might well have been part of that much earlier structure.

Pre-1583, the nucleus of the original village, including church and churchyard, had been a crowded, huddled together community. When military practices changed in the sixteenth century, the crowded security no longer mattered and the village began to expand. What today has become a bank, the inn and farm 'Lamberts' can look back on some 400 years of ownership from when Lambert Fredebölling became landlord in 1586. Alas, the main house was one of the fire casualties of 1945, but has been rebuilt on the old foundations.

Another of the war casualties of 7–8 April 1945 in that original hub of the village was still covered by a straw roof, lacking a chimney. Smoke would have risen from

Quonen, one of the old houses in the oldest part of the village, fell prey to the flames in 1945. A straw roof and no chimney as in earlier more primitive centuries.

the open fire through a layer of round staves up into the smoke room, where hams and sausages were 'cured' to last through the long winters. Finally, the smoke would have dissipated through the straw roof.

My First and Only 'Scooter'

It must have been on a later occasion when Uncle Anton remembered an old scooter that might be of use to me. I do not know how I got there, but my father's birthplace Eversberg stands on a mountain with its own ruins of a small castle. It would have been rather a long walk.

Perhaps I got a lift, but I remember scootering back down from the boar mountain all the way to Meschede, always one foot on the ground, pushing. The other foot rested on the crossbar near the ground, the rather small entirely wooden wheels wobbling well-worn and turning only under duress. It is difficult to imagine how many generations of children had worn out those wooden wheels.

The word scooter later became a byword for chic transport when Teds and Rockers ruled the roost. In my case, the word ought to be used with some reservation—you could not 'scoot' along on it. Basically, it consisted of two narrow wooden planks with a movable metal join at almost right angles. Each of the planks held a wheel, one at the end of the horizontal footplate and one at the bottom of the down-plank with a strut on the upper end supplying the handlebars. Even the early downhill part from Eversberg meant constant hard pushing. By the time I reached Meschede, I caved in. I capitulated and waited for the bus service that ran between town and village.

It was my first major outing on my own. I think it was also the only time the 'scooter' was used.

The *Rathaus* (town hall) in Eversberg, at my father's birthplace.

30

The Poles' Dilemma in Victory

It was then, when POWs suddenly became the victors, that human nature was tested to its basic core. Forced foreign workers who had been poorly dressed with little interest in personal presentation suddenly became again the people they had formerly been, often smart and personable.

In the days immediately following the arrival of the American 3rd Army, someone, probably Uncle August or Aunt Anna, had lit a cast-iron stove by the chimney that had survived the fire in the ruins of my grandparents' house. Maybe some iron cooking pot or pan had survived also. Standing close to the brick-built chimney, it would have offered a chance of a meal on returning from their forest hiding place. Early garden produce may have been available and chickens were forever finding hiding places to lay and brood their eggs instead of their prescribed roosts inside the house.

It was on that hot stove that my little sister badly seared her upper thigh, leaving her in intense pain. She had simply ventured too close. The doctor who came to help and soothe that pain was one of the Polish workers with whom I had played on one of the farms, learning Polish words we thought were swear words. Conversing with such prisoners was forbidden, but it must have been difficult to keep track of children. I have since realised that some of the words I learnt and still remember mean 'I love you'. Like most of them, this particular individual had been dishevelled in tattered clothing, but now he was a fine gentleman in an immaculate shining uniform. Bright red is the colour that has stayed in my mind, but then red trousers were a part of the Polish military parade uniform.

After the years spent with craftsmen and on farms in the village, in Remblinghausen, it was quite remarkable the way most Polish former prisoners reacted once they had been liberated. Stanislaus on the farm right next to my grandparents' place obviously realised the plight the former occupants were in once the house had gone. My mother often told of the times when she had visited the ruin and he had called to her from across the boundary fence and pointed to a particular hiding spot on her side: '*Für Kinder*' he had said ('For the children') and she had found some food stuffs or delicatessen he had saved for us either from the farm or from the Red Cross parcels the prisoners received, or maybe from American rations.

I found out only later some of the actions and reactions concerning Polish behaviour. In the last days before the artillery bombardment of the village on a nearby road, a column of retreating German army vehicles was attacked by aircraft and a Polish prisoner calmly ploughing in a nearby field had been hit and killed on the spot. He was buried in the village cemetery.

During the attacks on the village, a father took his badly wounded son to a German field hospital on an outlying farm. A splinter in the skull could not be operated on, however much the pain, the father was told by the medical orderly, 'Get used to it.'

As soon as the Americans reached the area, a former Polish prisoner took one of the GIs aside and persuaded him to take the boy and his considerable headache to hospital in the nearby town. In spite of the bumpy ride past bomb craters and around *Tanksperren* (tank barricades) in a jeep, they managed it, and the boy's splinter was removed and he survived without lasting harm.

In the village, an American officer told the Poles that for three days martial law would reign. That meant they could take revenge without consequences if such was desired, but their top-ranking officer ordered there should be no reprisals.

'We have been treated fairly here under the circumstances, so we will behave like civilised people!' There was to be no retaliation. One of his men is said to have complained: 'But I only want to beat up my farmer'.

The farmer in question survived unharmed by hiding and staying out of his former farm labourer's way for the next few days.

While other former prisoners like the French were glad to return home, the Poles had no such happy solution. Poland became part of the Eastern Bloc. I was involved in one such case when the adopted child of a farmer in the middle of the village married a former prisoner. The liaison would have had dire consequences had it been known before the end of the war, so now it came as a surprise, though perhaps not to everyone. The couple had decided to emigrate and start anew in Australia. Everyone was aware that the wedding meant a permanent departure.

I was known to have a camera, as I had the spring on my father's old box Agfa fixed by a watchmaker in the nearby town and I had experimented with a film or two. My first photographic assignment ensued when I was asked to photograph the happy couple and family for posterity. Film and developing were paid, but of course, I lost the negatives. I often wondered if my amateur efforts were worth perusing in later years.

Today I understand that my photographic subjects were not the only such couple of formerly supposed enemies to get married after the end of hostilities. They emigrated to leave any mistrust or bad feelings behind them. Canada and Australia were the favoured destinations.

There was, however, one former Polish prisoner who had spent his time on an outlying croft with a family and their young daughter. He declared being left with his child was only what German girls deserved. The boy grew up without a father.

Stanislaus from the neighbouring farm, who had helped us out in the desperate early days, delayed his departure back to his country for as long as possible, but eventually he, too, had to return to protect his family back home. There seemed to be an arrangement that he could leave Poland for a set time each year to bring in foreign currency, so for many years, he returned to the village, working on various farms for the time he was allowed to be absent.

The Poles were handed a double-edged sword with the German capitulation. In theory, they were among the victors, but their homeland was now under the brutal fist of another dictator. Still they were sent home.

Notably different behaviour by comparison must be reported from former Russian prisoners who generally preferred to become bandits, live rough in the hills and forests, even after the Americans' arrival, only coming out to barter for cigarettes and such. Others preferred the woods as bases for raids on lonely farms and cottages, demanding clothes, food, etc., and they were quite prepared to use force. Cattle and pigs were slaughtered out in open meadows.

They had guns and ammunition, mostly found in forests where they had been discarded by German military personnel before they changed into civilian clothes and rejoined their families. Those Russian fugitives became a problem at least for a while. One farmer was shot dead through his front door just as he was about to open it.

April 1947 with my mother and sister. This must have been before the Red Cross notice informed us that my father was alive in Russia. Women wore black in mourning.

31

Crutches of Hope

It has been said that war and hardship fill churches, and, indeed, most Sundays, the not inconsiderable interior of the village church was so full of worshippers, they stood outside its main door at services. Humans need somewhere to gather hope.

Uncle Emil had returned even before the end of hostilities, so had others in the parish. Former soldiers trickled back, quietly and nervous. News was passed on through the village grapevine every time someone returned, or a Red Cross postcard arrived with news. Many, like my father and Uncle Jupp, had been officially declared missing. Others had simply vanished—disappeared in a void of uncertainty. Neighbour Josef Nelle, for instance, was he alive and a prisoner of war? Would he return? Was there a grave somewhere?

People grasped at straws. Prayers and pilgrimages were the main options left to so many worried relatives. The fourteen Stations of the Cross, marking Christ's last journey and ascent to his crucifixion, regained their popularity. Churches display them as icons around interiors or they were built outdoors as strings of small wayside monuments with carved or painted scenes, often on hillsides, leading up to a chapel at the top, representing Golgotha, the last stop with the tortured body on the cross.

There were more famous places for such pilgrimages, but a smaller version had been built at an outlier of the village, at Sägemühle, not quite at the bottom of a steep incline. Six houses and a chapel plus a millpond and the ancient sawmill that gave the place its name.

I remember the saw or lumber mill chugging away, a large tree trunk on rails slowly moving under the horizontal saw, turning the trunk into planks. A by-product was the manufacture of farmer's implements like wooden rakes. Even then it had the air of antiquity about it, though it has been grandly and lovingly preserved and protected by local enthusiasts since then. With its origins in the thirteenth or fourteenth century, it has become a protected cultural monument.

Close by stands an octagonal chapel, the finest in the parish with a fine baroque roof structure or helmet expertly covered in slate. It is dedicated to the '*Vierzehn*

Nothelfer' ('Fourteen Helpers in Need'), fourteen saints that were deemed especially effective in interceding with the Lord on behalf of humankind. All but one of the saints were martyrs in early Christianity and their help has been sought at least since the Middle Ages and the Black Death. They were particularly revered in the area between the fourteenth and sixteenth centuries.

On occasion, I attended catechism or acolyte lessons in the chapel's small confines. It is believed that, just like the village church, this splendid building once marked a stop on an ancient pilgrim's route that found its final destination in Santiago de Compostela in north-western Spain.

We had attended several such physical and devotional exercises at the fourteen Stations of the Cross by the old chapel, but this time a more distant and more popular venue had been chosen. A horse and traditional open coach were borrowed from a friendly farmer for a Sunday pilgrimage to the Kreuzberg, higher in the mountainous region. As a child with a mind of my own and an asthmatic disposition, I found the repetitive prayers and the slow devotional moves of such events somewhat of a trial. But then sacrifice was part of the reason of the exercise. In actuality, I was usually excused when asthma became too persistent.

Aunt Anna had at last persuaded her reluctant bachelor intended Franz, who, although in uniform, had never been posted far from home. As Uncle August with 'a shadow on his lung' was ill much of the time and men were rare in the family, Uncle Franz was asked or perhaps had been volunteered to take the reins. Franz Zimmermann was a carpenter and his name actually described his calling. '*Zimmermann*' means carpenter. Alas, he was not used to horses and farming.

The trip is a blur in my memory, though its auspicious beginnings could not be forgotten. Trouble started immediately at the steep road down to the Sägemühle. At the incline, the whippletree pressed against the hindquarters of the nervous horse and, unable to withstand the pressure, it began a break-neck downhill sprint in its attempts to escape the rear pressure. Pandemonium broke out on the open coach until finally one of the women pilgrims remembered there was a brake that could be operated, thus saving a calamitous situation and avoiding disaster.

Today, a new faster but gentler road bypasses the village, and the Sägemühle has become a pleasant cul-de-sac.

In spite of the hold of the church and its teaching, superstition also was rife in the village, and there were the people who would cater for it. Palmists, clairvoyants, and mystics set up their stalls. If there was a chance to find out what had happened to a loved one, it was worth the effort to explore. Payment would have been in kind, butter or eggs most likely.

Someone had heard of or visited a 'Seer' to read the future in the nearby town. A picture of the missing person was required and something personal, like a wedding ring in my mother's case. She went with one of two spinster sisters of Josef Nelle. A neighbour and friend of Uncle Jupp, he had not been married either.

Above: The millpond at Sägemühle. Before the bypass was built, the road featured dangerous curves around the pond and the octagonal chapel. Centre right another small chapel, the beginning of the fourteen devotional Stations of the Cross that led uphill from there.

Left: The chapel at Sägemühle did not escape war damage.

The village is officially an outlier of Meschede today. The town lies 5 km away on the old road. When the two women returned, there were mixed messages. My mother told how her ring had been suspended on a fine thread above a photo of my father. If the ring turned, the missing person was alive. If the ring remained still while suspended, there would be no hope. The ring moved, but the two women had been warned to expect the worst, just in case. When Miss Nelle's mother's ring was suspended above her brother's picture, the ring did not move. The forecaster tried again. There was no movement. The missing man's sister fainted clean off her chair. Her brother never returned. Later it became known that Grenadier Josef Nelle had died on 19 January 1943 in Luxembourg, aged thirty-six. Uncle Jupp would have been of a similar age.

During the war, my grandmother had had a dream that reverberated within the family for several years. She had seen a calendar of the one-day-at-a-time kind, the small sheets carrying a large printed number of the day, the day of the week, and the month of a given year, printed red for Sundays and holy days. In grandmother's dream, the days had flown off one by one until it came to a certain date—I think it was 19 September or November—while a voice mysteriously called out the date loud and clear. It must have been akin to an omen, especially with all the ladies in the family. The dreaded day arrived and passed without incident. Bad news from the front might take its time arriving, but eventually it was decided it had to be the following year that was meant in the dream—and then the following year.

Rumours kept circulating. How far the story had spread or who had spread it and why I cannot say, but someone had mysteriously worked out that the end of the world was to come about at noon on a certain day. Armageddon was imminent. After all that had happened—after all the depressing news—rumours, fears, and uncertainties were rife. Anything might be possible. Religion, in a close catholic community, was something we lived with every day and the end had been forecast in the Bible.

As we lived on the second floor in a house just a little down the road from where grandmother's house had stood before the fire, we had a grand view of the church and its tower clock. Our landlady's husband never returned from the war. I cannot say how many or who was with us. A mother and two daughters from Silesia lived in another room downstairs.

It is strange just how an idea like that can take hold given the right circumstances. At the time, we sat about the bare table, not knowing what to expect, though I have to admit that at eleven or twelve years of age, I was old enough to be harbouring my share of scepticism. After all, it was not how I envisaged things to proceed and we had lived through something similar already.

The church clock struck noon in the tense atmosphere and for several heartbeats nothing happened. I could not help myself; slowly my knee rose under the table, lifting it off the floor and causing it to move about. My sister still accuses me of almost giving her a heart attack that noontime whenever she recalls the event.

One of my earliest photographs, a Christmas greeting taken from the window of our temporary home. In front of the church, in the centre, the old school with its two classrooms and teacher's flat.

32

A New Beginning

Eventually, the glorious six months without schooling after the end of hostilities came to an end. We returned not to our usual school premises that had to be repaired, but to mixed classes above the village fire station where formerly and later the Kindergarten was held. Headmaster Bolte had lost both his sons to the war. It was heart-breaking to see the previously dapper and decisive man in such a state, or it would have been heart-breaking, had there been such feelings as compassion among us heartless scholars. For a short while, I thought he had suffered a breakdown, maybe he had, but like everyone else, he managed. Things eventually returned back to normal and we moved back to classes in the repaired schools.

Teacher Kortenkamp in one sense was perhaps less affected by the war. He and his family lived on the upper floor of the New School. They had experienced the village's bombardment in the sturdier cellar's, yet even their walls were blown in and people were hurt, one fatally. The boys were younger than the head teacher's had been, the youngest being my age. Ludwig, the eldest son, had been commandeered to meet at a collective station for military outfitting and training a couple of mountains away, though that was in the final days, right at the end of the war when sensible people realised that all was lost anyway. Supervision not being what it should have been in the chaos, the newly drafted young men of his age had simply decided to leave and go back home, using the familiar mountains and woodland terrain to avoid zealous commanders.

During the days the village was attacked with mortar fire, it had been Ludwig who went out to look for the doctor and the priest.

A woman from the village called on my mother and somewhat haltingly explained that her husband had decided to set up a grocery business, so it fell to her to alert people and, as they did not yet have the premises, to take orders directly from people of foodstuffs that could be delivered. She was almost ashamed to ask, but her husband had returned with only one arm and, like it or not, she had to help.

Would my mother be interested in a supply of cod for a traditional Friday meal? My mother must have found the money, for I remember the very tasty flakes of cod the size of slices of bread, the likes of which have been impossible to imagine for many decades since, now that with overfishing, cod never reach such grand heroic dimensions. For a while, the one-armed merchant held an open-air market on specific days in the centre of the village.

Our new village doctor visited me during one of my almost regular bouts of asthma. He tried a new type of treatment called a fever injection, but it seemed to have the opposite effect to the one desired. Instead of improving my lot, it made it worse. The young doctor sat with me for hours, he was that concerned, but eventually I pulled through and afterwards it seemed as if that narrow escape had been a watershed. My asthma did improve, and later, for decades at least, it hardly bothered me at all.

Photo Experiments

A camera being the only thing left from our former life, I began experimenting with photography. On the old box cameras, one did not press the shutter, one moved a small lever. Then one had to peer through a small dark red window at the back while winding the film on until the next number appeared on the film backing paper. In shade, that could be difficult and one might miss the next frame. With only eight images, 6 cm by 9 cm, each image had to count.

Bird photography took my fancy temporarily. I had the idea of capturing them on film at an old bird table in the garden below by securing the camera to a fence post. A long string tied to the exposure lever would depress that lever when pulled from a safe distance and hiding place. I could not find string fine and light enough to work without the weight itself moving the volatile lever.

Next I decided the birds could take their own pictures by attaching a crust of bread rigged up over a branch to the secured camera. It would severely shorten the fine thread required, which in theory would move the lever simply by the weight of the bird.

There were several disadvantages, the main one being the lack of weight of a blue tit or even a great tit or sparrow, which had insufficient leverage. Another problem was the string itself, which would twitch and move by the very nature of the action, thus ensuring instant flight of the shy models.

Of course, the camera had to be removed following each action to wind on the roll of film before again securing it. That by itself would ensure a long wait before a feathered friend again picked up the courage to participate. Finally, the simple lens could not cope with the short distance required.

I have to say in my defence that at the time there were no telephoto lenses, self-timers, or extension release cables and the safety pin shutter was too slow to allow for movement.

Occasionally, the winding mechanism would not hold tight and the film loosened in the camera. On one occasion, while removing a film under the bedclothes to avoid light spill during retrieval, somehow the filmstrip and the safety backing paper were separated, ending up in a knot of convoluting strips that in my wisdom I decided to

Another of my early photographs (6 cm × 9 cm), taken with the Agfa box camera south-west of the village.

protect as a ball covered in newsprint. That bundle I handed to the photo studio in the nearby town for developing.

Newsprint does not bar daylight and the film was well exposed. The developed work of art did show very hazy branches and a ghostly bird feeding box could be recognised, even some streaks of moving birds, all on a crumpled background of newsprint.

I have no idea where I scrounged the money for such extravagance, but even an older cousin was tapped for the price of a film when he visited.

Rations and Yellow Bread

Times were tough with rationing, and few necessities, not to mention luxuries, were available in empty shops.

For a time, our village bakers received an American supply of maize. Maize bread was better than no bread at all, but given a choice, it was a doomed idea. Yellow bread never was a hit, certainly not with me. My own favourite was sliced rye bread roasted, browned, and crisped on the hot metal surface of the cooking and heating range, then perhaps sprinkled with sugar.

Burnt-out houses were being rebuilt, but not always in the former sometimes cramped spaces. Several owners moved to larger plots on the fringe of the village or on their fields. Soddemanns, our former landlords by the churchyard, rebuilt the house and shop, expanding to the full width of the property, incorporating what had been our annex.

School meals were introduced and prepared at the New School. We took it in turns, the older boys and girls, to carry the cauldrons across half the village to the Old School. The meals, too, were of a new and different taste, but on the whole, they were a valuable addition and very welcome. We walked to school with containers and spoons as well as our satchels. The former Army-issue slightly curved field containers with a secure lid that might be attached to soldiers' belts were great and useful favourites, as well as the light metal cutlery that had short spoon and fork handles riveted together and could be folded or jack-knifed into each other.

Traditional trades were rekindled, but eventually many were doomed when times improved. Who would have a suit made to measure when one could just go and buy a fashionable cheaper one off the peg instantly? It was the same with dresses, shoes, and even furniture.

One by one, the midden disappeared from houses as the keeping of pigs and the cost of pig feed conspired with younger people's aspirations and sensitivity to their environment to ostracise such husbandry. Once it had been a symbol of pride and local standing, for the house with the largest midden also was the house with the most livestock and therefore wealth. Soon the old habit grown out of necessity of sharing a roof with livestock became a thing of the past.

There was a moment in German post-war history when in one sense all people really were equal. In June 1948, the currency reform replaced the old Reichsmark with the Deutschmark, at least in the US, British, and French occupation zones. Everyone received DM40. My mother often recalled how she suddenly had DM40 to spend. The event also rekindled earlier memories after the previous war, when inflation made nonsense of the value of money.

In the aftermath of the destruction and with Uncle Jupp's last letter accepted by all, it was agreed that Aunt Minna and Uncle Emil would build their house on the foundations of the old wattle-and-daub house. It was a make-do and hope bungalow affair erected of breeze-block walls, just one floor high and with a red tiled roof.

Uncle Emil's family were carpenters and they supplied the doors and windows and much of the wood. In the absence of paint, the doors were treated with blowlamps, a light scorching process that would bring out the natural pattern in the wood and also go some way to protect it from the elements, at least for a while. Perhaps my once cherished, but long since abandoned blowlamp had found its use at last?

Uncle Emil had trained as a baker, but had turned to driving for a living and driving higher military ranks in the Army.

War had been relatively kind to him as '*Feldwebel*'—something akin to a warrant officer—or so I thought until I saw his photographic memories. He had been in the trenches in the First World War in 1917, he just never mentioned it later. In the early days of the Second World War—a time some called 'the Glory Years'—as a serving soldier, he spent time in Alpine scenery on holiday with comrades. One picture has him standing beside an armoured vehicle at a large Army barracks, but he also spent time in Crete and Athens in the Mediterranean, where he met up with another noted member of the village, Alfred Kotthoff, the owner and publican of Schäpers, the Post Inn. The publican, too, survived the war, but with a permanently unbending knee akin to Aunt Minna.

One of Uncle Emil's observations had been that National Socialism was similar to Communism, except more elegant and refined.

Above: Uncle Emil Hütten, fourth from right, in the First World War.

Below: Wry smiles, Easter in the field, 1917. Uncle Emil is third from left. Was this a propaganda picture?

Another group image of young recruits in the First World War, with Uncle Emil standing fourth from left.

Uncle Emil in the trenches in 1917, seated second from right. A message behind them warns of mines.

Above: Another war. Uncle Emil, here probably at Krefeld, in a spoof scene of barrack-room humour.

Right: Uncle Emil seems to have driven all kinds of vehicles.

Uncle Emil's Christmas in Athens, Greece, 1941.-

With village publican Alfred Kotthoff (Schäpers) in Athens in February 1942.

33

Swapping to Survive

For a while, every available room in the village was taken up by people displaced from towns, especially from the large industrial towns in the Ruhr valley, the Kohlenpott. Not only was the village more crowded, people were dispersed to outlying farms and hamlets, too.

At the farm next to the ruins of gran's house, besides the large family of my friend Norbert, his three siblings, mother, and assorted aunts, a mother and son had moved into a room at the first floor front. The new boy was older than we. It was then for the first time I heard jokes being made about Adolf Hitler, which I thought rather forward, as previously nobody would have dared say such things. In hell, it was said, a new system of punishment had been devised. Sinners had to turn at least once about their own axis for every sin committed in their lifetimes. Goebbels and Himmler had a busy time turning, but Hitler, it was said, had been installed as permanent extractor fan in the hottest part of the Devil's kitchen.

Of course, there was rationing, but even so it would have been difficult to make ends meet. That older boy shouted to us from his first floor farm window. He had caught a sparrow, he insisted, and he was about to pluck and fry or cook it. 'Come up,' he shouted, 'if you don't believe me.' Norbert was not interested either.

If local people had their problems, those in the big towns found it even more problematic to get by. A new wave of 'swappers' moved on to the land, bringing anything portable that might be of use to a household in exchange for food. Anything edible was at a premium, but the most asked for item was the tough skin of pigs with hopefully a little lardy fat still attached. Such luxuries would supply the fat to fry potatoes, etc. People warned one another by sharing their experiences with such strangers.

At the small farm of Nellen, the two spinster sisters were still waiting for their brother to return, though a family with several almost grown-up children had moved in with them in the meantime. One of the sisters had answered a call on their front door, and while she went out back to the larder to look for something edible to swap for an offered light bulb or something, the caller had kept up conversation unnecessarily loudly. The reason had been, it was later thought, to gauge the time it would take to her return. The sister handed over some morsel and was thanked profusely. It was not until the evening that she realised that the bare lightbulb in their hall had been unscrewed and was missing. Lightbulbs were precious commodities and would have been swapped again at the next house of call.

There were shortfalls of so many things that when shops finally received any kind of supplies, the news would spread and people would queue up to buy and stock up again. My favourite memory is the story of the woman who queued up and finally managed to buy something new: somewhat perplexed on exiting the shop, she had to enquire what it was she had purchased. In her hand, she held a small blue, slightly curved plastic tablet as her trophy, but wondered what it would be useful for. She had bought a soap-saving device that could be pressed on to the side of a bar of soap, thereby wearing down only the opposing side of the bar during usage.

Mopeds were among the first and oft-belittled modes of transport once conditions improved and petrol became more widely available. Something called a 'Quickly', a cross between a bicycle and a motorbike—more akin to a bicycle with a small motor attached—made a memorable sound and added humorous comments to village life whenever one appeared. Even its name sounded 'foreign'.

Rather early one Easter morning, there was a fire in the forests above the village to the south. The official way to announce news to the populace was for a village crier to deftly ring his hand bell and shout a message at the top of his voice while running about the village streets, whatever time of the day or night.

Waking that early on hearing the noise and the word 'fire', I got scared for a moment when I saw sparks flying past my window in various directions until I realised they were fireflies on their innocent natural business.

Transport of various types could again be found on the roads.

34

The Gift of an Apple

With German capitulation on 8 May 1945 (now feted as VE Day), in the aftermath of the war, the movement of people did not stop.

At the Potsdam Conference in July and August 1945, the Allies dispensed justice to the defeated Germany and endorsed a so-called 'orderly and humane' expulsion of millions of ethnic Germans from Poland, Czechoslovakia, and Hungary. Perhaps understandable, all annexed territories were returned to or reintegrated into neighbouring states, and Germany's eastern border was moved westward. In exchange for territory Poland lost to the Soviet Union following the readjustment of the Soviet–Polish border, Poland received a large swath of German territory and it began to deport the German residents.

Ethnic cleansing on a grand and official scale followed. The once-harmonious coexistence of Czech, German, Slovak, and Hungarian people had been poisoned. German-speaking people were held accountable and collective guilt was pronounced on a population that lived in Sudetenland for instance, a mountain range 200 miles long and 20 to 40 miles wide, in the north of Bohemia and Moravia as well as covering part of Sudeten Silesia. Germans had lived there since AD 500. In 1946, an estimated 1.3 million ethnic Germans were deported to the American zone of the future West Germany and an estimated 800,000 were deported to the Soviet zone, later East Germany.

I watched such a convoy of '*Flüchtlinge*' arriving in the village. Open lorries turned up at the churchyard by the old school with their pathetic loads of mainly women and children, clutching a few bags or suitcases. From there, they were taken to the old school to await dispersal to their new 'homes' among local families. In their long old overcoats and dark shabby clothing, they were a pitiful sight. What do you grab and pack when you are told you are leaving your home forever and you can only take what you can carry? Warm clothes for the children? It is always the vulnerable and innocent who suffer when nations bully each other.

As a family, we had lost almost everything, but at least we were still among the people we knew in a place we called home.

In the village, there was no happy welcome. The strangers spoke with strange accents. They sang about giant mountains—the Riesengebirge—and told stories about a legendary giant called 'Rübezahl'. Rübezahl is the subject of legends and tales in Polish, Czech, and German folklore, and it is at home along the border between Poland and the Czech Republic. Silesia was emptied of its ethnic German population and added to Poland, and the capital Breslau was renamed Wrocław.

Our school class numbers were greatly enhanced. Mostly, the newcomers were quiet traumatized people who were out of their element, away from friends and families, displaced, dispossessed, and disheartened, while locals were hardly pleased with the encroachments either.

Evacuees eventually drifted back to their places of origin, but, of course, for the '*Flüchtlinge*', there was no going back. In time, the newcomers integrated, and the children grew up and intermarried with an injection of new blood into traditional stock. Deportations and migrations affected up to 16.5 million Germans.

One of the stories of displacement comes from a small village near Hirschberg, Silesia. From Polish origins, in 1281, the settlement was first mentioned as Hyrzberc. Subsequently it passed to Bohemia, then in 1526 to Habsburg Austria. Beleaguered in turn by opposing sides during the Thirty Years' War, Hirschberg was annexed to the Kingdom of Prussia in the mid-eighteenth century during the Silesian Wars. In 1871, Hirschberg became part of the German Empire. It was destroyed and rebuilt several times throughout its history.

In 1946, the area was acceded to Poland following the Potsdam Conference and its name changed to Jelenia Góra. All German residents who had not already fled west before the Russian advance were unceremoniously expelled and replaced with Polish settlers. Even the cemetery at the former German Protestant church was destroyed, along with parts of the old town.

Nearby Lauban was a famous centre for kerchief making—there was a saying '*Lauban putzt der Welt die Nase*' ('Lauban blows the nose of the world'). German inhabitants received a few hours' notice to take what they could carry and be ready. Cattle trucks and goods trains shunted them west from place to place and among others a mother with a boy and two young girls eventually arrived by lorry in Remblinghausen, where they were taken first to the old school and then to a large room above the fire brigade's building, a room that had served as kindergarten.

It is with a mixture of feelings, but also with pride in the nature of human kind that I must relate the story of one such a displaced child of my own age, Gisela, the elder of the two girls from Silesia, who was so moved by the plight of a boy who was ill so often that she handed over an apple—a rare luxury for someone like her—to give me cheer. After all that had happened, the simple goodness of a child in spite of everything still stays with me and colours my memories.

Gisela remained in the village and together with her local husband created a reputable family. Is it possible to ever say adequately 'thank you' for such a gesture of compassion from a child who had lost everything except her human heart?

35

Church Matters

Pastor Ruegenberg

Our ageing Pastor Ruegenberg had been a strict disciplinarian in my mother's days, a powerful man walking the aisles between school benches during studies, especially catechism, cane in hand, and woe the pupil whose attention slipped or who thought not to be observed. Hands had to be folded on desks in front of the students then, which made a quick stroke with the cane a likely possibility.

At his priestly golden jubilee in March 1944, several of the attending priests were former pupils of his. He suffered a stroke in April that year and most of his tasks were taken over by the younger Vicar.

Occasionally, Pastor Ruegenberg would wander about the village, and when we met, he would ask after my father: 'Is your father still not back from the war? He is supposed to fix my roof'. Then he would press my hand and watch me squirm under the pressure. I found that I began to have the courage and strength to press back.

The intellectual priest was a man of considerable studies, hence the many books and documents that were lost in the firebrand. He had paid the fees for several young men to train for the priesthood. There were murmurs that he had been warned by the Party for speaking out from the pulpit. Priests had disappeared if they spoke out against the excesses or misuse of Nazi power and did not toe the party line if their conscience dictated otherwise.

It was the parsonage barn that was the first to fall prey to General Patten's Army incendiaries, which in turn ignited and burnt down his home in 1945 and where two villagers and soldiers died in the shelling. It was rumoured that his large barn had been requisitioned by the *Wehrmacht* for the storage of petrol or other flammable material. At the time, he was sheltering at Cloidts House, the big house and farm at the edge of the village that once had been home to the ruling elite of the neighbourhood.

It was not the first time that the priest's house went up in flames. On the evening of 18 December 1883, it had fallen victim to an arsonist while it was occupied by a

Above: A priest's ordination would have been a blessing for a family, here in 1904. The picture must have been taken on the priest's lawn, as the big house of Cloidts features in the background.

Below: At the Golden Priest Jubilee of Pastor Ruegenberg (third from left) on 9 March 1944 several of the attending priests and religious dignitaries had been students of the celebrant. In the doorway at the back is the suspended 'friend of Hitler', Dr Lorenz Pieper (see page 207). Head teacher Bolte's daughter, Ursula, in white seems petrified.

The priest's house in early 1960s. It was the first to be hit and burnt down in April 1945 and was rebuilt, though without the large tithe barn at its side. To its left, a new building replaced our old condemned schools.

local farmer, widower Franz Gierse (Droste), who with his family of seven children plus servants had found shelter there when he himself had been the victim of fire just a few weeks earlier, on 21 November that year. The farm had been razed to the ground, though the livestock had been saved and it had been insured for most of the losses. In both instances, in farm and parsonage, the arsonist was identified as a servant girl with a grudge.

When street names had to be sorted later, the main village street became Jakobusstraße after the patron saint of the church and a lower road close to the Parsonage became Rügenbergstraße, remembering the priest who had served the village in a long and active life.

One third of the German population were Catholics in the 1930s. Even Adolf Hitler and his most ardent persecutor of Catholic clergy, the propaganda minister Joseph Goebbels, were brought up as Catholics. Catholic schools and newspapers had been closed. Catholic leaders had been targeted and murdered as part of Hitler's 1934 Long Knives purge. Monasteries and other Christian institutions were expropriated by the SS, Christian youth organisations were dissolved, and in schools, the crucifix was replaced by portraits of the Führer. In our school literature, the old Germanic gods and sun worship were remembered and hailed as part of the 'new times' (post-war schoolbooks featured stories by foreign writers as well).

At the infamous Dachau Concentration Camp, a dedicated clergy barracks was established in 1940. It held 2,720 prisoners of nine different nationalities. By far

A family with a visiting man of the cloth and the paraphernalia and animals of a pastoral lifestyle.

Traditional family group in one of the outlying hamlets, Höringhausen. The house fell victim to fire.

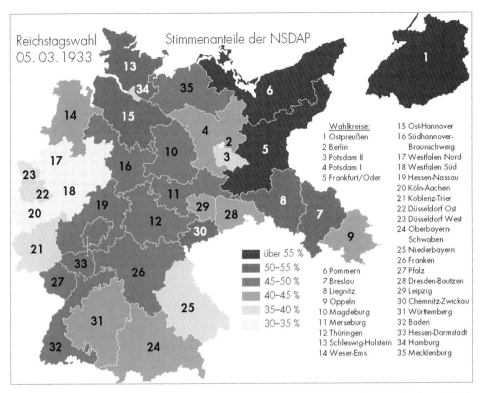

Westphalians—my countrymen—cast among the lowest percentage of votes for the NSDAP at the *Reichstagswahl* of 5 March 1933 at just 30–35 per cent of the population. (No. 18, Westfalen Süd).

the greatest number of 1,780 inmates came from Catholic Poland, but some 447 were German. Overall, more than half did not survive, adding to the millions that perished in the infamy that became known as the Holocaust. Of course, little of this was known at the time by the wider population and those that suspected it generally kept their heads down and avoided confrontation with its inevitable consequences.

The Astute Verger or Six Weeks of Bell Ringing

Character descriptions of my fellow Westphalians have long included the words stubborn as well as astute and sagacious. A good example of this comes from 1765 when Kaiser Franz I died, and a decree demanded the peeling of bells for the soul of the regent for six weeks continuously. That order came to the parish council and they passed on the message to the verger, but if they had expected the verger to simply buckle down and get on with the task they were rather disappointed.

The village priest recorded that the bells remained silent and he had been forced to announce a reminder from the pulpit. The verger, however, reminded the elders that he was still owed payment for ringing the bells four years earlier, on the death of Elector Clemens August—9 Reichsthaler and 12 Groschen were still due to him.

The elders had no choice but to agree to payment and the priest announced the decision to the congregation, adding the Groschen everyone in the parish would have to contribute within the next three to four days. If the money was not found, the bells would fall silent again. The bells started ringing—temporarily. Two men were sent to the verger when he had rung the bells for six days, tasked with the order of ringing the bells themselves. The verger referred to the elders of the village and they tried to persuade him to continue. Even a threatening letter to the verger from the dean of the monastery in nearby Meschede bore no fruit. Instead, the verger went directly to the dean and accused the elders, which resulted in a threat to the elders of a fine of 16 Goldgulden. That concentrated minds.

The parish council convened and twice summoned the verger to appear before them at one of the village hostelries, but the verger declined so the elders eventually went to him. Still he resisted their advances, so they went to see the priest for help. Only when the priest joined them in begging the verger to continue with the bell-ringing did he cave in, but with the strong proviso that his fees would be settled. They promised to pay his expenses as well and furthermore to protect him from any future problems or interference with his tasks. Verger Gerhardus Wilhelmus

When a bell needed attention or rehanging, the local smithy would be called to the task, *c.* 1965–66.

Görgens received the sum of 9 Reichsthaler and 12 Groschen, as well as 18 Groschen for expenses by 13 December 1766.

There is a codicil to this story. Today, the village elders would likely be held to account by the Noise Abatement Society. Only a few decades ago, the slits in the protective shutters that direct the bell sounds from the church tower had to be reset following complaints from a local hostelry whose guests were disturbed in their slumber by the bells. Now, the age-old traditional calls to prayer pass more gently over their heads.

Blessing the Fields and the Countryside

On *Fronleichnam* (the Feast of Corpus Christi on 3 June), traditionally most of the villagers would turn up for a procession through the surrounding fields, singing and chanting in Latin with Latin replies by the congregation. There were two designated routes, wide loops to the north-east of the village and to the south-west, some 4.5 to 5 km long. The one time I joined in, I found it most trying.

All the various societies would be represented with their flags and the priest would carry the host, protected under a canopy that was held aloft by staves on four corners by stout lads. Not an easy task on wet and windy days or in scorching summer heat.

It always was a special day for street decorations in the village and anywhere near houses. Neighbours would vie for the best designs down the centre of roads along the routes. In the days beforehand, baskets of flowers would be collected from meadows and gardens, many reduced to petals. Ladders laid down along the centre of fairways made valuable decoration aids, as the areas between rungs could be filled with colours and various designs and patterns. When lifted, the ladder would be moved along. At the next house, neighbours would continue the design schemes. This was where the priest walked, a considerable effort by devout women. Devotional images and statues would be placed outdoors and decorated along the route on miniature altars.

By 1939, flags without swastikas were forbidden and Corpus Christi was no longer a holiday, so people had to be careful and would only unfurl their flags shortly before and remove them again immediately afterwards. This happened one fine summer's day when teachers decided to give time off to students 'to celebrate the hot weather'. Children could now join the planned procession. At Sägemühle, the stout lady of the house Gierse is said to have unfurled her flag as the procession neared and hurriedly withdrew it once everyone had passed.

The flower-enhancing tradition reminds of somewhat similar activities mainly in Derbyshire, England, where wells are dressed with petals, leaves, moss, etc. into works of art, but that devotion can be traced back even to Pagan times.

At the 750 Year
celebrations of the
village, on 28 June
1992, some of the old
customs like floral
road decorations were
rekindled.

On *Fronleichnam* (the Feast of Corpus Christy), the congregation walks in procession
through village and fields, the priest under a canopy carries the Blessed Sacrament in a
monstrance. Here in May 1994.

Dr Pieper, a Lifelong Nazi

Born in my father's hillside hometown of Eversberg, some 11 or 12 km away as the crow flies, one priest courted controversy for most of his life, wearing the insignia of the NSDAP (*Nationalsozialistische Deutsche Arbeiterpartei*) even on his priestly robes to the end of the war. He had joined the Nazi party in 1922. In the year following, he claimed to have spent six months in Munich with Hitler, agitating on behalf of the party. The Church disowned him. He kept Hitler's portrait as proof, signed personally by the Führer '...in sincere admiration...', but it would seem that for a catholic priest—especially a suspended one—was in Hitler's entourage no longer a place.

Later, Dr Pieper was appointed official priest in charge at various lunatic asylums, though when in 1940–41 euthanasia was introduced, he is said to have contacted relatives of inmates and urged them to collect their loved ones before they could fall victim to state diktat. Attempted phone calls and letters of complaints to Hitler, Bormann, and Göring proved fruitless, but brought instead about Dr Pieper's dismissal. He retired to his hometown and concerned himself with the establishment of a museum of local history. Even the position of priest in his hometown was denied him (see image, page 200).

The Man of Pain or *Schmerzensmann*

A previous much smaller church had been pulled down in a rather dilapidated state following a climate change in about 1550, the little Ice Age, when hunger was caused by frequent poor harvests, followed by the harassments, plunders, and trials of the Thirty Years' War (1618–1648).

The new church was erected from 1753 to 1764. The interior was added in Baroque style in 1767–1769. With its figures carved in Baroque flamboyance, the ensemble has been feted altogether as the most important cohesive work in the Sauerland.

Under the high tower at the back of the church stands the late-gothic life-size figure of a *Schmerzensmann* or 'man of sorrow', a wood-carved Christ of pain in expressive realism with a crown of thorns, showing signs of maltreatment and flagellation, hands tied in his suffering—*ecce homo*. It is thought it stood in the earlier church and was banned to an attic when it became unfashionable with the Baroque style of the new church. Pastor Ruegenberg found it again in the church attic and restored it to the body of the church when he arrived in the village. Signs of repairs hint at attacks on the statue, possibly at times of extreme deprivation, when revenge was taken for bad harvests or other 'Acts of God'. To me, the distinctive statue represents the sadness and futility of war, the pain man inflicts on man as happened in my early days.

The *Schmerzensmann*, or man of sorrows, like the *Pietà*, a devotional image of the suffering of Christ, found its visual expression especially in the later Middle Ages. In Remblinghausen, such a wood-carved life-size figure was found neglected in the church attic.

As indicated by the fortunes of the *Schmerzensmann*, styles and perceptions of art change, even in religious expressions. When Pastor Ruegenberg first came to the village in 1908, the central spot at the high altar was taken by a crucifix that did not match in style to the rest of the interior. He was soon informed that his predecessor had not found the Baroque style of the Madonna that had previously occupied the space to be of sufficient piety. He had called her a '*Lebedame*', a woman of pleasure, and he had sold the statue. Thanks to the intervention of a teacher, at least she had not been destroyed.

Pastor Ruegenberg had no such qualms. He had traced the offending statue all the way west to Aachen and to a grotto in a private park. By paying all costs incurred and appealing to the purchaser's Christian conscience, he was successful and today the Madonna again stands in full glory on a global universe, treading on the head of the evil snake, about to be crowned by angels.

The earlier puritanical priest had also taken umbrage at the traditional depiction of St Agatha, who, according to the legend of her martyrdom, retains her severed breasts on a plate on one of the side altars. The worried Reverend had the offending items recarved into lemons.

His Eminence, The Bishop's Visit

Vicar Moog with his military experience had tasted real life in army barracks. No shrinking violet, we may recall his pastoral as well as his practical care during the attacks by General Patten's 3rd Army and the application of his first aid training to civilian casualties.

He took a special interest into youth movements and activities, and once he was back in his own building, the Vicarage where Aunt Minna and Uncle Emil had occupied the top floor and where we had witnessed the arrival of the American forces, he made one room available for youth meetings. It was there that we designed and built a replica of one of the oldest houses in the village to replace the stable in the Christmas display in our church. Like so many books and archives, the traditional stable had fallen victim to the flames in the priest's house.

I cannot vouch for the accuracy of the following story: on a parochial visit about his Diocese, the Bishop, being only human after all, was caught out on an open road by a call of nature and with no convenient tavern in sight, one of his entourage knocked on the door of a humble wayside cottage with a request to allow the Bishop to please use their convenience. The woman curtsied and stammered, but such a request could not be refused. She asked for a moment of time and closed the door.

It took ages, while the good man had to contain nature as best he could. Lots of activity could be heard in the house, preparations for so important a visit. Finally the front door opened again, and in flushed excitement, they bade the exalted visitor to enter. Their best room had been rearranged, furniture moved, leaving a large bare centre that had been surrounded by flowers, saintly statues, crucifixes, and framed religious images, while in the centre of the now-hallowed space stood their best chamber pot in splendid isolation.

It must have amused the exalted party for some time afterwards in the retelling, for it was our street-wise Vicar from whom I learnt the story.

In earlier times, when the black-robed priest walked through the village, following a boy with a censer and a small bell while wearing the acolytes' red and white regalia, everyone knew that someone was dying or close to death and that the priest was carrying the Sacrament to dispense the last rites. People would stand or kneel by the roadside and bow their heads; males would remove their headgear as a sign of respect.

Facts and Myths of Witches

Maybe it is a residue from earlier Pagan times, but the Christian religion does not preclude unholy belief in occult and sorcery as the possibility of attacks and subsequent repairs to the figure of the '*Schmerzensmann*' may explain.

On 19 January 1629, a woman from the village was accused and tried for witchcraft. She freely admitted that during a time of pestilence visitation, a woman in the village had taught her to befriend the devil by taking three steps backwards and renouncing God. Among other trumped up charges—apparently she had poisoned two calves—she had been visited by a strange lover and they had danced on a nearby mountain. The man had been dressed in green with a black hat with white feathers. The woman named a local shepherd who had played a rather long flute and several other women from the village who had been present. There were other such allegations, where only details differed. They usually flew to the hilltop dance, sometimes riding a goat with long horns or travelling in a golden coach.

Bullying and torture would eventually produce admissions, however nonsensical, to suffice for a guilty verdict. People admitted to having shapeshifted into animals or produced thunderstorms. How anyone could take such desperate ranting seriously remains a mystery unless we allow for lack of education and sometimes for human failings like greed or jealousy. It is interesting to find the names of many of the people named in those processes still attach to houses in the village today—at least they did in my youth.

The priest at the time seems to have been well versed in witchcraft. His last will and testament mentioned among several books on the theme the infamous *Malleus maleficiarum*—the *Hammer of Witches*—that was first published by clergyman Heinrich Kramer in 1487.

There is a tradition that witches were burnt in fields at a roadside opposite what is now the village sporting field, marked by a gnarled old lime tree, a small saints' chapel, and a wayside crucifix. By its situation in open fields outside the village, such a past seems darkly plausible.

My own family on my father's side was not exempt. A witch process was recorded in Bilstein, a village with its own castle, when one of my ancestors, a woman called Agnes Beckers, was burnt as a witch on 3 July 1590.

A small wayside shrine and a wooden crucifix stand overshadowed by a large old lime tree right opposite what has become the sports and football ground. They are thought to mark the spot where once witches were burnt outside the village.

36

Father's Return

At last, in 1947, when most surviving former soldiers had returned and hope had all but dwindled, a postcard from the International Red Cross informed my mother that our father was alive and a prisoner of war in Russia's Ural Mountains. It was the beginning of another anxious year, waiting for his return, but at least now there was real hope.

I do not remember how the message reached us on the day, though I believe someone returning by bus from nearby Meschede brought the news. My father was on his way home to the village, and he would arrive that afternoon. I was thirteen years of age, it was 1948, and only since that postcard arrived a year earlier did we know he was alive. It seems a kind of odyssey. Missing since 1944, he had been a prisoner for four long years, and including his call-up and service, he had been away for nigh on eight years.

What would he look like? What would he be like? Had he changed? He had been at home for only a few short weeks in my young life.

We still lived on the second floor with its high viewpoint into the village and with a bedroom on the first floor in the familiar neighbourhood just down from my grandparents' former house, where Uncle Emil and Aunt Minna were building with the sibling's agreement.

An Onion and Two Potatoes

My mother never was demonstrative in her affections, always shy and concerned what others might think. 'What will the neighbours say?' was a familiar expression.

It was a quiet, almost embarrassing homecoming, impressed on my mind and recorded almost like a film sequence, though there are missing moments. The lorry puffing up the road with what looked like a few vagrants at the open woodblock-piled back, but they were very probably workers returning from their shift (in the absence of petrol, vans and lorries were fitted with wood-burning stoves that supplied the steam energy and moving power. It never occurred to me then, but probably my father would not have had the money for the bus?)

On that occasion the lorry stopped in the street and the poorest of the 'vagrants' climbed down laboriously, shouting something to the driver or the others—an old man with stubble and greying short trimmed hair, in quilted trousers and a long quilted jacket, dirty and well mended, wearing one leather shoe and one wooden clog. On his belt—or rather the piece of string that held up the trousers—dangled a small pouch.

Approach to the first floor was by an outside flight of steps. My mother hesitated momentarily before rushing downstairs and bringing the stranger indoors before embracing him. Showing her feelings in public would be like making an exhibition of herself.

It is strange, but I cannot remember if I shook his hand—I must have. He came upstairs with us and flopped unto a chair. The pouch on his belt carried all his possessions: an onion and two potatoes, some 'makhorka' (Russian tobacco), and some bits of Russian newsprint to roll it in. Makhorka reputedly only tasted right if it was rolled in Russian newsprint.

My father's prize possession, however, was a small homemade book of brown sacking paper—from tobacco sacks, it turns out—containing scribbled recipes collected from various comrades from various parts of Germany. It had kept them occupied on the long evenings in the Urals, exchanging and collecting recipes, lovingly recording them and dreaming of home and of full bellies. If turned about to start reading at the back pages, the little pocketbook contains seven pages of addresses of fellow prisoners, written not always meticulously and by different hands. In some cases, there is a cross and a date marked next to a name.

What had happened to the sturdy jovial man with black wavy hair smiling from photos? At a casual glance, the stranger looked quite well nourished, though that was deceptive. On pressing a finger into his flesh, it remained a depression—water caused by malnourishment accounted for the swollen limbs.

Mother later recalled a day or two after his return when she had accompanied him by bus to the town of Meschede and the administrations to report and register his return, ashamed of his poor attire. As they passed a steaming midden on which a couple of fish heads had been carelessly abandoned, my father had stopped and only with some difficulty had my embarrassed mother managed to pull him away. 'If this were Russia,' he had said, 'they wouldn't last two minutes there. They would still improve the taste if added to a cooking pot.'

Eventually, we learnt more of his return journey. They had been in transit for days, stops and starts; not being informed, certainly not of their destination, they had been put on cattle trains and shunted to various locations until it dawned on them purely by the direction of the sun and stars that they were moving westward. Sometimes the train had been left in sidings for days without guards, when it was

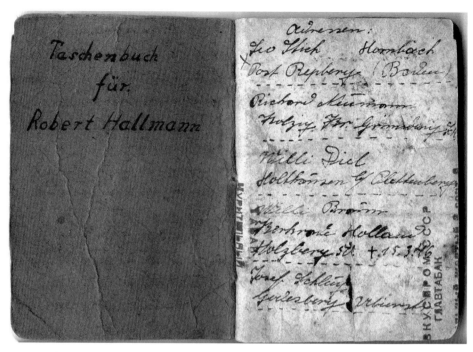

It is a sad memento from the years as POW in Russia, 1944–48. A small handmade and handwritten booklet with two beginnings, not a diary—from one end, it contains cooking and baking recipes collected from all over Germany and from the other end it recollects addresses of comrades. Marked against some of the names are dates and crosses.

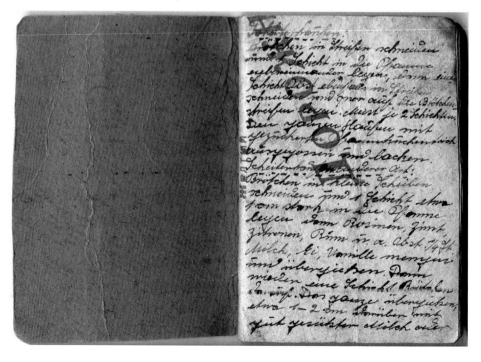

a kind of Russian roulette whether to take a chance and go out foraging into the countryside and risk being left behind should the train set off again suddenly.

Driven by his survival instinct, my father had gone out. On the whole, the local population had not been much better off than the POWs. When potatoes were planted as ordered under the communal farm system, the locals were likely to dig them up again at night for their own consumption. Onions were a staple diet and they would hang out to dry in bushels under low roofs outside houses. My father had been caught helping himself to just such onions when he had been 'arrested' by a countrywoman with her shotgun.

'SS,' she had said and prepared to execute him on the spot when a local man intervened and convinced her that this was just an ordinary soldier, not an SS-man. My father had never made it further up the promotion ladder than receiving two stripes—an *Obergefreiter*. It had been pure luck that he rejoined the cattle trucks before they were shunted off again. I never heard him complain or speak ill about the actual Russian population. Perhaps a small insight into Russian distances is the fact that a train journey from Ufa, where he had been kept, to St Petersburg today is said to take two and a half days.

When the trucks finally crossed the border back into Western Germany, a great swell of song had risen from the relieved travellers: '*Großer Gott wir loben Dich…*' ('*Great God we praise thee…*').

Not long after his return that small handmade recipe book was put to good use. Potato balls the size of large fists formed of mashed potatoes and fried in an open pan do not at first glance constitute great culinary feasts, but perhaps they had to get all that enforced fasting out of their system. My father had invited a comrade from his time as a prisoner of Russia and the two sat on our simple *chaise lounge* at table, demolishing about six or seven potato balls each. It seemed an impossible task. The sofa agreed, suddenly splintering and breaking in the middle.

Of the years out in the Ural in ice and snow and endless forests, we learnt very little. It was not his style to dwell on the past, nor did telling of his experiences come easy to him. He began to write down his memories once later in life, but stopped again after two or three pages. Why did I not encourage him?

The now and the future were more important. If only I had been more astute and asked more questions or offered to write it, but at that stage, I myself had not taken up the pen and put thoughts to paper seriously.

Very occasionally, a story would come back to haunt him. He had become a prisoner with a wounded knee. As despatch rider on the Eastern Front in the vastness that is Russia and where roads were poor and petrol scarce, he had suffered a fall from his horse, resulting in a wound that would not heal with the lack of medication. Urine was the means of cleansing wounds and maggots were positively encouraged to invade open infections—they kept the wounds clean and free from puss.

There had been no barbed-wire fences about their confinement camps as there was no need: who would survive an escape across that distance? They had been employed in the felling of trees, being marched out in the mornings and herded back in the evenings. If someone fell by the wayside, it was too bad. With his bad knee and general weakness, my father had collapsed on the way back one evening. There he would have stayed had it not been for comrades who had carried him back to barracks where he recovered. There was great camaraderie among the survivors.

One of my father's best friends had the misfortune to find himself behind the Iron Curtain when he finally returned to his family. For many years, my parents sent food parcels and clothes to East Germany, especially at Christmas time. Even their letters were censored. On few occasions, my parents arranged meetings of sorts by dropping hints in letters. The 'meetings' of course could only take place with the hideous wired and mined 'wall'—the Iron Curtain—between them and only a furtive wave of hands when there was no border police about had to suffice by way of communication across the divide, at least from the other side. It was not until the East German couple were past retirement age that they got permission to travel to the west and visit.

Prisoner of War, 1944–1948

Russians call it the Great Patriotic War—1941 to 1945. The Soviet Union lost some 26.6 million men and women in total. The date of German surrender was 9 May 1945, and it is now a national holiday (Victory Day)—the day of a grand military parade in Red Square, Moscow.

The city of Ufa in the Ural Mountains of the Republic of Bashkortostan is today described as one of the largest towns in Russia—an economic, cultural, sports, religious, and scientific centre and an important transport hub—located about 1,340 km south-east of Moscow. There are three military burial places of prisoners of war in or about the city (officially, 635 burials, and according to the archives of the Ministry of Internal Affairs, names, military ranks, nationality, year of birth, and date of death of all prisoners of war who died between 1945 and 1948 in Ufa are known). 'Germans, Poles, Czechs, Latvians, Japanese, Austrians, Magyars (Hungarians), and Romanians died in the camps of the Ministry of Internal Affairs, special hospitals and workers' battalions in the city of Ufa'.

Prisoners had begun to arrive in the winter of 1942, but at the fall of Stalingrad in February 1943 alone, some 94,000 survivors were captured.

Dmitry Kolpakov wrote on the occasion of '70 years of Victory' in 2015. Interviews with people who somehow had been involved with the prisoners give various insights, but it is clear that there was no great communication between them and locals. 'They called us gay beggars'—which probably would be better translated as 'happy beggars'—remembered an informant, likely when prisoners compared the locals to the standards they were used to from home.

Prisoners of war in Russia had little contact with the population. They worked in factories and built houses and later tried to shut out the memories by not talking about it.

According to witnesses, the rank system of hierarchy prevailed, among German prisoners at least. According to an official statement, officers had separate rooms with beds, while 'rank and file [ordinary ranks] slept on two-story bunks', most still wearing uniforms without insignia, '... until their officer confirms, they will not do anything'.

One interviewee recalled: '... they did not celebrate Victory Day with us'. When asked if there were ideological fascists, the answer was 'Probably among the officers were. But we did not care. And their ordinary soldiers did not have any politics at all'. 'I remember if they had a holiday, someone brought an accordion, sang, danced'. It would seem that kind of diversity from boredom and homesickness has been the lot of prisoners of many wars and many ages.

Local historian Margarita Ageeva mentioned in her memoirs the winter of 1943, when for the first time prisoners were taken along the streets under escort:

> ... prisoners were taken to work, they built houses at the intersection of Lenin and Stalin streets. A grey mass of people walked along the road, they were guarded by soldiers with rifles and dogs. People ran to see with shouts: 'The Germans are leading! [being led?]. The prisoners are dirty, hungry, thin'. They threw stones at them, and others, including my older sisters, and they were 11–12 years old, seized the moment and piled pieces of bread and potatoes to the prisoners. The Germans, in response, waved their lowered heads and smiled with the lip [edges?] of their lips.

Some of the German prisoners built new houses. Apparently, prisoners were collected from camps by entrepreneurs or officials who applied to and paid the camp commandant. It was 'purely business'. The largest employer of prisoners was a plywood mill, where high-strength aviation plywood was produced; in Russian references, it is recorded as 'veneer'. There prisoners worked according to qualification and skills, with engineers being especially valued.

When asked did they lose people, the delicate answer was '... on the "veneer" about five hundred people. But if you count Sotsgorod, 21st trust, "Dubitele", Kirzavod, BNZS and others ... [overall from the various camps]—thousands'. This wood mill must have been where my father was employed, felling the trees, where they were marched to work into the forests and back in the evenings.

It was not only the prisoners who suffered privations and hunger: '600 grams of bread they were given per day. And on the "veneer" they rolled logs—hard work. In 1946 food was worse than in the war—there was absolutely nothing to eat. In August 1946, an endless rain began, falling into snow in autumn, and the harvest was lost. The year was lousy, first of all it affected the Germans'.

Perhaps it is not surprising that my father never complained about the people of Russia—they were poor themselves. This was the time under extreme Communist edict of communes where amounts of seeds or seed potatoes had to be planted, tended, and harvested communally by each village. The Bolshevik Party had seized power in November 1917 and abolished private ownership of land. Industry, too, was gradually nationalised in a utopian dream that does not allow for human nature. Leader Nikita Khrushchev mentioned the failure of communes in 1959: '... everyone wanted to live well and yet work as little as possible for the common good.'

Numbers of German prisoners in the Soviet Union vary. According to Soviet sources there were 2,389,560, German statistics mention over a million more: 3,486,000. They had to work 'to re-build what they had destroyed.' Molotov had coined the now historical phrase that 'no German prisoner will return to his homeland until the restoration of Stalingrad'. In spite of being forced labour, among the Russian people, they seem to have gained a good reputation. One commentator mentioned that the Germans did not know the meaning of the word 'hack-work'. German labour discipline became a household name and even gave birth to a peculiar meme: 'Of course, it's the Germans who built it'.

Sister Marianne's first Communion on 24 April 1949. A photograph taken with the fire-tempered Agfa box camera as the family returned from the service. On the right walk my mother and Aunt Anna in new hats, and my father no doubt under a borrowed hat called a '*Zylinder*'.

37

A New House

Today, we have helpful insights for post-traumatic stress disorder, but immediately following the two great wars, there was no help, survivors just had to cope. German survivors had lost a war that was not of their doing or choice, but they were the losers, they were guilty. The Reich that was meant to last a 'thousand years' had been terminated prematurely and whichever side you were born on was your bad luck. You had lost. Whatever they had witnessed, whatever they had experienced, whatever they had done or been ordered to do, they would have to cope with the memories.

My father-in-law from an English family had been part of the Somerset Light Infantry, and as a young man, he had been sent to Bengal, Turkey, and Palestine by people who dreamt of grandeur and business. Theirs had been a company of neighbours; young people from the same locality would look after each other and fight better together than assorted strangers.

Afterwards, many had migrated to the valleys of South Wales when there was work to be found in the coalmines. My father-in-law was a weak man when I knew him, not especially venerated by his sturdy sons. When I asked for the hand of his daughter, he preferred me to ask her mother. Later I learnt of his military history: his best friend, a neighbour whose family lived just at the end of the road, had died in his arms somewhere in some faraway land. I never found out the exact circumstances, but he had not been able to walk that short distance and tell his friend's family about it, even after so many years.

My father coped similarly by shutting out the past, but he concentrated on the future. Action was the way forward. It did not take him long to pick up on his former business. There was plenty of work still from war damage on roofs neglected for years that needed urgent repairs, and a new apprentice joined the family. At thirteen, I still had several school years ahead of me, but there was really no excuse for me not to help out and get accustomed to the life that was mapped out for me as eldest and only son.

My school reports were pretty good, though that was not a first requirement to get a roofing business off the ground. That demanded hard work and commitment. I do believe my father was impressed all the same—I was top of my class—it might even be good for business. That make or break experience with the fever injection seemed to generally have improved my health and reduced my frequent bouts of asthma.

Unfortunately, I had taken up friendship with the goat herders at the western end of the village, some of whom went to my class in school. After school, they were in charge of the family goats that provided milk and maybe cheese for people who had houses and stables but lacked their own land. The waysides were lush and plentiful, but it meant the goats had to be watched and moved on to new parts, though tethering was possible within reason. It meant those boys led quite an outdoor life, but also that they were never short of mischief.

I hate to remember the time I came home with my short corduroy trousers caked with the drying poo of cows that left any material cloth odour rich and rigid. Heifers, almost grown cows before they were old enough for their first calves, were lively beasts, strong and fleet if necessary, so sneaking up on them, grabbing a tail, and hanging on when they took off became a dare that meant he who could hang on the longest was the winner. Heifers were powerful runners when spooked.

It was after returning from one such outing that my father took me to task in the evening.

'Where have you been?'

'Out, with friends.'

'I said we were working at the new school.' He named a new building outside the village.

'Yes,' I said, perhaps not totally oblivious of where this conversation was leading.

'I said we were going to work there.' He gave special emphasis to the 'we'.

'Yes, I thought you meant you and your apprentice.'

'I meant "we", and that includes you.'

He sat down on a chair, pulled me towards him, and bent me across his knees, then preceded to give my behind a few half-hearted slaps. It did not hurt, but I left the room. I was ashamed. I had never given any thought to his experiences the many years he had been away or how without help he was rebuilding his business. He was a master roofer, which meant he was qualified to take on and teach apprentices, though for that I was still too young. Maybe I simply was not used to take instructions, other than what passed in school.

I did go to work with him, joining them after school, carrying slates up ladders, walking across structural beams at height, whatever could be expected of an untrained boy. We were putting a roof on a brand-new building, a new school for children in a catchment area well outside the village from where previously all children had to walk, cycle, or be brought from miles around. Times were improving, but only by hard work and application.

My father shaping the rough slate into the traditional roof-shape, *c.* 1960.

Looking down from the roof beams, we spotted a rabbit running hither and thither in a meadow below as if drunk, not at great speed, but obviously there was something amiss.

'Go and fetch it,' my father tried to encourage me. 'Might be good for the pot.'

I hesitated, only to watch a car stop by the roadside, two fellows entering the meadow, catching the rabbit without great difficulty, killing it with a blunt stick and taking it back to their car. My father looked at me with disappointment.

'Myxomatosis,' I said, 'there has to be something wrong with it. Would you want to eat it?' He did not argue the point.

Uncle Jupp's sad statement, his Last Will and Testament in a letter from the Eastern Front, was acknowledged and accepted as genuine and lawful by the siblings, and Uncle Emil and Aunt Minna built their bungalow on the actual foundations of the old burnt-out house.

Aunt Anna and her new husband Franz adopted Uncle August, the bachelor who now owned the estate. Uncle August began to have problems mentally and he would never marry. Together they decided to build at the top of my grandparents' plot a little nearer to fields and forest in the traditional style, still allowing for pigs and cattle and a large traditional barn door for the passage of laden wagons. A row of sturdy oaks along the eastern boundary of the property fell to the axe and saw in support of the building.

It was up to my father to choose a building plot. He enclosed a slice above what was now Aunt Minna's home and started planning our own house. The first casualty became the knotty and melancholy growth of the arbour and its moss-covered green bench seat. A temporary shed to house new equipment and materials needed for the roofing business took its place.

I drew up a dream house with an open fireplace in a large central room, off which most other rooms led, a kind of atrium, but without the opening in the roof allowing for daylight. I do not think I had considered the lack of light when another floor would be added, and anyway, the style of houses with the apex roof space above it made such a salubrious layout impossible. However, it was the idea my father took to a local architect who produced the blueprint. My central room became a small hall, off which six doors led to various rooms and an entrance space with a staircase up from the basement and again up to a separate upstairs flat. Another flight of stairs led to the roof space and mindful of the past and self-sufficiency the then still very useful flame-tight smoking or curing room for hams and sausages. At ground floor were spaces for a workshop, pigsties and cellars, and later, a shower room for the work force.

One of the more genial traditions of the village was neighbourly help. When a new house was built, digging foundations was one task freely undertaken by able-bodied men from the neighbourhood—cases of bottled beer being payment in kind.

Täubchen—or the Embarrassing Brickmaking Episode

I had to be useful for something. There were shortages of everything, so my father hit on the idea of manufacturing our own roof tiles. With so much destruction everywhere, there was and would be a great demand for roof covering. A cheaper alternative to the labour intensive traditional slate roofs was required. Slate was trimmed individually by hand mainly during the long cold winter months when roofs were covered by snow. Not only that, slates were cut depending on the size of the raw material. Delivered from quarries sliced in its irregular sharp-edged state, slate was extremely rough on hands. Unlike the British system of rectangular shapes, all of the same size, the slates were trimmed by hand to a special pattern with the very specialised roofer's hammer on a curved iron T-edge. The result would facilitate the easy drainage of the roof.

Those hand trimmed slates then had to be graded against a measuring device. Roofs would sport the largest stones at their lower edges and gradually the size of the slates would reduce towards the upper edge and the ridge. It is work of great pride and craftsmanship, but all I ever managed was grading the trimmed slates.

Simply hanging tiles would be a faster and cheaper alternative. A shed was hired or borrowed from a farmer right in the centre of the village, next to the looming Tuckelsburg, an experienced man was hired in the nearby town who would come up every morning, prepare the mixture of sand, cement, etc., and via a simple machine press the mix into forms that would dry and harden in the sun and air. I should have learnt eventually, but to begin with, it fell to me to take over from the workman at the end of his shift and after school to shovel any leftover mixture into simple wooden frames to be air-hardened into bricks as a by-product.

It was during just such activity that I was quite uncomfortably interrupted by the appearance of a young lady only slightly younger than I, but obviously far in advance at mental and physical development, as females at that age tend to be. She lived in a large house that stood slightly uphill within sight across the yard and a meadow. It was the building of the new *Genossenschaft*, the farmer's collective, where seed corn and seed potatoes and such were available. Later it housed the first bank in the village.

To me, the fair maiden's appearance, carrying large buckets with little water, was rather unexpected. She was preparing to bathe, she confided, but at her home there was not enough water pressure to fill a bath, so she had to collect from lower down in the village before heating.

It was true that there was often a water shortage in dry summers before the village invested into a larger underground reservoir collecting from a natural spring in the hills to the south that would especially improve supply on higher parts of the village. I was totally out of my depth, blustering, stuttering, and mumbling.

Never for a moment did it occur to me that somebody might actually be interested in me and she most probably was not, but that did not mean she might not relish my awkwardness. Older fellows had named her '*Täubchen*'—turtle dove. The statuesque minx, soon to be probably the most coveted beauty in the village, totally upset my equilibrium.

Thoughts like stopping what I was doing that was of no great intellectual worth anyway and as any good knight errant of old would have done, offering to carry the slopping pails for the struggling maiden to wherever that led, crossed my mind in fast confusion. Another little voice warned me of making a fool of myself when other villagers would hear of it and arrive at the wrong conclusion. Or maybe the right one? Then again, the maid in question was of a most alluring and mysterious kind, and at that age, circumspection is not always foremost in a boy's mind.

By the time I calmed down, she had left and was on her way across land I did not even know had a footpath. How else would she have crossed the wires and fences? My agony was rekindled and stirred again later when she waved from a small upstairs window and without suitable binoculars I could never be certain of her state of dress or undress. I consoled myself with the thought that I had been saved from making a fool of myself.

The tile making and with that the brick making did not last. The small labour-intensive output, once the general economy in the country picked up again, made the effort uneconomical.

My few bricks were used, not where I could point them out with a creator's pride, but in inferior interior walls in the cellars when my father built the house that is still home to my sister.

In theory, I did have a girlfriend by then—literally the girl next door from our wartime dwelling, whose house, like ours, had fallen prey to the phosphor shelling. The fact that I was disturbed by the brazen passer-by speaks for the unexciting attitude I had towards this convenient liaison. Our parents became friends and seemed to approve of our friendship, though we were not really suited. Probably it was the convenience of proximity that had pushed us together.

Primitive desires were totally thwarted by the ingenuity of seamstresses. Daughters remained virginal by the simple parental device of a surfeit of buttons, neck to hem, that frustrated an ardent admirer's tryst at closeness and protected virginity like a medieval chastity belt. Boasting and posturing by some older self-proclaimed stallions only added to the dreaded fear of what could lead up to pregnancy.

That lack of love and excitement eventually became apparent and it was the girl, though younger, who sensed and distanced herself, thus saving me from a greater embarrassment later. Her more grown-up insight freed me to pursue my own path and live life the way it should be lived without early pressure.

It was not until I met a beautiful Myfanwy in the Welsh valleys many years later that the miracle of love finally caught up with me.

Country Ways

Later, the jovial, yodelling, and storytelling joker Uncle August, stalwart member of the male voice choir, had a breakdown, shunned women, and became somewhat of a recluse. Perhaps his mental problems had begun when the first, and to my knowledge only, serious feud arose between the siblings. Aunt Anna and Uncle Franz had decided that my father's plot for our house was a little too generous. He had taken too large a slice of land in their opinion, enough for a house and a large roofers' storage shed as well as a small garden.

Pushing Uncle August forward as the new owner, they did not confront my father directly in a civilised manner, instead they shouted across the meadow from their building site some distance away. All the exchanges were held in the vernacular, of course.

Perhaps the space between had already been divided into more saleable building plots, but the complaint was that not enough space was left for that. At one time, physical threats supported by a waved axe were shouted, though nobody actually ventured away from their premises in person. All passers-by would do was grin and perhaps offer to suggest other implements for a good skirmish.

Keeping in the background at the time, I found the animosity embarrassing and I did not get involved. My mother tried to keep peace between the two sides and eventually the feud was resolved when my father changed the angle of his enclosure a few feet at the back. At the front, the house could not be moved.

Aunt Theresa, who already had her house in another village with Uncle Engelbert, never received a building plot or the equivalent thereof.

Such public displays of animosity were rare in the village, though not unheard off. When on a neighbouring farm a young wife joined the household, the woman who had led that household previously had no intention of stepping down or aside. She might have been an older sister to the groom or an aunt, but the demonstrations of her standing up for her rights could on occasion become very vocal and public when she chased the new arrival cursing about house and yard, around and around, a ladle or some other household implement raised in her fist. Her not especially lithe quarry would take it in sensible good humour, shouting to passing witnesses that she had 'honey in her bottom' as the reason for the pursuit.

Little more than a year had passed since my father's return from the deprivations of the Ural Mountains, when the house was almost ready for occupation. One morning after breakfast, he pushed back his chair and beckoned to me: 'Come on, today we're moving house'. With that, he lifted his end of the breakfast table. I could but respond and lift the other side, laughing. My mother hastened to clear the dishes first, collecting and securing what she could—he was in too much of a hurry. We manhandled the table through the door to the top of the stairs while my mother and little sister still grabbed cups and dishes to save breakages. It was only a short walk to the new house and the rest of the move was accomplished in similar self-help fashion. There was not much to move anyway.

Traditions and customs prevailed. Here a '*Brautwagen*' (a bride's wagon) has been waylaid in one of the outlying hamlets by stringing a rope across the road. Transporting the bride's things to her new home was a reason for rejoicing, especially between farming families. Only a few glasses of schnapps would buy free passage, *c.* 1934.

Above and below: A bride's wagon right in the village, *c.* 1953–54, when the daughter of a farmer was to marry the eldest son of a farmer-publican. A bedstead on the wagon and a cow tied on behind were traditional ingredients for such a public journey.

Wedding of my sister Marianne and Alfons Rettler in the village church, 15 May 1964.

My father's first car was a three-wheeler lorry. In winter, when wheels compressed the snow on uncleared roads to two rills, leaving a high ridge between them, a three-wheeler became especially troublesome, when the single front wheel had to career about that improbable spine of snow, even worse so on cold frozen mornings. We still had large amounts of snow in those winters. Another problem became the hooks at the rear to either side of the loading space that released the backboard like iron fingers sticking out sideways.

With most vehicles driving slowly, especially laden ones, and little traffic anyway, it had become an often seen practice for cyclists to hang on to the sides at the rear of lorries on uphill stretches with one hand while manoeuvring the handlebars with the other. I can vouch for the dangerous exercise, having been guilty myself in later years. My father abandoned the three-wheeled lorry for a larger less dangerous four-wheeled one when somebody sued him, having been caught by one of those outward reaching levers and tearing a limb. Had he been hanging on for him to have been in such close contact?

Maybe my father had a lightweight motorcycle as well, for I remember a warning from our good-natured village policeman that if I was seen again driving without the necessary training and papers, he would be forced to take action.

Winters were harsher then. I managed to acquire a well-worn pair of skis—from where I know not—but treated with beeswax and lashed to our sturdy hobnailed boots, they were still able to afford limited exercises on the picturesque slopes. Alas, as the landscape was mostly divided into fields and meadows by small landowners, there were barbed-wire fences to beware of on what otherwise might have been fine downhill runs. My favourite way of making the best of those winters were long treks across country on back roads, lanes, and on forest tracks.

In March 1949, I made a note in my diary: 'Bone doctor in the morning, ski in the afternoon'. I had dislocated a joint, possibly an arm, and my father decided the traditional ways would be best and teach me a lesson in the process. Roofers, apart from trimming slate under a protective awning, would have to wait for thaw to be able to work on roofs again. He drove me to an isolated farm where he knew a certain countryman to be working. We found the labourer with a wide reputation for traditional healing. Earning extra money while in a farmer's employ would have been frowned upon, so he made certain we could not be seen behind a farm building before he felt about the affected joint with practiced fingers, then a sudden pull and twist and the bone was back in place. It must have been a successful cure for me to be back on skis by the afternoon.

Parish workers spread grit on a slippery road. To the left the old vicarage where Aunt Minna lived in the upstairs flat and in front the rails by the roadside guard the old fireman's pond where GIs went fishing for souvenirs.

Winter could mean problematic travelling for outlying hamlets.

A new priest must have hankered after the past as by the 1950–60s, the clock seems to have been turned backwards when first communicants were dressed like old men and the girls like Victorian ladies? Here they are photographed by the chapel at Sägemühle.

St Martin's Day, 11 November 1952, and the children are celebrating with lanterns and there is even a bishop on a horse. The Roman soldier who became St Martin famously shared his cloak with a poor man.

Farming used to be labour-intensive before mechanisation. This happy group are about to encourage yield by spreading artificial fertilizer, mid-1950s.

Harvest time kept people busy. Potato pickers at a local farm, mid-1950s.

A harrowing experience. The rough ploughed fields had to be smoothed again for new seed.

The farm of Kotthoff, Vellinghausen. A pride in horses, though their decline was inevitable.

Tractors would soon replace the strong and patient horses.

With the war-ravaged inn, now 'Landhotel Donner', as a backdrop and the *Wirtschaftswunder* bringing progress, the priest is no longer blessing horses, he is blessing tractors.

In this year, the tractors were blessed near the church and war memorial in front of the old school, attended by a large congregation and with the *Musikkapelle* in attendance.

The man who collected the milk urns and returned them empty.

38

No Fun in Wartime:
Schützenfest Restarted in 1948

More than a hundred villagers of the parish of Remblinghausen had got together to found a '*Schützengesellschaft*', a company of marksmen, a kind of rifle club or shooters' guild with conviviality in mind. The notion of banding together to protect the village would have been an old folk memory, a tradition from the Middle Ages to be rekindled, though with less serious intentions. A plot of land was secured, a hall was erected, and on 5 June 1920, the first '*Schützenfest*', literally translated as 'Marksmen's Festival', was celebrated. My grandfather, Adam Schütteler, was member No. 19. Music was provided by the village's own music band that had been founded as early as 1914 and led by author, poet, verger, and musician Jost Hennecke. That festive occasion became the highlight of the summer seasons until 1939, when such frivolities had to stop. The men would be taught to shoot with a purpose and the main hall was reserved for sports and party events like Hitler Youth rallies. An annex became a barracks for Polish prisoners of war.

After all the upheavals and destruction, life was beginning to reassert itself. A heavy weight was lifted from the psyche of local people. Fun was long overdue, and while some were still in mourning or living with the uncertainty of missing loved ones, eventually the spirit rekindled, not least among the young.

Following the Second World War, permission was sought from the military authorities to re-found the group *St Jakobus Schützenbruderschaft*, a brotherhood of marksmen under St Jacob, the village's patron saint. Guns were not allowed so soon after the end of hostilities; still, without shooting, it would not be a shooter's fest and tradition had to be upheld or at least rekindled. In 1948, the *Schützenfest* was re-inaugurated. A tall slim tree trunk like a telegraph pole was erected with a spread eagle baked with reinforced dough at the top and a clown puppet similarly, so they would break up and allow winners to be chosen. The clown would be placed lower and was easier to hit.

Probably the first Schützenfest march down the main street, following the policeman and the *Musikkapelle* on 5 June 1920. The horse was called 'Blitz'.

The Schützenfest Committee, and in the centre, the man who would be 'King' for a year in 1926. More stars and medals would be added every year until the chain of office became unmanageable.

The committee and winner of the crown, *c.* 1929

The antidote to the formal winner of the shooting contest, the *Geck* (Fool? Joker? Dandy?) is a fun character of the festivities, here with entourage in the 1920s.

Right: Schützenfest, 1933. Following the band through the village. To the extreme left is a glimpse of the house of my birth.

Below: Firing at an improvised bird. Great interest for spectators.

Committee and 'King' in 1938. The following year, such frivolities as Schützenfest would be banned. Uncle Emil is seated second from left.

After the war, the brotherhood reformed. Even children had their own Schützenfest, 1948–9, dressed as their grandparents. It is as if we tried to get back to earlier, happier times.

Guns were forbidden after the war, so the Schützenfest had to resort to crossbows (1950).

Committee and 'King' in 1953. A new freedom and joviality seem to have broken out.

Above: They have got their man, though the new '*Schützenkönig*' seems perplexed at the honour. Still, there is a gun pointing at his back, 1955. A rare picture with my father looking in third from left at the back.

Left: When Bacchus reigns, forget health and safety.

Crossbows and bolts were allowed, so it was back to the past. I do not know where they were found or if they were specially made for the occasion, but everyone agreed that crossbows provided not nearly the fun without the ear-splitting bangs. Nor had the crossbow bolts the power of rifle shots and the eagle had to be lowered, vandalised, and have bolts removed before it would allow itself to break up and provide a winner to be accorded kingship for a year.

The *Geck* or clown—today he is called a *Vizekönig* or viceroy—had to be lowered as well to allow the crossbows to do their damage (the British once rather successful tradition of the longbow might have been a better choice, but the lack of safety precautions when unaccustomed inebriates handle a longbow might have presented a serious problem).

Of course, at that first post-war almost spontaneous occasion, there was no brass and no dance band, little or no sustenance except the liquid variety and that would have been of rather limited choice. Yet the elation alone of having passed through fire and survived was almost enough to suffice. The damaged hall had been provisionally repaired, though even the damaged version would hardly have impeded the atmosphere. All I remember is the motley march up to the hall and following it a little ways, but the evening for all its shortcomings apparently had its entertainment value in its very deprivation, especially afterwards when it faded into folklore as the night of the Cuckoo Waltz.

The only musical entertainment available was a lady with an accordion and a repertoire of maybe three tunes, of which the Cuckoo Waltz was the most suitable to be danced to, but it did not matter. Again and again that night, the dance had been a waltz. However deprived people may have been, such dearth of choice hardly dampened the enjoyment. It is perhaps understandable that in future years that particular tune, if played at all, elicited a smile on many of the populace, even those who had missed that memorable evening.

Later, when guns were allowed again, it might be a problem to find a winner when such prowess could not be afforded by everyone, as the accompanying expenses would mount up. Then volleys would have to be introduced to help a reluctant underachiever, or somebody who lacked accuracy due to early inebriation.

Before the wartime authorities forbade such festivities, the jubilant celebrations of honouring the new '*König*' had been such that, on one occasion, at least the attending musical band marched all the way into the village to deliver the new celebrity to his home with suitable pomp and decorum, when it was realised that the actual person of the new king was still happily loitering by the base of the tall shooter's pole. They had to march back and repeat the whole process in the spirit, if not under the influence of Bacchus.

Of course, both 'King' and 'Viceroy' retain their positions for a year until the Saturday of the following year's festivities, after which new incumbents shoot to the fore.

The past can never be fully recreated. Before the war, Uncle Emil had run a successful stall at the *Schützenfest*, setting up targets in a booth for shooting practice

Schützenfest 1969, when a neighbour became King. Middle row, third and fourth from left, my father and mother. Adherents of the Geck or Viceroy are fans of the Remblinghausen football eleven.

In 1973–74, my sister and brother-in-law were queen and king for a year. Here at the start of the royal progress. My father hidden, my shy mother laughing in her embarrassment. The King's Chain of Office is lengthening again.

The village fire brigade, *c.* 1928. Seated in front two publicans well apart on either end of the bench.

March of the fire brigade, 1920–30s.

A *Musikkapelle* or brass band was formed in 1914 under the guidance and leadership of local sage Jost Hennecke (standing centre back with straw hat), *c.* 1930.

with cheap prizes of paper rosettes, flimsy paper dollies, paper flowers, windmills on sticks, etc. Nostalgia decreed that custom should be brought back, and at a future occasion, Uncle Emil was persuaded to manage it again. Uncle Emil was no longer the jovial young entrepreneur and the attempt was a flop. People simply had advanced beyond such cheap and jolly frippery.

Today, the brotherhood counts in excess of 600 members, by far the largest organisation in a village that has become known for the surfeit of clubs and societies it supports. All kinds of other village festivities share and fill its hall's ample space throughout the year.

The fire brigade was founded in 1924, though as early as 1884, firefighting equipment and ponds are mentioned in village records, quite understandably as fire was one of the likeliest destroyers of property while open lights and candles were used in such fire-prone surroundings.

The village music band—*Musikkapelle*—had its most dynamic time from 1918 until 1939 when all festivities and processions were forbidden—music had been too involved with religious celebrations. Only at funerals of uniformed personnel and at war memorial services was music allowed, but it was decreed that on leaving such events, lively marches had to be played. A new band was inaugurated in 1981.

Most of the males of the village must have turned up for this later group photo. Jost Hennecke still takes prime position standing centrally behind the big drum.

MGV 1926 (male voice choir, founded 1926) in an early group photo out in a natural setting. Relaxing in front (second from right) is Uncle August. Standing front row, third from left is choirmaster *Lehrer* Kortenkamp (in glasses). Third from right is a flamboyant *Lehrer* Bolte. Back row, second from left is Jost Hennecke.

MGV 1926 on an outing in 1954. Front row, third from left, is the author. Squatting, second row, first from left, is Uncle August. Standing back from left are Mr and Mrs Kortenkamp.

A church choir had existed after a fashion since 1900, but in 1926, a male voice choir was founded and teacher Kortenkamp became its able and long-time director. Even the author exercised his tuneless bass voice while living in the village. Today, the male voice choir is complemented by a ladies' choir and a plethora of other groups.

As *Lehrer* Kortenkamp's favourite subject was music, on special occasions, people would gather from far and wide to attend his organ recitals.

Founded in 1920, FC (Football Club) Remblinghausen is still today a pride of the locality. The club's emblem is a wild boar, and they have carried the title '*Wildsau Elf*' (Wild Boar Eleven) with pride ever since in 1951 a local businessman challenged and managed to entice players of the then runner-ups in the German Football League, Preußen Münster, to come to the village for a friendly match. Payment would be a feast of wild boar. Frantic activities ensued about the parish and its eighteen chapelries to trap and catch one of the creatures that still roam freely on the heights and in the forests of the Sauerland. The Prussians came and played, and in the last minutes, the organisers were successful. Footballers feasted on wild roast and the village team had a new nickname.

Mr Kortenkamp was organist from 1923 to 1971. A fine artist on a fine organ, he would draw audiences to concerts from a wide area to listen to compositions by the likes of Johann Sebastian Bach or the more recent celebrated Max Reger.

Remblinghausen's Football Club, *c.* 1920–21, included two uncles—middle left is Johannes and bottom right is August Schütteler.

Above: When grandfathers and great-grandfathers played for the village.

Left: Announcing friendly matches in the village in 1952, when the team was known as the Wild Boar Eleven. Poster typesetting/typography by the author.

Above: *Kameradschaftlicher Verein Remblinghausen* (the Veterans' Society), founded 1900. Today, the society is largely active in charitable work.

Right: More traditional customs. When a niece married a carpenter in October 1988, members of his guild in their traditional costumes attended outside the church to put the newly wed pair through various tests.

Left: Preparing for a lifetime of hard labour, but all in good fun.

Below: Young folk tried to rekindle old customs.

39

Belated Facts of Life

In a village permeated by animal husbandry, the physical side of procreation, at least as far as beasts/livestock were concerned, was part of daily life. Cockerels and chickens went about their natural ways and dogs cared little about human presence. At one time, there lived a large hound somewhere in the village; he would start his daily routine by visiting a rather small bitch on a farm in the neighbourhood. As soon as the natural, if somewhat comical transaction had been concluded, he would disappear again until the following morning.

Horses' genes, at least during the war, were passed on by their own specially prized representatives from Wallachia. Bulls in fields fulfilled their function in full view, while cows on occasion attempted to mount their sisters in a kind of harmless, maybe frustrated behaviour. Young bullocks, if they mingled with calves or heifers until they were old enough for market, would be allocated the indignity of a sacking tied about their middle and held in place by string knotted on their backs in the style of aprons as barriers to physically prevent them from passing on their untried genes.

As many households—'*die kleinen Leute*' ('the little people')—kept cows, often by tradition in the same building as humans, the question of regeneration had to be solved by leading their mobile milk supplies to a nearby farm for insemination. On the farm across the road from *Oma*'s plot and later from our house resided a rather good-looking and handsome young bullock that was coming into his prime. This was at a time when house cows went out of favour and it may well have been one of the last ones left at a neighbour's home.

When her time came, the poor old bovine was led to the farm by a boy only slightly older than myself. The farmyard had by then been newly cobbled in the pristine modern fashion, and of course, the possible by-products of any bovine meeting or even passing would be undesirably close to the house. The actual meeting took place near the road. In passing, I stopped to help should the need arise.

The young bull was eager enough, in an almost belligerent kind of way, rippling with muscles and testosterone as he was led out. The cow had been through this ordeal on many a previous occasion and behaved more like a docile sufferer, preferring to walk away given a chance, bored and just waiting to return to her straw to continue her mastication. She was certainly no eager lover.

Unfortunately, it had been raining and cobblestones can be rather slippery in such circumstances. Added to that the inexperience of the Romeo, the union seemed to be doomed to failure, when school friend Karl handed the reins of the cow over to a third person while he took it upon himself to give nature a guiding hand.

The bull, in his clumsy eagerness, remained an unguided missile, even with help, as his hind legs slipped and slithered on the wet cobbles. Unfortunately, Karl, in his heroic attempt, instead became the recipient of that generous encouragement of life, or rather his trousers did, before he could take evasive action. Bulls simply are not designed to walk upright. The unimpressed cow moved forward out of harm's way. At the time, it seemed rather comical, such a powerful apprentice suitor's expression, sitting back on his haunches deflated, squatting on glistening cobbles in extreme bewilderment.

Where there are milk goats, there is the opportunity of business by providing the services of a male goat. Several plot-land-style provisional buildings sprang up in the area of the goat-herders. One of them was occupied by the family of the unfortunate school companion who had suffered the exploding hand grenade. Besides offering the services of the male goat, his father collected the unenviable reputation of forsaking his religion and taking up the staff and mitre of bishop in some new unfathomable sect. Still people had to flock to him with their goats. The two vocations may seem strange bedfellows, for even the relatively poorly functioning human nose could not fail to detect the testosterone charged aroma of the billy-goat's ambience from an unfair distance. In the village the owner was known simply as 'the Bishop'.

During the latter school years, it was felt that some sort of sex education was warranted to set us on the right path in life. It was a large mixed group of pupils both older and younger than my class and the sensitive and delicate subject fell to the naturally kind and gentle *Lehrer* Kortenkamp to instruct us in the facts of life and procreation long after such subjects had been discussed, hinted at, joked about, and occasionally experimented with. That is not to say that some 'strange facts' circulated at times.

Our interest centred not so much on the subject as on the way the teacher would approach it. A straightforward and to the point explanation might have been helpful, but nobody expected anything like that. Burning questions that were on many pupils' minds were not likely to be resolved and nobody would have dared to ask. The subject was simply taboo. Sex was a closed door.

By nature, that teacher was no disciplinarian and on this subject happened to be more shy and tongue-tied than many of his pupils as he looked over his thick horn-rimmed glasses, hoping against hope to wake some semblance of sanity in our wooden-top heads.

Few parents would talk to their children on such matters and theories abounded. It was left to children to whisper sometimes physically impossible wisdoms, opinions, and observations. One young addition to a large family insisted that women possessed just one central breast as he had observed when he had accidentally surprised a sister at her washtub. Of course he could cite precedents like cows and goats. There were also the braggarts who claimed to speak with experience, yet got things crucially wrong. Fear of the results of sexual activity kept the girls virginal and the boys nervous.

The teacher began by asking what we thought awaited us in the big wide world out there? Subsequent conversations developed something like this: 'Now don't act the innocent with me. It's all perfectly natural'. The teacher, taking heart, had obviously decided to boldly approach the subject: 'Don't be so backward. Try a little harder. Come now'. He could also be sarcastic at times. 'There's nobody tries as hard as our gamekeeper,' offered the shock-haired Werner. Everyone knew he had been spoilt on his father's large farm as the youngest of the family. Then he added wistfully, almost secretively: 'I've seen him'.

'Oh, what have you seen?' encouraged the teacher. At last the subject seemed to get some reaction. 'What's with the hard man of the woods?'

'Oh, it's not in the woods. His windows are low enough to look in and he was being hard with the maid.'

'You mean you have been snooping in other people's windows?'

'It's our house and our windows. And he leaves the curtains open.'

'A hart is a deer, you know, with horns,' suggested Herbert with a bland expression. He never did get good marks for spelling.

'Maybe he is a voyeur?' added little Willi.

'My,' said the teacher, 'that's a big word for someone so small. Where on earth did you learn that?'

'From my brother. He's a sailor, you know—at sea. He goes on voyages. And he says it's hard sometimes, when there is a gale blowing.'

They were deliberately being obtuse, decided the teacher. Just to draw out the agony.

'Her name's Gayle,' said Werner, throwing the hair out of his face with a sharp shake of the head. 'And she blows…'

'Yes, well, I don't think we want to hear about your gamekeeper!' The teacher interrupted before the direction of the lesson could take a turn for the worse. 'You're going to be let loose on an unsuspecting world soon. At least some of you. And women are not fair game. They need to be treated with respect. Blowing kisses is rather forward, but can be fine when there is an understanding between two people.'

'She's not blowing kisses, is our Gayle, she's blowing…'

'That's enough about your gamekeeper. Order in class.' Thick red veins were beginning to appear on the teacher's forehead and temples.

'Why can't we talk about the gamekeeper?' asked Herbert innocently enough. "Gamekeepers knows about those things. And farmers…" Herbert's father was a saddle-maker who worked on farms occasionally, but until now they had not taken the unsuitable Herbert along.

'Thought we were supposed to talk about sex,' mumbled Werner. 'This is boring. I only meant she's blowing hot and cold. All she ever says to me is "get lost".'

The teacher felt he was winning and ignored him. A different approach was needed: 'Long before you were born your parents got married.'

'Not so long before,' coughed Alfred, who had checked up on such things. The teacher ignored him.

'It takes two to create a life, though why anybody would want to bother creating you lot, I cannot understand.'

'They don't have to be married for that,' insisted Werner. 'But it makes you fat. Our maid is getting bigger by the day.' The teacher's face was beginning to redden again. His veins stood out like cords. It was difficult enough without someone constantly lowering the tone.

He had reckoned without the wisdom of Siegfried: 'The Mother of God had an immaculate one. Perception, I mean'. Siegfried was quite pleased with his contribution to the lesson.

'But isn't that part of creation, that things grow?' Herbert seemingly tried to add a note of sophistication. 'It's in the Bible.... The ripeness of pomegranates ... being fruitful?'

The teacher calmed down visibly. 'Herbert,' he said gratefully, though not entirely sure where the wily joker was leading, 'you surprise me. Such wise words from you? But you're right. As the seed grows in the ground, so the baby…'

'I hope not,' said Herbert.

'Pardon?' said the teacher.

'I hope they're not just growing because of a baby.' Theo surreptitiously glanced in the direction of Liselotte, though his look had not gone unnoticed.

'Talk about ripeness.' Siegfried added to the conversation without suppressing his stare. The tension rose again. Most of the male students now looked in the direction of the girl who, somewhat bored and leaning forward with her head between her hands, her elbows resting on her school table, which was really rather too small for her ample person. Dark blond plats covered her ears like earmuffs, ensuring that nothing disturbed her private world. Because of her oblivious attitude, her early development, and the more than usual fullness and tautness of her blouse, she had become a symbol of grown-up-ness, a sort of un-Holy Grail to which many of the male inmates of that room aspired, or at least of which they dreamt before they fell asleep. She on her part was vaguely aware of her effect and would not dream of being seen outside school with any one as young and juvenile as her classmates. A couple of buttons had slipped their buttonholes and her collar stood just slightly apart, nonetheless.

For long moments, everyone sat still, but instead of the expected explosion on behalf of the teacher, his attitude changed. He sighed. He would have to start again with a different approach. The teacher resorted to literature. He spoke about the stories told to us as children, which turn out to be merely fairy tales, examples and fables, traditional characters that we outgrow as we got older and wiser. He obviously had intended to reach out in sober debate, to leave childhood behind via the stories we all knew. The '*Klapperstorch*' (stork), pairs of which could often be found nesting and roosting on disused chimneys, were traditionally the deliverers of babies, flying in with the new additions to surprised families gurgling in white sheets that were carried in their long beaks or were knotted over them, particularly in caricatures and jokes. The mother's stay in bed, which coincided with that time, was explained jovially by the story that the stork had pecked at her leg.

Our teacher obviously hoped to get around to dispelling such notions via the now obsolete St Nicholas and the Christkind (the Christ child) in their present-distributing roles, which inhabited early stages in our development: 'You are almost grown-ups now,' he suggested. 'The world awaits you with bated breath. Well, perhaps. Childish things are left behind. You'll be parents and maybe grandparents in time and your children may sit here in this school.'

We were assembled in the New School. There was silence in class, as the teacher continued: 'Sense and responsibility take the place of childish notions like Knecht Ruprecht, Saint Nikolaus, the Christkind.' It was as far as he got.

Herbert interrupted with a contribution: 'or the *Osterhase*,' he threw in for good measure. The *Osterhase* (Easter hare) came with a willow-weave basket on its back, delivering colourful eggs on Easter morning.

In the silence that followed could be heard the heartrending sob of one of the girls, the younger of two sisters who grew up among a protective clutch of older brothers and sisters on their farm at home. Her sister sat in stunned silence. Their childhood illusions had suddenly and brutally been shattered. No Saint Nicholas? No Christkind? Tears stained the young face in her anguish. The tangible moment when childhood ends is seldom experienced that publicly. Her world had collapsed. The sound of the school bell announcing the end of the lesson had seldom been more appreciated. It was also the end of our sexual enlightenment.

The 'Christkind' had in many families taken on a position of such significance, it had surpassed the biblical story, though the imagery of the baby in the crib and the stable, shepherds, animals and kings were a part of traditional Christmas. The sweet child had evolved into a folk figure distributing largesse. Sentiment as expressed in the 'schmaltzy' carol 'Silent Night' was banned in the village church by our more pragmatic modern Vicar. Many years later, I was still taken aback when at a festivity in a Welsh mining village in the Rhondda Valley, I found myself dancing to that very tune, which had been adapted and jazzed up for the dance floor.

Today, the whole idea has been further degraded into pink-cheeked Father Christmases in their Coca-Cola-red cloaks. A metamorphosis and dilution of the historical famine-busting giver of gifts to poor people, the bishop of Myra (in Turkey), Saint Nicholas has been profitably adopted by commerce.

Job Advice

When I was asked by professional job advisors what I intended to do with my life when I left school, I announced 'Forester'. I wanted to be a gamekeeper/protector out in the open, but I was soon advised that with few such jobs available, I would only stand a chance of employment if my father were also a gamekeeper. Referring to my desire to work outdoors, the official advice was to become a land surveyor.

My head teacher had other ideas. He visited my home to persuade my parents to send me on to university. Without a background or tradition of such studies in my family, even I did not give the notion any serious credence. After all, we had been through and in my father's newly-built house, I would have to earn a living, rather than go studying. My father's stern and frightening sister, Aunt Sofie, sent a no-nonsense message: 'Just don't cost your dad any money!' At the same time I could not see myself as a roofer, either.

As many of the old traditional needs became obsolete, old farmhouses were transformed into modern homes, giving opportunities for artistic expressions as here in Mönekind, winter, 1960s.

40

Wirtschaftswunder

Germany had been divided among the Allies into a Russian zone to the east and an American, a British and two smaller French-occupied areas to the west. We were in the British zone, just, close to the American sector. The Russian zone became the German Democratic Republic in October 1949.

In 1948, my father returned, but it was also the year that the old Reichsmark was replaced by the Deutsche Mark, putting a stop to rampant inflation. West Germany's chancellor was the sharp-faced Konrad Adenauer, but largely it was Minister of Economics Ludwig Erhard who became known as father of the German economic miracle. There was a pool of skilled workers made up of returning soldiers and displaced people from parts of former Germany ready to be put to work. Maybe it was the very fact that a downcast and defeated people buckled down to work, rather than dwelling on the past and its total wartime devastation, quite different in attitude from that of victors who feel elated and deserving of their gains, that gave Germany the push that was turned to an advantage.

The first two years following the end of hostilities were marred by a directive to the US forces of occupation in West Germany to 'take no steps looking toward the economic rehabilitation of Germany'. Instead, thousands of top German researchers and engineers were transported to the US and to the Soviet Union. Much of Germany's coal and steel industry was dismantled and exported. Allies confiscated and removed all German patents to enhance their own industries.

The Potsdam Conference's decisions and their consequences eventually slowed down and living standards began to improve. Germany's economy picked up comparatively rapidly.

The Marshall Plan, which had been rolled out in 1948 to help Europe's countries to recover and of which Britain got the largest share, eventually was extended to Western Germany, too, though its actual impact has been debated ever since, as the recovery was already underway. The utter devastation of industry and most cities was a spur, rather than a hindrance. The European Common Market was founded in 1957.

Old habits and survival experiences were not easily abandoned. With all that had happened, keeping your own pigs made sense, though the idea of acquiring a goat was eventually dropped in our new house. Right behind the basement wall was a small enclosed space as the outside wallowing place for two pigs, bought just past piglet age. There was a connecting opening in the outside wall from and to the sty for warm summer days. Pig feed must have been bought in, for I do not remember the usual cauldron in the new house that produced the beloved warm mixtures.

The pig slayer was a man of short dapper stature, who was called when the time came in late autumn. I was never present at the actual deed, but I did wonder how the not always steadfast little man managed to aim his bolt and then manhandle the carcass on to the scraping ladder. His bare skull carried the scars of a close encounter with his own means of despatching while in a state of inebriation when the device had been held upside down and the bolt shot upwards, glancing his skull in its close proximity.

The village in the 1970s. Top right, beyond the houses, is the sporting field. Centre left of church, a new school building stands out.

Right: View into the smoke room in my parents' attic.

Below: Apologies for the quality of this snapshot of a one-armed man ploughing, but not for its inclusion. Josef Gierse returned from the war minus one arm. A proud man, he simply took up the task and carried on. He had a family and little choice. How do you judge the valour of a man?

The Gierse family and a neighbour on a special occasion.

In the back of the basement cellar was a brick-built or cemented bath-like addition where much of the larger chunks of meat were preserved in salt for and through the winter months, while in the roof space attic was a fire-secure room especially rendered airtight to serve as smoking room, where hams and sausages would be made to last through the preserving properties of beech wood smoke.

In earlier times and in older houses, smoke had simply risen from the central open fire to accomplish the same task through the rafters.

Apart from those men who did not return from the war were some who came back damaged with missing limbs. Wilhelm Gierse, the tall and sturdy farmer in one of my earlier pictures (page 62), bringing in the harvest with the dubious help of the Dr Padberg family and me, did not return. His brother, Josef, returned with only one arm, yet there was no alternative, he carried on the family subsistence farming literally singlehanded. Imagine ploughing, sowing, reaping with only one arm and with the family cows or heifers as power sources. Everything had to be done with just one arm. He was a strong and proud man who resented having to ask for help.

Pedalling up an Autobahn

A new teacher had been added to the ageing complement of teaching staff. *Lehrer* Meiworm was to cut his teeth on us uncouth scholars. Being young, blond, and possibly handsome, he was an instant success with some of his charges. It was said that female pupils collected at his lodgings in the mornings, just for the pleasure of walking him to school.

We boys were introduced to a wider world thanks to his fresh energies. At school holiday time, bicycle journeys were arranged for instance along the Rhine. For most that would have been the first time, certainly the furthest, from home they had ventured. My well-worn bicycle was newly acquired by my father from a large family of painters and decorators in the village. Their youngest son was one of my classmates. Having spent his pocket money in the first flush of excitement away from home, Willie hit on the idea that I had not paid sufficiently for the bicycle I was riding and therefore I owed him. I simply ignored him. The threatened vandalism to the mobility of my wheels, however, never materialised.

Siegfried had relatives in the Rhineland, relatives who owned a farm, so that became an overnight stage in our travels. While we all made ourselves comfortable in the hay of a large barn, Siegfried claimed or was offered preferential treatment among his relatives, an attitude that did not endear him to his peers. The exercise of daylong pedalling must have turned him into a deep sleeper, for the following night, he never noticed the blackening shoe polish someone cruelly managed to apply to his face. For reasons I could never fathom, I was later told that the next night a similar fate had been planned for me, though why the plan was adopted was never revealed, nor what had prevented its execution. I remember much rain on that trip, which did not aid morale.

One of our less heralded achievements during that adventure was for our two-wheeled caravan to happily pedal along while passing drivers took demonic delights in swearing and hooting their horns in passing. The reason for that eventually dawned on us: we were travelling blissfully on the wrong side of a motorway where bicycles were not allowed. Manhandling transport and baggage up a steep embankment; we reached the relative safety of a bridge carrying a lesser road more conducive to our mode of transport.

There were picture opportunities at places such as the steps of Cologne Cathedral, whose lofty twin spires rose from the devastation of its surroundings even more remarkable and awesome as survivors of the relentless bombardment the area had witnessed. To me, those ruins somehow reminded of the low dwellings surrounding it at the time of its construction. The cathedral's majestic rise from the ruins of Cologne made its height appear even more dominant. In that sense, our awe must have been akin to the experience of its medieval contemporaries.

There followed other cycling trips in subsequent years, not school organised but with various friends and one on my own once my friend Hermann and his family

Most of my school group on the steps of
Cologne Cathedral, 10 June 1949, with the
new teacher Meiworm.

had returned back to Aachen. I walked streets and parks with a drawing pad and
charcoal, though my interests well outstripped my talent.

Aachen also was the new domicile of the doctor who had once sat by my bedside
for hours after administering a fever injection. He was well remembered in the
village, not least as his young wife was rumoured to have been a nun before she
romantically eloped to be with him in matrimony. I found her and their lively little
daughter. The lady took me to meet the doctor in the large bright hospital where
he now worked. He had changed his calling. Hopefully the experience of my initial
reaction to his treatment had nothing to do with his decision, but he had retrained
as an eye specialist.

A Mountain's Demise

The threat behind the Iron Curtain and the belligerent Soviet Union during the Cold
War period so close to the east of us brought with it suspicions and rumours. If
and when the expansive Russians would invade the west, it was feared, the most
probable route of attack would be a corridor that rolled right across us in the
Sauerland.

A hill near the village by the big house of Cloidts had in past times been quarried for quality diabase or dolorite, but in rather small quantities, indeed, I remember watching local men in the old quarry laboriously hammering cobblestones from the tough material.

One farmer found the diabase in one of his mountains was of considerably larger quantity and that was needed for the repair of Western Germany's war-neglected roads and railways. At one time, two trainloads of local stone a week would head for Switzerland, and train lines in northern Germany and Holland welcomed the diabase from Remblinghausen.

Apart from affording big game hunting trips to Africa, one of the dividends of the new income for the mountain's owner was his purchase of a second farm in Canada to escape to just in case of a Russian invasion.

In Remblinghausen, the sudden bonanza meant work for many of the locals just as farm horses and labourers were replaced by machinery and traditionally trained artisans found it impossible to earn a living. People were able to buy ready-made shoes and off-the-peg clothes, even ready-made furniture. Many traditional artisan crafts were lost. A former shoemaker would become a foreman in the quarry. It operated from 1956 to 1992. In its last two decades, it employed about sixty people.

At my parents' house, it meant the constant daytime rumble of large heavily laden lorries passing through the centre of the village would shake the very foundations and could be felt even indoors.

On the hill behind the big house of Cloidts, an open-cast quarry was worked in the 1920s. An especially strong wagon had been built to transport hand-loaded stones.

Roughly 300 million years ago, volcanic activity, then under a sea, pressed up liquid diabas through older layers of slate and dispersed it in rills and pockets, to eventually become a most useful resource for road and rail builders.

Village and quarry, *c.* 1970. The sporting field lower right.

Right: View from
the depleted quarry
towards the village.

Below: An old
postcard of the farm in
Drasenbeck that would
erase a mountain.

The same farm with farmer, son (on right), and gamekeeper in July 1992.

Once the quarry was exhausted and the lorries stopped passing, a new smart bypass was designed and built to avoid the village and the steep incline down to Sägemühle.

West and East Germany reunited in 1990 and the perceived threat from the east was lifted.

A Broken Collarbone

With Aunt Minna building her house and another family moving out, too, the Vicarage was taken back by the Vicar, though why a single man required a whole house I could never fathom. He had set aside a first floor room as a kind of youth club and meeting place. It was there that for a few times in my life I wore boxing gloves with some seriousness. For a short time, a young blacksmith was recruited to keep our exercises in proportion and to follow certain rules when enthusiasm might get out of hand.

To celebrate Christmas in the traditional way, the village church needed a new crib, or rather a new stable to house the crib and the child and Mary and Joseph and the animals and shepherds. The carved figures had survived in the Verger's house next door, but the stable was needed.

Did it have to be the usual broken-down shack, or would it be possible to offer the child one of our houses? Our Vicar, *Herr* Moog, who had walked around the village during the nights of the shelling and given general absolution to his flock, readily agreed for us to build a replica stable. Hanses' old house would be a picturesque effort. It was called the Old House of Remblinghausen then, though an even older one has since been identified.

There was a surrender to tradition. Apart from the odd run-down barn, there were no more thatched roofs in the village. Our new old house, complete in detail with black beams and white squares, would have a traditional straw roof. We had budding carpenters among our number and the homemade effort allowed for some unexpected talent to emerge. It became an exercise of considerable merit that lasted for many a Christmas, expressing our pride in our home village.

The young priest had seen military training. At one time, he tried to warn us about the dangers of unprotected sex with talk of '*Nahkampfsocken*' (close combat socks). I had not heard the expression before, nor have I heard it since, but 'close-combat-socks' seem to make sense in context of the battle of the sexes. I was rather surprised at such talk from a man who had taken the vow of celibacy.

Now that Hitler Youth had been abolished, Christian youth work was again encouraged. Out in the hills and woodland and beyond the farthest hamlet on the outskirts of the parish stood an old rough wooden hunting lodge, which the Vicar

Early in the 1950s, we built a stable for a Christmas scene display in the church. Having set up the camera, I joined in just before the magnesium flash would explode. My eye and ear are just visible between two boys on right.

acquired on our behalf. He had it improved and secured by local craftsmen, but a lot of work was done by delegations of youths from the village. Of course, everything had to be carried there, food had to be prepared, though sandwiches were usually the preferred solution. Overnight stays were possible on rough bunk beds. Even an outside privy had to be dug as part of the character building exercise.

Each visit was an adventure, if only because of the isolation and distance. It was not all that far away from the former mine where men from our village had dug for silver as long-distance perambulating commuters in a previous century.

Outside organisations would occasionally share the hut and be spending time there. It was during the stay of one such group that it was decided to make a neighbourly surprise visit. All hush-hush, of course, a surprise would be all the more effective if it were timed at twilight. By the time we arrived in the far beech woods on the side of a hill, light was indeed beginning to fade. Approaching from different angles and trying to avoid privies, cooking areas, and such, we sneaked up as silently as possible. The windows showed light. The strangers were inside. The likely idea was to suddenly begin a pandemonium of noise about the hut and then watch the surprise reactions.

I like to think it was the very time of day that contributed to the accident, but it was I who spoiled the fun when I stumbled over a protruding root or a fallen branch, breaking a collarbone. Of course, one did not know that at first, only that something serious had gone wrong.

Such an anti-climax. Instead of being scared out of their wits by the shadows in the night, the incumbents of the forest hut were called on to help with the unexpected casualty. I wanted to walk, but I was overruled. I had not been diagnosed yet, so it became an exercise of a different kind. A stretcher was improvised from a blanket and two staves of wood and I was carried by four of my erstwhile conspirators who took it in turn to shake and stumble me some considerable distance to the nearest farm on the rutted track.

A phone call eventually brought out our hard-pressed village doctor who was not best pleased, but diagnosed the broken collarbone, placed a thickness of wadding under my arm, and tied my elbow to my body before affording me the privilege and luxury of transportation back home to the village in his motorcar. The collarbone healed, not as expected break to break, but slightly overlapping, leaving a bump.

Somehow, the enthusiasm for a youth shelter that far from home seems to have taken a dive after that unfortunate episode.

Marlene Dietrich in Remblinghausen

With wartime restrictions removed, an entrepreneur with a van brought films into the village that had been forbidden by Nazis, setting up his projector and loudspeakers in one of the inns in the centre of the village. We were regaled with the once-forbidden fruit, saving the 5-km journey to Meschede while the publican rested and watched quietly from behind the bar, tinkling glasses now and then. It was there that I watched a flickering version of Marlene Dietrich playing Lola Lola, a sexy cabaret singer, in the 1930's film *Der blaue Engel* (*The Blue Angel*). 'Falling in love again' was its most memorable tune. It had brought Miss Dietrich international success. Born in Berlin, she wisely left for America to become Hollywood's highest paid female star for a time, shunning German state efforts to entice her back to her home country. Henceforth she was *persona non grata* in Hitler's Germany.

Friendship and Aspirations

I used to write verse, simple rhyming stanzas that nobody ever saw—in some of my peers' eyes, a very suspicious activity. Nor did my position at the top of my class and my avoidance of my father's artisanship gain me friends in some quarters. Maybe my striving and acceptance of the finer offerings of civilization, like opera, may have marked me out as someone who punched above his station. From nearby Meschede, special trips were arranged to an opera house to experience such dubious and alien delights as Verdi's *Don Giovanni*. Personally, I saw no problem in wanting to experience all that life and civilisation had to offer.

My friend Hermann was an evacuee from Aachen on the German, Dutch, and Belgian border. The family had found temporary quarters in attic rooms of the new school. On one visit, expecting he would come to play out as usual, Hermann was playing a violin under his father's strict instructions. With tears in his eyes, he persevered, having to stay indoors and practice. On a subsequent visit, I found to my surprise that he did not want to come out because he actually enjoyed the practice.

In the sensible mode of the times, he became an apprentice carpenter, though the violin remained his all-abiding passion. That to some marked both of us out as different.

Our teacher *Fräulein* Fischer, who, like Hermann's family, also lived in the new school, was sister to the priest in my father's hometown of Eversberg. That must have been how my friend heard of a work of art—*a pietà*—a sculpted scene from the Passion of Christ that features Mary cradling her son's dead body following the crucifixion. The most famous expressions of the scene were created by Michelangelo and can be found in Rome. We decided it would be worth a trip out on our bicycles one fine day.

Rev. Fischer was happy to show off the work of art from around AD 1500 and mentioned his surprise to find two young fellows interested in such an old object of veneration. Personally, I was not overwhelmed with the carver's colourful achievement, but as we both were earning apprentices' wages by then, we politely wondered if there was a cost involved in the viewing. 'A half-pound of butter would be much appreciated,' replied the feisty priest, alas that was a payment neither of us could furnish him with.

One dark evening, we stood in the centre of our village back-to-back, awaiting a threatened attack from peers who for some reason decided we deserved a beating. We could not just let it pass, so we challenged all comers. When you stand up to bullies, they remarkably easily disappear.

Hermann's passion was seriously impeded when in an accident at his workplace, he lost the tips of several fingers on his left hand. No longer could he reach the catgut strings with his damaged fingers. Still he persevered, retraining and switching hands with bow and violin, but was advised that whatever his training, he would never reach the exacting standards required of a professional musician.

His love of music never wavered. My friend spent his life making music in orchestras—as a trombonist.

View into the village from my parents' kitchen window.

41

In the Steps of Gutenberg

I must have been a great disappointment to my father, though there was no real pressure. A tougher boy from my class became his apprentice, joining a journeyman roofer he already employed.

Perhaps he simply realised that I was not suited for the roofing environment, and without much fuss, he took a small sketchbook of mine and visited an acquaintance in the nearby town, at the largest of the traditional printing houses.

There was no immediate vacancy, so for about six months, I became a delivery boy, trundling packets of printed material on a bicycle front and back about town and sometimes to clients miles out in the countryside, before I signed the contract as a typesetter apprentice.

Roads still left much to be desired, and in the town, much new building also meant new road layouts and occasionally pockets of mire that had to be crossed while balancing parcels and boxes of pristine printed matter. A box of precious wedding announcements or invitations toppled off my bicycle frame on a wet and miserable day. I returned to the bookbinding department where my vulnerable box had been prepared for delivery. Our bookbinder was a pleasant and helpful fellow and probably mine was not the first accident of such nature. We just about managed to save an acceptable number to deliver without a total reprint. I became very careful after that.

Once my training began in earnest, I loved the new job as typesetter, though it meant standing upright all day in front of rows of shallow drawers with special divisions for alphabets and word spaces, capitals and lower case, italics, bold, and sometimes small caps, adding letter to letter to fill lines of often-minute text under the watchful eye of a master compositor.

Later, much design would be involved. One day a week, I attended a trade school several stops away by train, which would necessitate rather early starts by bicycle to the train and a long walk at the other end to reach lessons on time (I inherited Uncle Emil's bicycle for my transport needs, the frame number of which is still impressed in my brain as a constant reminder of vigilance).

It was at that trade school that I first realised that I had limits to patience for time wasters and bullies. One day some of the apprentices took it into their heads that it would be a wheeze if we did not return from lunch break as a group. The whole class hid behind a building, watched our teacher enter the premises and presently leave again, having been confronted with the puzzle of an empty classroom. Several thought that was hilarious and we could leave early for home. When the same was suggested the following week and peer pressure seemed to prevail, I decided that I was not going to such length of travel and transport to be prepared for a working life and then miss out on the actual lessons and I did not hesitate to say so. It actually came to physical grappling with the largest of the deserter fans. We were in class still and I had wrestled the commanding bully across desks on his back. My right fist was raised when the teacher entered the room. I was embarrassed, but nothing was said and when soon afterwards that same teacher asked the class to put someone forward for a presentation, they voted for me, so perhaps I was not the only one who preferred to learn instead of shirking.

Once, in the company of other apprentices, on passing the open front door of a hostelry, we were stopped in our tracks by a noisy and flickering monotone image, rectangular and maybe 6 or 7 inches wide on a box at the far side of the interior. I do not remember what the subject was or even that any of it made sense, but it was our first glimpse of that new-fangled invention of television.

In the village, word made the rounds and neighbours would be invited to a display of the new replacement of the radio. Many of us piled into a large room at a neighbouring farm where a sharp-eyed salesman had set up and ensured reception of a small black and white television set. Little did we know how it would grow and make its way into every home.

Lunch hour at work was a great time for exploring or just hanging about somewhere in the neighbourhood with our sandwiches. Double flights of steps led up from the pavement to the front doors of buildings in our street, possibly the result of flooding in earlier centuries. Walking up to our premises there was a stationary and office equipment shop to the right, with offices behind, passing the stairs to the upstairs living quarters of the boss's family to the left and behind it a rather large kitchen. Behind that, we went straight on into the composing room and the print works that extended out to the edge of the River Lenne, a contributory to the River Ruhr. Before joining the Rhine, the Ruhr eventually passes through the coal-mining district. It gave its name to the industrial area that had seen so much of the devastation of wartime and now contributed greatly to Germany's revival—the Ruhr District.

Not that we apprentices were concerned with such seriously economic affairs, when the generous proportions of the beautiful daughter of the bakers next door received more of our surreptitious attention, even though we would not have admitted such behaviour had anyone commented on it. Nevertheless, the freedom of her behaviour as she bent and interacted with younger siblings might have been interpreted by some as to be privately meant for our benefit.

I often wondered at the stoic contribution to adolescent wonderment when a watchmaker's wife in the town would rearrange the shop window displays about lunchtime, leaning forward in loose-fitting garments at a time when brassieres still seemed to be surplus to the female wardrobe. It must have appeared somewhat curious to passers-by watching the heads of several wide-eyed apprentices moving in unison from side to side in rhythm with the lady's generous activities while pressing their noses close to the large expanse of glass.

The printing premises had in previous times seen the publication of a local newspaper, a constant and regular income in earlier days. Times change and the premises would no longer be able to cope with what would then have been a major undertaking, though many people still dreamt of bringing back those days.

One inescapable aspect was the close proximity of the boss's family with all commercial activities. While our congenial boss dealt with all things print-wise, shop and shop assistants were largely under the leadership of the boss's beautiful and capable wife, the '*Chefin*', and his spinster sister.

The boss's mother also had apartments upstairs. Once my spelling prowess had been recognised, I might be sent upstairs on special occasions to proofread tracts of printed matter with the elderly lady, always comfortable interludes. Long lists of names of local or national voters could turn into demanding if tedious litanies.

More curiously demanding were the times before Christmas when I was sent upstairs with the questionable task of writing verse of comment or description or humour about the various characters that made up the company, a delicate task when considering how I had to work and live with colleagues, employees and superiors afterwards who had been at the sharp end of a lampoon that rankled on a personal level. It gave me a certain power of getting even, as well as trying to be amusing to the greater assembly, though I shudder at the memory of so many innocently bland platitudes that had to be endured.

Those questionable works of poetic zeal would be read out at a festive occasion by a well-disguised Father Christmas, usually the boss's learned younger brother whose calling was that of a dentist. Occasionally, I had to later absorb the grumblings of dissatisfied older colleagues who were not wholly impressed with the witticisms I had revealed about them, but of course, as it was the boss who had instigated the occasions when Christmas presents and bonuses were handed out, their grumbles had to be moderated.

Later in my years as compositor, I must have been in an especially jovial mood one day when I felt sorry for the lonely maiden that was the boss's spinster sister and I went into the shop, simply took hold of her, and kissed her.

'What's that for?' enquired the nonplussed maiden with astonishment, but I felt an explanation of simple shared happiness would be too difficult to fashion into sensible words.

The 5-km distance cycling home up to the village in the evenings included some rather steep stretches on the old road, forcing times to think and overcome boredom.

I realised I had a strong desire to write, but I was also aware that at that stage of my experiences I simply did not have sufficient knowledge. I had to wait until retirement before picking up the pen with greater seriousness.

On one special company occasion everyone was invited to an outing to a hunting lodge or clubhouse in a woodland setting on an autumnal afternoon. Food and music would be provided. A large wood fire to procure the glowing ashes was needed for the kind of traditional event that still draws crowds today. *Kartoffelbraten* means potatoes in their jackets placed into and raked from the still hot embers, peeled and filled with dabs of butter, grilled or boiled sausages, with mustard, and, of course, cases of bottled beer. An accordion player would provide the atmosphere to help the party go off with a swing.

Suddenly people hastened into the wooden building where our boss had decided to lift his wife up into the small ceiling opening to inspect the roof space for whatever reason. There were no stairs and no ladder. Of course, what goes up must come down, and so the handsome and fashionable lady lowered herself feet first back down where many hands were offering but our boss insisted that it was his job and his alone to catch her for a soft landing.

Steadiness is not helped by a few bottles of *Warsteiner*—the nearest local lager brew—and as the beautiful vision descended, he grabbed a little too clumsily, catching the clothing but not the shapely contents, which slid through his welcoming arms to the floor, exposing the latest range in exquisite female underwear and to some degree the lady's modesty.

The embarrassment was tangible as she fled the building to a seat outside where the darkening hour somewhat diffused the awkward situation. Only I went over to apologise and to pretend that I had been too dismayed to even look. Whatever I said must have had the desired effect, for the lady calmed down and re-joined the general frolic and banter.

It was only later, when the party broke up, that she insisted to drive me home to my village, which was not necessarily the furthest anyone had to travel. My boss, she declared, could walk to become sober.

The fragrant ride in comfort was beautiful and she stopped the car before we reached the village. When she kissed me, I was too bashful to reciprocate—or maybe I dreamt that—but on similar such evenings in future, my boss insisted he join us on the homeward journey.

Passing shop, offices, and household kitchen at the printing premises on the way to the composing and printing rooms meant that household employees could not always be avoided and would be known at least by sight and name. There was a potentially embarrassing day when my boss took me aside and informed me that the young kitchen and children's maid had, when pressed for the identity of the lover responsible for the predicament of pregnancy, named me.

'I don't think I have ever as much as shaken her hand, leave alone been alone with her,' I said truthfully.

'That's what I thought,' he said, 'she picked you as a better prospect.' It was never mentioned again.

Right: Setting up type in the composing room. Knickerbockers were a belated fashion.

Below: At a private party with employees of Fr. Drees, Printers. Again I had set up the Agfa camera and told everyone to huddle together for the picture, which was reacted to with gusto; after all, there are the boss's wife and sister in the throng. I had secured a magnesium satchel away from flammable material, probably with the aid of a broom handle, and lit the flame-carrying paper strip, switched off the light, and opened the lens before piling in from the left. The magnesium would explode with a bright flash. Not everyone could resist making use of the dark, before I closed the lens and light returned to the room.

The Wandering Journeyman

Lower down the little stream that filled the pond and once drove the sawmill in Sägemühle stood a water mill, driven by a traditional waterwheel, nestling by a babbling brook, lonely and picturesque. The most direct route to the village was via a steep and narrow cutting and up around the octagonal chapel before the long steep road to the village, which itself lies on a slope.

Among dark and towering fir trees, that narrow track worn by countless iron-rimmed wheels down to slippery bare rock among steep sides as high as a man spelled hard work in history. Even then, the mill building was in a bad state of repair. Moss grew on the thatched roofs of outhouses. As elsewhere, small labour-intensive undertakings lost out to larger industrialisations. Picturesque does not mean profitable. The stream that winds its way through the meadow flanked by wooded hills was an enchanted place. To me it was a secret valley, the setting for stories and scenes as evoked in the music of Franz Schubert in the song cycle '*Die schöne Müllerin*' ('The beautiful Miller's Daughter').

The romantic notion of the wandering bachelor, the '*Geselle*' or journeyman who travels the countryside, following streams and brooks to the next mill for employment encapsulates the old system and culture of the various guilds that at the conclusion of an apprenticeship further education is sought from many sources.

In this way, skills were spread and standards raised. Even Gutenberg, the inventor of individual movable type, had his helpers who then spread his invention abroad. In Franz Schubert's song cycle, we follow such a '*Geselle*' on his travels through life and love, wherever mill wheels turn.

When the time came for my own move out into the wider world, I placed an advertisement into our printing trade paper. I received nineteen offers of work from all over Germany. It was not easy to choose.

'Look here,' said my boss with a grin, 'an advert from Haarlem in Holland. They're looking for compositors, too. You'd have to learn another language to get on there.'

'OK, I'll go to Haarlem. That should be fun.'

There were problems in my parents' marriage. My mother had been crying and the atmosphere was not the usual placid normality. I believe my father blamed my mother for the way I had turned out.

Both my parents had to sign a form agreeing my leaving to work abroad as I was not yet twenty-one. 'What if I don't sign it?' said my mother.

'Then I'll have to wait 'til next year,' I said.

Although I was quite prepared to take the bus to town and the railway station, my father insisted on driving me there with my suitcase. Along the way, he pronounced that my mother had done a poor job in his absence. She had spoiled me and should have been much tougher/harder in my upbringing. I could not let it rest.

'There are various ways in bringing up a child,' I told him, 'with the rod or with gentle persuasion. My mother chose the gentle path. If she had not, would I be able to go abroad to earn my keep in a job of work I take pride in doing? They would not have me if I was not able.'

He became thoughtful then and later my mother asked me: 'What happened on the day you left? What did he say? What did you say? He was a different man when he came back.' Their relationship had returned to the better. As for me, I knew that I would be back only as an independent success. If things were to go wrong, I would not have returned for hand-outs.

So I myself followed the tradition, seeking different—far-flung in my case—places of employment until I settled in London. After Holland, I set type in printing houses in Wales, England, and Ireland before stopping off in London on my way back to employment in Germany, changing from typesetter to typographer and designer.

One of the directors of a Bond Street, Mayfair, advertising agency addressed me with 'You are German? I was torpedoed by the Germans'. It was the only time it was mentioned. More important was my ability to do the job. I was accepted and stayed on for two years before I went freelance and worked independently for the rest of my working life.

Above left: Haarlem in Holland cherishes its own alleged inventor of printing. The author in front of a statue of Laurens Janszoon (Laudje) Coster, complete with the inevitable Dutch bicycle.

Above right: Uncle Emil in later years, here with a visitor from Wales, my future wife, Maureen, on a walk in the Sauerland hills.

42

Travels with My Father

I once watched my father at a remembrance service outdoors by the memorial to the dead of two world wars, among a small group of former soldiers standing to attention, right hands raised palm forward to the side of the head as soldiers do in saluting. The sombre sounds of '*Ich hatt' einen Kameraden…*' ('I had a comrade…'), a tune with the moving words describing the death of a fellow soldier played by the youthful *Musikkapelle* (the village brass band) in that now peaceful setting among leafy trees, facing the three crosses with their writhing bodies in a depiction of Golgotha.

My father tried his best to stand upright and still, except for his shaking saluting hand that would not or could not obey and be still. They stood only a few yards away from where in 1945 our school portrait of the Führer had lain broken and speared by a sabre.

He loved to travel, first whenever he could manage to look up one of his former comrades from the *Wehrmacht* or more likely from his time as prisoner of war in Russia. They would have formed strong bonds during those cold deprived years.

With his son abroad, he would bring my mother, visiting London and wherever I was staying, when I had my chance to show off and be the guide. He even brought my mother and my sister as well as a sister-in-law to our wedding in Wales. In other years as the family grew, we would explore Wales or the Highlands of Scotland where he took great delight on tourist routes to wait for a gust of wind that might reveal if all those continental travellers' stories that guessed at the dress sense under a Scotsman's kilt were true.

He also loved to have company on his travels, taking pride in showing off the mountains of southern Germany and Austria, drives into France and Switzerland with my wife and daughters, always allowing for our enjoyment.

My father and I, 1993–94.

GI's at the Eagle's Nest

On the southern tip of Germany close to the Austrian border, Berchtesgaden in Bavaria, 30 km from Salzburg, used to be a favourite hangout of Adolf Hitler's.

The Berghof, where he claimed to have had his best and perhaps most sinister ideas, and where he wrote much of his bestseller *Mein Kampf* once he had been released from prison, had been vastly extended into a second *Reichskanzlei* (Imperial Chancellery), where foreign dignitaries could stay and were welcomed. Other Nazi leaders also enjoyed retreats in the vicinity.

Allied bombers devastated that favoured retreat on 25 April 1945, not as a strategic necessity, more to make a point. At the end of the war, the SS set fire to the Berghof. When French troops and GIs arrived on 4 May, it was still smouldering.

Above it, the *Kehlsteinhaus*, better known as the Eagle's Nest, was a present for Hitler on his fiftieth birthday in 1939. It is the highest part of the once-sprawling system of buildings and tunnels, most of which have now been eradicated or closed to avoid neo-Nazi pilgrimages.

We visited with my father. Buses took us on the dizzy winding road clinging to the side of the steep mountain to a place from where an original brass lift takes the visitors up to what is now a restaurant and lookout area. The far view over the crags and mountains was breath taking when we arrived, but only for a brief moment before vapour moved in and we found ourselves isolated in the clouds; I barely had time to set the camera and grab a picture. Historical records reveal that it was actually rarely visited by Hitler.

Above and below: Kehlstein near Berchtesgaden, once a gift for the Führer, now a restaurant with a breath-taking view—clouds allowing. GIs came up from nowhere and vanished again into the clouds.

It was with some surprise, though, that I noted a troop of American GIs arriving up out of the mist as if from nowhere, turned away from the building that today is a favoured tourist restaurant and in single file disappeared over a crag among the jagged and towering rocks back into nothingness, obviously on a high mountain all-weather exercise.

Cruising on a Russian Ship

In February 1977, my father invited me to join him on a cruise—Southampton, La Coruña, Vigo, Lisbon, Funchal, St. Cruz, Lanzarote, Casablanca, Cadiz, Southampton—as my mother had decided she preferred to stay at home. Of course, his journey began and ended in Zeebrügge, with me joining and leaving at Southampton. Nothing unusual in that, perhaps, except that the ship was Russian, MS *Gruziya* of the Black Sea Shipping Company, a small cruise ship, with a Russian crew, but for him, it was a kind of sweet redress, remembering the four hard years he had spent in Russia's Ural Mountains as prisoner of war.

His attitude and treatment towards the crew that now served us did not remind of that. In fact, I do not think he ever divulged the fact he had been such a prisoner, just the fact that the tables were turned was enough. I was delighted to accept, catching up on half a lifetime's separation. Yet still I did not ask about his wartime memories. In all that time, we never talked about that part of his past. It simply was the past and looking forward to the future was the more promising attitude. We were happy in each other's company and he quietly did all he could to assist me in my passionate hobby of photography.

Most of the passengers came from Germany, results of the '*Wirtschaftswunder*' that had caused a defeated people to pull themselves up by their shoelaces and start afresh, just as my father had done. It seemed so easy the way he could make friends when simply addressing strangers.

There were also passengers from other continental countries, but most of those also spoke German. On a previous cruise, a Dutch lady had taken to the microphone one evening during the on-board entertainments and directly invited all their German neighbours to come and visit her beautiful country. There was one proviso: 'Would they not come all at once like the last time, please?' The Dutch couple and my father became staunch friends for the rest of his life.

In 1992, the village celebrated 750 years since it was first mentioned in documents. For a week, it seemed, the whole population, got into the spirit, the through road was closed and a holiday declared, while much of the village became a pop-up museum. Once loved and used items and vehicles were brought out of attics and barns, crafts and traditions from past and present were re-enacted, the many clubs and societies displayed their pride, music played, and choirs sang.

Above: The 750 Year Celebrations. A radio interview about village affairs at the back of what once was a post inn (30 June 1992).

Below: Washerwomen. With the roads closed, all sorts of old habits and traditions were remembered and relived (4 July 1992).

Above left: Village view from where my grandparents' house used to be (August 1990).

Above right: The village in August 1990. The inn and farm in the centre has become a bank and the Tuckelsburg at the left has been demolished.

Church approach, May 2018. The old Post Inn, left, where we sheltered temporarily during the shelling in 1945 has changed little, though the cellar door at the front, where we first sought shelter after fleeing our burning building, has been filled in.

After the war, the village of Remblinghausen counted some 1,600 souls, today there are 1,860, including the outlying hamlets. Both the old school and the then-new school have been demolished, as has the Tuckelsburg, which in more affluent times had become an eyesore, though not in my eyes. When it counted, I was not there to defend it. The new bypass leaves the village quiet again and lovers of nature come and visit the rural peace of the Sauerland.

The Village War Memorial remembers the dead and missing of both the First World War and the Second World War.

Let no one say a country does not pay for its follies. These are the dead of two wars from just one small parish.

Bibliography

Ageeva, M., (ed.), *Ufa: Pages of History*, Book Two, (Ufa: Inesh, 2014)

Bell, Lt-Col. Edgar V. H., *War Diary of Detector 6*, January–June 1945, 4point2, last modified 23 July 2001: www.4point2.org/belldiary.htm

Huyskens, A., *Der Kreis Meschede unter der Feuerwalze des zweiten Weltkrieges - Aus den Erlebnisberichten vieler Mitarbeiter aus dem ganzen Kreisgebiet zusammengestellt und dargestellt im Auftrage der Kreisverwaltung* (W. Bertelsmann Verlag, Bielefeld, 1949)

Kolpakov, D., *70 Years of Victory* (Moskovsky Komsomolets, 2015)

Kortenkamp, G., various research material and results, unpublished

Kortenkamp, L., *Remblinghausen—Beiträge zur Geschichte der Gemeinde* (Herausgeber: Ludwig Kortenkamp, 2015)

'NSDAP election results of 1933 in Germany's constituencies.'

'NSDAP Wahl 1933' (Map of % of votes cast) Wikimedia: By derivative work: DoveNSDAP Wahl 1933.png: Korny78-NSDAP Wahl 1933.png, CC BY 3.0: commons.wikimedia.org/w/index.php?curid=5486833